Programming with Rust

Programming
with Rust

Donis Marshall

✦✦ Addison-Wesley

For information about buying this title in bulk quantities, or for special sales opportunities (which may include electronic versions; custom cover designs; and content particular to your business, training goals, marketing focus, or branding interests), please contact our corporate sales department at corpsales@pearsoned.com or (800) 382-3419.

For government sales inquiries, please contact governmentsales@pearsoned.com.

For questions about sales outside the U.S., please contact intlcs@pearson.com.

Visit us on the Web: informit.com/aw

Library of Congress Control Number: 2023947453

ISBN-13: 978-0-13-788965-5
ISBN-10: 0-13-788965-8

1 2023

Pearson's Commitment to Diversity, Equity, and Inclusion

Pearson is dedicated to creating bias-free content that reflects the diversity of all learners. We embrace the many dimensions of diversity, including but not limited to race, ethnicity, gender, socioeconomic status, ability, age, sexual orientation, and religious or political beliefs.

Education is a powerful force for equity and change in our world. It has the potential to deliver opportunities that improve lives and enable economic mobility. As we work with authors to create content for every product and service, we acknowledge our responsibility to demonstrate inclusivity and incorporate diverse scholarship so that everyone can achieve their potential through learning. As the world's leading learning company, we have a duty to help drive change and live up to our purpose to help more people create a better life for themselves and to create a better world.

Our ambition is to purposefully contribute to a world where:

- Everyone has an equitable and lifelong opportunity to succeed through learning.
- Our educational products and services are inclusive and represent the rich diversity of learners.
- Our educational content accurately reflects the histories and experiences of the learners we serve.
- Our educational content prompts deeper discussions with learners and motivates them to expand their own learning (and worldview).

While we work hard to present unbiased content, we want to hear from you about any concerns or needs with this Pearson product so that we can investigate and address them.

- Please contact us with concerns about any potential bias at https://www.pearson.com/report-bias.html.

Contents

About the Author

Donis Marshall has over 20 years of experience in designing and building enterprise software utilizing Microsoft technologies for leading companies across industry segments. As a Microsoft MVP and MCT, he has trained developers and engineers for many years. Donis is the author of the *Programming Microsoft Visual C#* (2005), *Programming Microsoft Visual C#* (2008), and *Solid Code* (2009).

Introduction to Rust

Welcome to *Programming with Rust*.

Your journey along the Rust super-highway begins here. Fasten your seat belt and prepare to enjoy an amazing journey of learning and exploration. Along this journey, you will uncover the benefits of Rust and how the language is positively changing the perception of modern programming languages. Each leg of the journey will inspect a different area of the language. In this manner, you will explore the entire language and emerge as a Rustacean, a professional Rust practitioner, and hopefully an active member of the growing Rust community.

The goals of this chapter include the following:

- Providing an overview and description of Rust
- Reviewing the Rust programming style
- Listing the many benefits of Rust
- Identifying and explaining Rust terminology
- Reviewing the key elements of a Rust application
- Creating your first Rust program

Introduction

Rust is a general-purpose language for creating safe, secure, and scalable applications. The language has features from several programming paradigms, as described shortly. Rust was originally designed as a systems programming language. However, it has emerged as a more versatile language capable of creating a variety of application types, including systems programming, web services, desktop applications, embedded systems, and more. Although it may sound cliché, what you can accomplish with Rust is only limited by your imagination.

Different! That is an accurate assessment of Rust. Although the Rust syntax is based on the C and C++ languages, the similarity with other C-based languages often ends there. In addition, Rust is not different *just* to be different; it is a difference with a purpose.

Rust's borrow checker is an excellent example of a difference with a purpose. The borrow checker is a unique feature within Rust that promotes safe coding practices by enforcing rules related to the single ownership principal. No other language has this feature. For that reason, the borrow checker is a foreign concept to many developers but nonetheless invaluable.

In many ways, Rust represents *lessons learned*. Some of the unique features in Rust are lessons learned, or instances of a lack of success, from other languages. The willingness of Rust to depart from the normal script when necessary is a major feature of the language. Many programming languages struggle with effective memory management, for example. That is the purpose of the ownership feature in Rust—effective memory management.

Let's be candid for a moment. Learning Rust can be frustrating at times. It requires an investment of time and the sacrifice of some brain cells. However, you will find that your investment in learning Rust is more than worthwhile. For example, learning to work with the borrow checker, not against it, is invaluable.

My goal in writing this book is to increase the number of Rustaceans—individuals with a high proficiency in the Rust programming language. My hope is that you will become an active member of the Rust community with your new mastery of the language. You have now officially started the journey toward becoming a Rustacean.

Functional Programming

Rust embraces a variety of programming paradigms, including functional programming, expression-oriented programming, and pattern-oriented programming. Let's explore these various paradigms, starting with functional programming. Since Rust is our focus, I will present just a review of these programming models in this book.

What is functional programming? It is a programming model where functions are the essential building blocks of the language. With functional programming, functions are first-class citizens. You can use functions wherever a variable is normally found: a local variable, function parameter, or as a function return. A function can even perform operations on other functions, described as a higher-order function.

Rust is functional programming *light*. The language does not include every feature found in functional programming, such as lazy evaluation, a declarative programming style, tail call optimization, and more. However, Rust does support a functional style of programming.

Functional programming languages typically restrict procedural programming capabilities, such as global functions. As they are not incongruent, Rust allows for the comingling of procedural- and functional-style programming.

Pure functions are the centerpiece of functional programming. As a pure function, a function is fully described through its function interface. There is a direct correlation between the function parameters and a specific return value, without side effects. In addition, the results of a pure function should be repeatable. For example, a function that relies on an internal random number, making the results unpredictable, is not a pure function.

Immutability is an important ingredient of functional programming, which is a core tenet of Rust. Pure functions, for example, lean heavily on immutable state to eliminate side effects. Pointers, global variables, and references are generally omitted from a pure function to avoid side effects that can leak from a function.

To summarize, functional programming offers several benefits:

- Added flexibility, with functions as first-class citizens
- More transparency, with the focus on functions and not individual lines of code
- Immutability, which makes programs easier to maintain by removing common problems such as side effects within functions

Expression Oriented

Rust is also an expression-oriented language, which is a programming style where most operations are expressions that return a value, instead of statements that return nothing. Expression-oriented programming is a close cousin of functional programming. All functional programming languages are also expression-oriented languages.

So what is a statement, and what is an expression?

- Statements do not return a value, but they can cause a side effect. The possible side effects are unlimited, including database manipulation or updating a shared variable. Indeed, the purpose of some statements *is the side effect*.
- Expressions are one or more operations that return a value, with minimal or no side effects. Pure functions are examples of expressions.

In Rust, expressions are preferred, even transfer of control statements such as the `if` and `while` statements are actually expressions.

The many benefits of expression-oriented programming include the following:

- Without side effects, expression-oriented programs are easier to maintain.
- The value of an expression is fully defined through its interface. This makes expressions more transparent.
- Because expressions are interface driven, they are more testable.
- Expression-oriented programming makes documentation easier. Without side effects, the expression can substitute as the documentation.
- Expressions are more easily composed.

The ability to combine the various programming paradigms is another of Rust's advantages.

Listing 1.1 provides an example of both functional and expression-oriented programming in Rust. The factorial function is a pure function with no side effect. As an expression, the factorial function returns the result of the factorial calculation.

Code Listing 1.1.   Factorial is a pure function and expression.

```
fn factorial(n:i32) -> i32 {
    match n {
        0..=1=>1,
        _=> n*factorial(n-1)
    }
}
```

Pattern Oriented

Typically, professional programming in Rust involves an abundance of patterns. Fair to say, patterns have a ubiquitous presence in Rust coding. This nod to pattern matching contributes to the uniqueness of the Rust programming style. Rust source code simply looks different from C++ or Java, for example!

Pattern matching is often associated with switch statements. For example, C++, Java, Go, and other languages have a switch statement. This is single dimensional pattern matching largely based on string or integral expressions. In Rust, pattern matching is extended to instances of user-defined types and sequences.

Rust has a *match* expression instead of a switch statement. However, pattern-oriented programming extends well beyond the match expression. Every instance of any expression in Rust is an opportunity for pattern matching. For example, even a simple assignment or conditional expression can result in pattern matching. This provides interesting ways of reimagining your code.

Pattern-oriented programming in Rust offers several benefits:

- Patterns in Rust are highly expressive. This allows you to collapse complex code into simpler expressions.
- In Rust, pattern-oriented programming is a complementary model to expression-oriented programming.
- Rust supports exhaustive pattern matching, which is more dependable and less error prone.

The `display_firstname` function demonstrates pattern matching, as shown in Listing 1.2. The function parameter is *name*, which is a tuple. The fields of the tuple are *last* and *first*. In the match expression, patterns are used to destructure the tuple, extract the first name, and print the name.

Code Listing 1.2. The `display_firstname` function displays a first name.

```
fn display_firstname(name:(&str, &str)){
    match name{
        (_, first)=> println!("{}", first),
    }
}
```

Features

Professionals regularly select Rust as their favorite programming language in a variety of recent surveys. Much of this recognition pertains to the unique features found in Rust.

Let's explore the core features that contribute to Rust and its popularity.

Safeness

Safeness is an important crosscutting feature touching almost all aspects of the language. Safe code is robust, predictable, and not prone to unexpected errors. With these attributes, Rust provides a solid foundation where you can confidently develop applications. Immutable variables, the single ownership principle, and other features contribute to this objective.

In addition, Rust enforces safe coding practices at compile time. The ownership model with the borrow checker is a perfect example of this approach. At compile time, the borrow checker performs a series of checks, including ownership. If the ownership check fails, the borrow checker presents an explanation and the compilation does not complete successfully.

Several factors contribute to safe code in Rust:

- Immutability is the default, which prevents inadvertent changes
- The enforcement of proper lifetimes to prevent anti-patterns, such as dangling references
- References for safe pointers
- A "resource acquisition is initialization" (RAII) strategy for variably sized resources, such as vectors, for dependable memory management

Ownership

The ownership feature provides safe memory access using the single owner principle. This principle consigns a single owner to variables, and never more than one owner.

This approach prevents sharing ownership of the same memory. Race conditions, unstable variables, and dangling references are some of the potential problems mitigated with this approach. There are exceptions for sharing ownership as presented later in this book.

Let's use a car analogy to demonstrate the single owner principle. Here are the basic facts: There is a car, and Bob is its sole owner.

Now here are two scenarios:

- Bob has the car.
- Ari occasionally wants to drive the same car.

As the owner, Bob can always drive the car, except when he has loaned it to someone else. If someone else (Ari) wants to drive the car, there are two possibilities: Bob must either sell or lend the vehicle to Ari. Either way, Bob loses possession of the vehicle, at least temporarily.

Here are the steps if Bob lends Ari the car.

- Bob drives the car.
- Bob lends the car to Ari. Ari drives the car. When Ari is done, he returns the car to Bob.
- Bob drives the car.

The borrow checker is responsible for enforcing correct ownership, including lending, at compile time. We will unlock the mystery of the borrow checker later in the book with the goal of making the borrow checker your best friend.

Lifetimes

Lifetimes is a feature in Rust that prevents accessing values that are no longer available. A reference is a basic pointer in Rust. If allowed, improper access to dropped values can cause hanging references and potential program failure. The result would be vulnerable applications that are both unstable and unpredictable. Rust eliminates this problem with the lifetimes model.

The borrow checker manages lifetimes. You are notified at compile time of invalid lifetimes. These sorts of problems are better isolated at compile time, not at runtime.

When there is ambiguity related to lifetimes, lifetime annotations are hints to the borrow checker about the proper lifetime. If determining the lifetime is trivial, lifetime annotations are not required. The borrow checker will just know. This is called lifetime elision.

The benefit of the lifetimes feature is a stable memory environment without the worry of hanging references.

Fearless Concurrency

Fearless concurrency is important and worthy of inclusion in the list of major Rust features. Fearless concurrency provides a safe environment for concurrent programming. In many ways, this safe environment is created from the benefit of the beforementioned features. For example, the ownership model in Rust largely eliminates race conditions in concurrent programming.

When transitioning from sequential to concurrent programming a process called hardening is often undertaken to ensure a safe environment for multithreaded code. Removing global variables, as shared data, is typically one step in the hardening process. Fearless concurrency eliminates the need for hardening.

Concurrent programming is often considered the bogeyman of coding. It can add complexity and make applications less maintainable. Worst of all, problems in concurrent programming are often not found until runtime. Fearless concurrency creates a safer environment for concurrent programming.

Zero-Cost Abstraction

Zero-cost abstraction is a feature of Rust features. Yes, you read that correctly. For that reason, it is the final feature mentioned here. Zero-cost abstraction is the policy that Rust features should not incur a performance penalty at runtime, if avoidable.

Generational garbage collection is an intrinsic feature of several popular managed languages, including Java, C#, and Go, for managing dynamic memory. Garbage collection can be costly and nondeterministic. As such, you never know when garbage collection may occur. Compare this to Rust, where there is no memory model. Absolutely none! Ownership, as described earlier in this chapter, provides deterministic memory management without overhead. That is an example of zero-cost abstraction.

Rust Terminology

Many technologies, including programming languages, have their own terminology. Familiarizing yourself with that terminology can be helpful when communicating with peers and others in the larger Rust community.

For Rust, the motif is crates, as in shipping crates. Here are some of the important terms in Rust. These will help you *talk* Rust.

- **Rust**: Let's start with the most important term: "Rust" itself. Rust is not an acronym or a special technology term. The name Rust comes from the term *rust fungi*, which is a robust pathogen that attacks living plants.
  Graydon Hoare, the original Rust designer, has been credited with this statement: "I think I named it after fungi. Rusts are amazing creatures."
- **Crate**: A crate is a compilation unit in Rust. Executable, library, or external crates are the most common.
  Executable crate: An executable crate is a binary executable that can be launched independently of other crates.

Library crate: Library crates provide services to other crates and do not execute independently.
External crate: External crates are external dependencies. For example, Crate A references Crate B, but Crate B is not within the same package. Therefore, Crate B is an external crate, or dependency, for Crate A.

- **Packages**: A package consists of multiple crates that provide a specific service. Packages can consist of multiple executable crates and possibly a single library crate.
- **Modules**: Modules in Rust are similar to namespaces from other programming languages. You can use modules to create a hierarchical program structure within a crate. Modules also help to avoid name collisions.
- **Cargo**: There are several *cargo* entities within Rust, which extends the crates motif (cargo in crates).
  Cargo tool: The Cargo tool is the Rust package manager.
  Cargo.toml: The Cargo.toml file is the manifest and configuration file for Rust.
  Cargo.lock: The Cargo.lock file is a record of all dependencies with their specific versions.
- **RS**: RS (Rust source) is the extension for Rust source files.

Figure 1.1 shows the interrelationship of various elements of Rust.

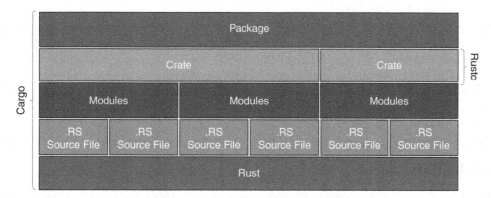

Figure 1.1.   The interrelationship of various elements in Rust

Tools

The Rust environment hosts a variety of tools that span a variety of services, from compiling Rust source code to publishing crates. Understanding these tools will improve your productivity. There are too many tools to list here, and more tools will be introduced throughout the book.

This is a list of the more important Rust tools:

- **Rustup tool**: The Rustup tool is the Rust installer. It also installs the toolchain. You can download the Rust installer at https://rustup.rs. Follow the directions there to successfully install Rust.
- **Cargo tool**: Cargo is a multipurpose tool with package manager as the primary role. Ancillary services include compiling code, formatting source code, and creating new crates.

Here is a Cargo statement that creates a library crate:

```
cargo new --lib mylib
```

- **Rustc tool**: Rustc is the Rust compiler. Rustc can compile a Rust source file (.rs) into an executable or library binary.

    Here is the Rustc statement to build a simple crate:

```
$ rustc source.rs
```

- **Rustdoc tool**: The Rustdoc tool compiles document comments embedded in a Rust source file into a help document, rendered in HTML.
- **Clippy tool**: Clippy is a comprehensive testing tool consisting of several lints. The tool identifies common problems and best practices that can benefit your code.
- **Rustfmt tool**: The Rustfmt tool reformats source files to adhere to the style guidelines for Rust.

Cargo is the pivotal tool in the Rust environment. You can use Cargo for many of the tasks required to maintain your environment and packages.

A Note About Security

In the security-conscious world in which we now exist, secure coding practices are an imperative. Few applications are immune to security considerations. In the modern era of computing, applications exist everywhere, including mobile devices, IoT devices, wearables, enterprises, and the cloud. This increases the potential impact of a security failure.

Rust provides a safe coding environment that reduces the attack surface, making development in the language inherently more secure. There are fewer vulnerabilities for cyber attackers to identify and possibly exploit.

Summary

This chapter introduced the software paradigms associated with Rust and many of its notable features.

The availability of the various paradigms provides flexibility and a *best-of-all-worlds* approach. The following Rust features complement the various programming models and define the important attributes of the language:

- Safeness
- Ownership
- Lifetimes
- Trustworthy concurrency
- Zero-cost abstraction

You now have a foundation in Rust, including its toolchain. In the next chapter, you will complete your first Rust application and further explore important tools, such Rustc and Cargo.

2

Getting Started

This chapter introduces the core concepts required to create, compile, and run Rust executables and libraries. This includes completing your first Rust application—the illustrious "Hello, World" application. When learning a programming language, this application is often the first example. It is a great tool for learning a new programming language. The first documented example of this familiar application is found in the book *The C Programming Language* from Brian Kernighan and Dennis Ritchie back in 1972. Who are we to break tradition?

Several variations of the "Hello, World" application will be presented here while we explore different "getting started" topics.

We will also continue exploring the Rust toolchain in this chapter. Knowledge of the tools in the toolchain, such as Cargo and Rustc, is essential to productive interaction with the Rust environment. For this reason, components of the toolchain are introduced here.

Preliminaries

Before we create our first application, Rust must be installed. Rustup is the Rust installer and toolchain manager. Rustup manages the proper installation for specific platforms.

By default, Rustup installs the latest stable build, also called a channel. At the moment, Rust is on a six-week release cycle. The upcoming release schedule is published at Rust Forge (https://forge.rust-lang.org/). The following are the three available channels:

- **Stable**: The latest release
- **Beta**: The next version available with the upcoming release
- **Nightly**: The nightly build, which includes experimental features

You can also request that Rustup install specific versions of the Rust environment. This is especially useful if your organization has not upgraded to the latest release.

Different methods are available to install Rust. Each requires a different level of user involvement, from minimal to moderate. For a standard installation, choose a minimal approach. However, more involvement is required if you want to customize the installation.

Rust and Windows

When installed on the Windows platform, Rust requires the Microsoft C++ Build Tools from a recent version of Microsoft Visual Studio. Linux developers are fortunate and can simply skip this step. If Visual Studio is installed, you may already have the Build Tools. The availability of these tools can be confirmed with the Microsoft Visual C++ Redistributable.

If necessary, follow the instructions here to install the Visual C++ Build Tools:

https://visualstudio.microsoft.com/visual-cpp-build-tools/

You are now ready to install the Rust language.

Installing Rust

The most straightforward approach to installing the Rust language and toolchain is to visit the Rustup website. This is the minimal approach for a quick install of the standard Rust environment. You are presented with minimal options and documentation. Here is the web location:

https://rustup.rs

Alternatively, visit the Install Rust web page for more documentation and options, such as selecting either a 32-bit or 64-bit installation. Here is the location of the Install Rust page:

www.rust-lang.org/tools/install

For even more details, visit the Rust Getting Started page. This page documents how to install Rust, with some options, and it provides some helpful "getting started" commands for the Cargo tool, the Rust build tool and package manager. The bottom of the web page lists various editors and integrated development environments (IDEs) available to Rust developers:

www.rust-lang.org/learn/get-started

Rustup installs the Rust toolchain locally in these directories:

- **Windows**: \users\{*user*}\.cargo\bin
- **Linux**: *home*/.cargo/bin
- **macOS**: /users/{*user*}/.cargo/bin

A great practice is to *trust but verify*. This would include your Rust installation. This is easily accomplished with either the `rustc` or the `cargo` tool, both included in the newly installed Rust toolchain. From an operating system command line, enter these commands:

```
rustc --version
cargo --version
```

The proper response is the current version of these tools:

```
$ cargo --version
  cargo 0.00.0 (a748cf5a3 0000-00-00)

$ rustc --version
  rustc 0.00.0 (a8314ef7d 0000-00-00)
```

If either command returns an error, the implication is that Rust is not properly installed or the environment variables are not set correctly.

Advanced Rustup

As demonstrated, `rustup` is an excellent tool for the general installation of Rust. It can also install a specific version of the Rust environment. This could be advantageous for various reasons, such as product requirements, reproducing problems found in older builds, or maybe developing on a code branch based from an earlier version of Rust. The `rustup install version` command installs the indicated version of Rust. For example, Rust 1.34.2 is a version from way back in 2019. Assuming this version is required for some reason, `rustup` can install that specific version, as follows:

```
$ rustup install 1.34.2
```

You can also install Rust from one of three channels, as mentioned earlier. The default channel is the stable release. Here is the syntax for Rustup to install Rust from one of the channels.

```
$ rustup
$ rustup install beta
$ rustup install nightly
```

After installation, you can use the `rustup self uninstall` command to uninstall the Rust environment.

Now that Rust is installed, it's time for our "Hello, World" application.

"Hello, World"

Listing 2.1 shows the "Hello, World" application. Without a transfer control statement, it runs sequentially, displays the text "Hello, world!", and then exits.

Code Listing 2.1. The "Hello, World" program

```
fn main() {
    println!( "Hello, world!");
}
```

Let's examine the program.

First of all, the source code for the executable crate is saved in a file with an .rs extension, such as hello.rs. This is the standard extension for Rust source files.

Functions in Rust are preceded with the `fn` keyword. The function name, parameters, and return value follow, if any. Here is the syntax of a function:

```
fn  func_name(parameters)->returnval
```

Snake case is the naming convention for functions in Rust. For this convention, each word of the function name starts with a lowercase letter and individual words are separated with underscores.

The `main` function is the entry point function for a Rust executable crate and the starting point of the application. In Rust, our `main` function has no function parameters or explicit return value.

Code for a function is encapsulated within curly braces, {}, which demarcates a function block. For the `main` function, the program concludes at the end of the `main` function block. It is the primary thread for the application.

In the `main` function, the `println!` macro displays the "Hello, world!" message and a line-feed. Function blocks can contain expressions, statements, and the macro. Macros in Rust have an exclamation point (!) after the name. In most instances, expressions and statements are terminated with semicolons.

Compile and Run

Rust is an ahead-of-time compiled language where a crate compiles to a true binary, not an intermediate language requiring a virtual machine for execution. Rust is not a managed language. Once compiled, Rust binaries can probably execute anywhere else, even where Rust is not installed.

As stated earlier, `rustc` is the Rust compiler and is included in the Rust toolchain. It is installed by default with the remainder of the toolchain. `rustc` can build different types of binaries, depending on the platform. For Linux, the binary format is Linkable Format (ELF file). `rustc` can also create portable executables (PEs) when building a binary for the Windows platform.

Here, the `rustc` tool compiles the "Hello, World" crate to an executable binary:

```
rustc hello.rs
```

When the executable crate is compiled, two files are generated:

- *cratename*.**exe**: This is the executable binary.
- *cratename*.**pdb**: This PDB (program database) contains metadata about the binary, such as symbolic names and source line information. Debuggers, such as GDB, read this PDB file to present user-friendly diagnostics information to developers.

From the hello.rs source file, `rustc` creates the hello.exe and hello.pdb files.

The `rustc` compiler is talkative, providing verbose warnings and error messages. References may also be provided for more detail. Here is the compiler error message displayed when the `println!` macro is improperly used without the obligatory exclamation point:

```
error[E0423]: expected function, found macro `print`
 --> hello.rs:2:2
  |
2 |     println("Hello, world!");
  |     ^^^^^^ not a function
  |
```

```
help: use `!` to invoke the macro
   |
2  |     print!("Hello, world!");
   |          +

error: aborting due to previous error

For more information about this error, try `rustc --explain E0423`.
```

Despite the talkativeness of the Rust compiler, it is simply impractical at times to display all relevant error information during compilation. When this occurs, an error identifier is provided. Using the `rustc --explain` *erroridentifier* command, you can display additional error information. The additional information entails a detailed explanation of the error, suggestions on correcting the problem, sample code, and more.

Cargo

You can use the `cargo` tool to compile Rust crates and create binaries. This is in lieu of using the `rustc` compiler directly. `cargo` is a versatile tool that can perform various tasks, including creating and managing packages, compiling binaries, maintaining a secure environment, and managing dependencies. For compilation, `cargo` delegates to the `rustc` compiler.

Because of the flexibility of this tool, Rustaceans often prefer `cargo`, instead of `rustc`, for compilation. In addition, this means learning only one command-line interface instead of two. Since most Rustaceans are probably using `cargo` already for something, such as creating new packages, it is simpler not to switch to a different tool. Keep in mind, though, that the `rustc` tool will continue to be used, just indirectly.

The `cargo new` command, shown next, creates a new package for either an executable or library crate. The default is an executable crate. A library crate can be created with the `--lib` option.

```
cargo new name
```

The `cargo new` command also creates a directory structure for the new package. Initially, this includes a root directory and src subdirectory. The tool will add more directories as needed. In the root directory are two files: .gitignore and cargo.toml. Either the main.rs or lib.rs crate is placed in the src subdirectory, depending on whether this is an executable or library package, respectively.

You can also create a package within an existing directory. From that directory, issue the following command, and a package is created at that location:

```
cargo init
```

The .gitignore file lists directories and files excluded from GitHub. This initially includes the target subdirectory, which contains the compiled binaries, and the cargo.lock file.

Cargo.toml is the manifest and configuration file for the package. The TOML suffix is a reference to Tom's Obvious Minimal Language and is a standard format for a readable configuration file. Cargo.toml contains important configuration details about the package, including the name of the package. The `cargo new` command creates the initial cargo.toml, as shown in Listing 2.2.

Code Listing 2.2.   Sample cargo.toml file

```
[package]
name = "packagename"
version = "0.1.0"
edition = "2021"

# See more keys and their definitions at https://doc.rust-
          lang.org/cargo/reference/manifest.html

[dependencies]
```

Within the cargo.toml file, the following information is presented:

- **name**: The package name is derived from the `cargo new` command.
- **version**: The three-part semantic version (major.minor.patch).
- **edition**: The current Rust language edition.
- **dependency**: Dependencies are documented within this section.
- **comments**: The # character indicates a comment to the end of the line.

The `cargo new` command creates the cargo.toml file. Information can be inserted manually in the TOML file, such as license information, a brief description, and the location of the documentation.

In addition to the cargo.toml file, the `cargo new` command creates a source file in the src subdirectory. For an executable crate, this is the main.rs file that contains sample code for a "Hello, World" application. Of course, feel free to replace this with your actual code. Listing 2.3 shows the main.rs file generated by the cargo tool.

Code Listing 2.3.   Source file generated by the Cargo tool

```
fn main() {
    println!("Hello, world!");
}
```

You can compile the crate with the following command and create a binary executable:

```
cargo build
```

This command must be executed from within the package. The `cargo build` command performs an incremental build. Changes to the crate, modifying the dependencies in cargo. toml, and other reasons may force a full build instead of an incremental one.

The `cargo build` command creates a *packageroot*/target directory. Within that directory, a debug or release directory is created, depending on the type of the build target for the binary. The `cargo build` command defaults to building a debug target. A debug binary has few, if any, optimizations, which is ideal for debugging. The release binary is most often optimized for either performance or size. The `cargo build --release` command creates a release binary that is placed in the release directory.

You can run an executable crate with the following command:

```
cargo run
```

This must also be done from within the package. If the binary is not already built, `cargo build` will be done first. For this reason, some skip the separate build step entirely for executable crates and rely entirely on the `cargo run` command.

Library

When you use `cargo` to create a library, the primary difference is the creation of a lib.rs file, instead of main.rs and a "Hello, World" application. The lib.rs file contains sample code within a function that performs a trivial mathematical operation. All of this occurs within the context of a unit test. The following command creates a new package with a library crate:

```
cargo new --lib packagename
```

Unlike executable binaries, libraries are not self-executing. Placing the source code for the library within a unit test provides a mechanism for executing that code. You can execute the library crate with the following command:

```
cargo test
```

This command will run unit tests in the crate. For lib.rs, this provides the opportunity to execute and test the source code in the library. As a result, the `cargo test` command displays whether the unit test passed or failed.

Listing 2.4 shows the lib.rs that `cargo` creates, with sample code.

Code Listing 2.4.   Cargo-generated lib.rs file.pub

```rust
fn add(left: usize, right: usize) -> usize {
    left + right
}

#[cfg(test)]
mod tests {
    use super::*;

    #[test]
    fn it_works() {
        let result = add(2, 2);
        assert_eq!(result, 4);
    }
}
```

Let's explore the lib.rs crate. The file starts with the #[cfg(test)] annotation. This annotation asks the cargo build command to ignore unit tests and not to include them in the resulting binary. Within the file, each unit test is labeled with the #[test] annotation. The sample unit test performs a simple addition. The result of the operation is compared to the expected value within the assert_eq! macro. You update the code in the unit tests to reference the specific public functions of your library. There should be a unit test for each public function in the library.

Listing 2.5 provides an example of a library crate with two functions. The get_hello function is public and returns the "Hello, world!" string. The test_get_hello function is a unit test and tests the get_hello function.

Code Listing 2.5.   Example unit test and target function.pub

```
fn get_hello()->String {
    "Hello, world!".to_string()
}

#[cfg(test)]
mod tests {
    #[test]
    fn test_get_hello() {
        let result = get_hello();
        assert_eq!(result, "Hello, world!");
    }
}
```

You may want to create an executable crate that uses the library. The cargo.toml file for the executable must be updated to reference the library. Listing 2.6 shows the updated cargo.toml that references a local version of the hello library in the dependency section. The change in the file is highlighted in bold.

Code Listing 2.6.   Updated cargo.toml with hello dependency

```
[package]
name = "use_hello"
version = "0.1.0"
edition = "2021"

# See more keys and their definitions at https://doc.rust-lang.org/cargo/reference/
  manifest.html

[dependencies]
hello={path = "../hello" }
```

With the preceding cargo.toml file, the executable crate can access the public functions of the library. The syntax for accessing functions in the library is *libraryname*::*function*. The code in Listing 2.7 calls the get_hello function found in the hello library.

Code Listing 2.7.   Calling `get_hello` in the hello library

```
fn main() {
    println!("{}", hello::get_hello());
}
```

You can now use the `cargo run` command to run the executable crate and display the "Hello, world!" string.

Comments

So far, the source code in this chapter has not contained comments. Comments appear in source code for a variety of reasons, including identifying the author, highlighting license information, documenting functions, explaining complex algorithms, or simply providing important context.

Rust supports C-style comments. The `//` characters start a comment until the end of the line. You can frame multiline comments within the `/*` and `*/` characters.

In Listing 2.8, comments are added to the "Hello, World" source code to identify the author, source file, and the purpose of the application. Both multiline and single-line comments are shown.

Code Listing 2.8.   "Hello, World" program with comments

```
/*  Author: Donis Marshall
    Hello.rs
    Hello, World program
*/

// Displays hello, world message
fn main(){
    println!("Hello, world!");
}
```

Rust also supports documentation comments. Documentation comments are compiled into an HTML page using the `rustdoc` tool. This tool is automatically included in the Rust tool-chain. Compiling the documentation comments creates several HTML files in the {package}/target/doc/{package} directory. The main HTML file is index.html and can be opened in any browser.

For documentation, there are single-line comments and multiline comments—both support markdown. Single-line documentation comments use the `///` characters. Multiline documentation comments are enclosed within the `/**` and `**/` characters. Documentation comments apply to the next entity in the source file, such as a struct or function.

Let's look at another version of the "Hello, World" application—as a library crate. This library exposes a `hello_world` function that returns a greeting in various languages. The function accepts a parameter that selects a specific language, using the major-minor language code, for displaying "Hello, world!" Listing 2.9 shows the function with documentation comments.

Code Listing 2.9.   **Multilingual "Hello, World" program with comments**

```
/** Display hello based on the
     language (major.MINOR) provided.
     Languages support: enUS, enUK,
     frFR, and hiIN.
**/
pub fn hello_world(language:&str)->&'static str {
    match language {
        "enUS"=>"Hello, world!",
        "enUK"=>"Good day, world!",
        "frFR"=>"Bonjour le monde!",
        "hiIN"=>"नमस्ते दुनिया!",
        _=>"Hello, world!"
    }
}
```

The `//!` characters precede documentation comments that apply to the parent entity, instead of the next. This is most often the current crate. Here is documentation for the hello library crate with markup included:

- The markup highlights the first line in bold:

    ```
    //! <b>Hello library crate</b>
    ```

- The paragraph tags insert linefeeds:

    ```
    //! <p>Author: Donis Marshall
    //! <p>Apache 2.0 License
    ```

You can also add sample code to your documentation comments. This can provide invaluable guidance to users of the application. The sample code within documentation code can also be executed as unit tests. Place the sample code in the Examples section. Sections are designated with the `///` # characters. Notice there is a space between `///` and #. Bracket the code snippet with three backticks (`///` ```) before and after. Listing 2.10 shows the sample code.

Code Listing 2.10.   **Sample code within documentation comments**

```
/// # Examples
///
/// ```
/// let greeting=hello::hello_world("hiIN");
/// ```assert_eq!(greeting, "नमस्ते दुनिया!");
/// ```
///
```

The `cargo test` command will execute both normal and documentation unit tests. In addition, the following command compiles documentation comments using the `rustdoc` tool, generating the index.html file and other related files:

```
cargo doc
```

Figure 2.1 shows the index.html file in the browser from compiling the previously shown documentation comments.

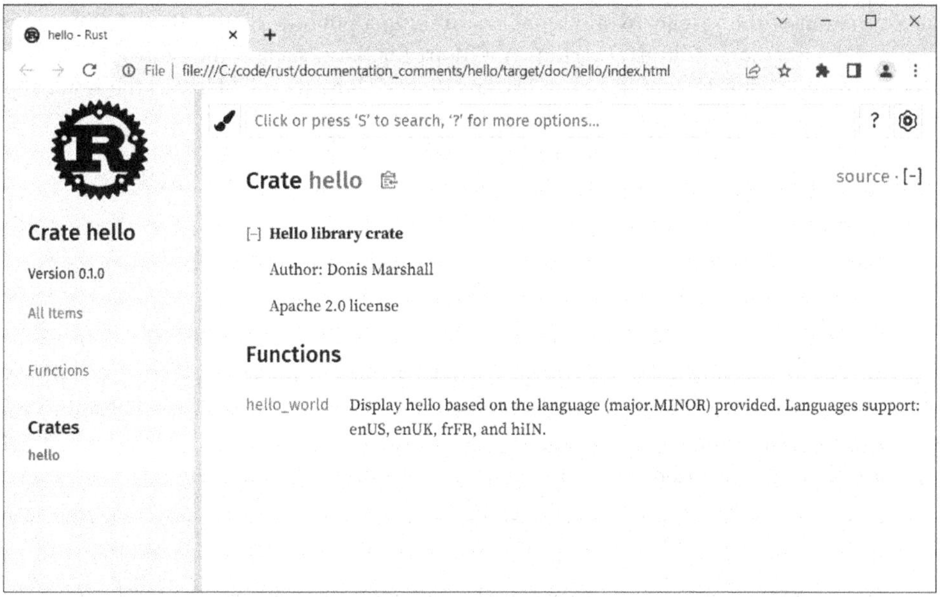

Figure 2.1.   Index.html file result from compiling documentation comments

Figure 2.2 shows the documentation comments for the `hello_world` function.

Figure 2.2.   Documentation comments for the `hello_world` function

Published Crates

Several approaches to creating a "Hello, World" application have been shown. Next, we will create a variation of the "Hello, World" application using a published crate. Rustascii is a public crate found in crates.io and displays various ASCII art for Rust, such as the Rust logo. The `display_rust_ascii` function of this crate displays "Hello, Rustaceans!" Here is the result of the function:

```
   ____                         __
  / __ \__   _____/ /_
 / /_/ / / / / / / / ___/ __/
/ _, _/ /_/ (__  ) /_
/_/ |_|\__,_/____/\__/
Hello, Rustaceans!
```

You must first locate the rustascii crate in the crates.io repository. Fortunately, crates.io has a search feature at the top of the page. Searching for rustascii will locate the latest version of the crate. When the crate is found, a brief description, current version number, and other helpful information about the published crate are provided, as shown in Figure 2.3.

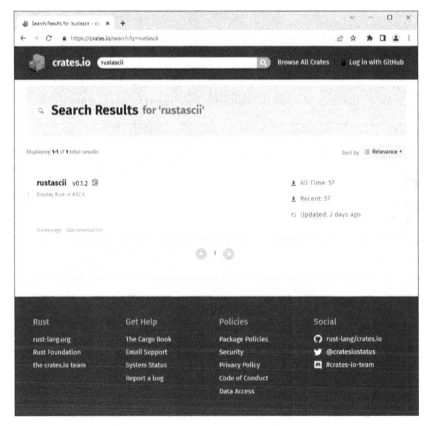

Figure 2.3.   The rustascii crate in the crates.io repository

In a package using an external crate, you need to update cargo.toml to reference the crate. You should enter the name and version of the crate in the `dependencies` section. Find the icon for a clipboard within the rustascii page in crates.io. Select the clipboard to copy the dependency information identifying the current version of the rustascii crate. Finally, paste that information into the `dependencies` section of the cargo.toml file, as highlighted in Listing 2.11.

Code Listing 2.11.   Cargo.toml file that includes a rustascii dependency

```
[package]
name = "use_rust_ascii"
version = "0.1.0"
edition = "2021"

# See more keys and their definitions at https://doc.rust-lang.org/cargo/reference/
  manifest.html

[dependencies]

rustascii = "0.1.1"
```

After updating the cargo.toml file, call the `display_rust_ascii` function in the rustascii crate using the `::` operator. The syntax is *crate::function*. Listing 2.12 shows sample code in an executable crate.

Code Listing 2.12.   Displaying "Rust" in ASCII art

```
fn main() {
    rustascii::display_rust_ascii();
}
```

When executed, this crate calls the `display_rust_ascii` function in the rustascii crate to display the greeting.

Main Function

The `main` function is the entry point function for executable crates. Execution starts at this function. The `main` function prototype has no parameters and returns either a unit or the Termination trait. In Rust, a unit is an empty tuple, which is `()`. This is the default return.

From the `main` function, you can return an integer value to the operating system using the Termination trait. The default implementation of the trait returns `libc::EXIT_SUCCESS` or `libc::EXIT_FAILURE` as an exit code. These values are most likely 1 and 0, but that is implementation specific.

Instead of returning from `main`, you can call the `exit` function (`std::process::exit`) to prematurely exit an application. However, the `exit` function immediately terminates the application without performing cleanup for the functions currently on the call stack, possibly preventing an orderly shutdown. The parameter of the `exit` function sets the process return value for the operating system.

Command-Line Arguments

Command-line arguments are sometimes used to affect application initialization, configuration, or flow control. This is an often-used technique to receive direction from a user. Entered at the command line, the arguments form a zero-based collection of values. The full path of the application itself is usually provided as the first command-line argument. The details about command-line arguments may vary between different environments. Be sure to review the specific documentation for a particular operating system.

The following command line has three arguments:

```
myapp arg1 arg2
```

For the `cargo run` command, append the command-line arguments. The first argument, which is the full name of the application, is set implicitly. Therefore, arg1 and arg2 of this example are actually the second and third command-line arguments from perspective of the application:

```
cargo run arg1 arg2
```

Command-line arguments are provided as input to the `main` function in many languages. However, the `main` function in Rust has no parameters. Command-line arguments are instead read programmatically using the `std::env::args` function, which is found in the `std::env` module. The `args` function returns an iterator to the sequence of command-line arguments. Furthermore, iterator functions, such as the `nth` and `collect` functions, are available to access the command-line arguments. The `nth` function returns a specific command-line argument, if available. The `collect` function returns the arguments as a collection.

Listing 2.13 demonstrates various ways to access the command-line arguments.

Code Listing 2.13. **Various approaches to accessing command-line arguments**

```
fn main() {
    // display arg 0
    if let Some(arg)=std::env::args().nth(0) {
        println!("{}", arg);
    }

    // iterate and display args
    for arg in std::env::args() {
        println!("{}", arg);
    }

    // collect and display args
    let all_arg: String=std::env::args().collect();
    println!("{}", all_arg);
}
```

Summary

Beginning with how to install Rust, this chapter provided the foundation for Rust programming that will underpin the remainder of this book. We will continuously build upon the base established here. Many of the concepts introduced, such as traits, dependency management, iterators, and more, will be revisited later in the book with extra layers of details.

Tools explored, such as `rustc`, `rustdoc`, and `cargo`, are the everyday ingredients of the Rust environment. These are tools that must be fully understood to effectively navigate Rust. You now understand how to accomplish the standard repertoire of tasks using these tools.

Crates.io expands the capabilities of Rust programming. The crates found in the repository often provide unique solutions. As importantly, the repository grows every day with new solutions and capabilities. Anyone in the Rust community can contribute a crate to the crates.io repository. This includes you!

Next, we will explore the Rust type system. Until you have a better understanding of the type safeness and immutability and the various types available in Rust, your applications will be limited in scope and functionality.

3

Variables

For a programming language, the type system encompasses the available types with their features and characteristics. Of course, the Rust type system has some unique characteristics that further the overall objective of the language: safeness, security, and scalability.

The type system impacts every aspect of the programming language. Mutability, for example, has a broad impact on the language. The type system is the thread that binds an application. For that reason, it is essential to have a thorough understanding of the sweeping type system in Rust.

Rust is a strongly typed language. As such, variables are statically typed. The variable's type is determined at declaration and cannot be changed afterwards. Even with type inference, a variable is assigned an inferred type, which will never change. This avoids the type of problems common to languages with weak typed systems, including errors from the misuse of variables. Also, Rust is more flexible at inferring the correct type than other languages, including indirect inferences.

Immutability is the default in Rust and contributes to the safeness and security of the language. By default, variables are immutable. This prevents inadvertent changes and increases transparency.

Rust provides a full complement of standard types and operators. In addition, you can create custom types or aggregate types for modeling more complex problems. You could model an accounting system, a blockchain, or even the space shuttle!

Another benefit of the Rust type system is the wide variety of type sizes. These help developers efficiently manage memory utilization, especially in applications where every bit matters.

Terminology

The terms *type*, *variable*, and *memory* are related and frequently appear in this chapter. Actually, these terms have been mentioned a few times already. Memory is where data resides. Variables are named memory storage, and they remove the need to reference data using memory addresses. Symbolic names are much easier to remember! Memory has no intrinsic format. A type describes the memory layout of a value, such as an integer or float value.

Variable binding is another important term in the Rust type system. A declaration, such as the `let` statement, creates a binding between the variable name and a memory location. Put another way, memory locations are bound to variables. Rust supports flexible binding. A full exploration of binding is found in Chapter 15, "Patterns."

Variables

Variables resolve to a memory address that identifies a specific memory location. The variable name is more descriptive and consistent than a raw memory address. This is not only helpful when coding but invaluable when maintaining or debugging an application. When you're writing self-documenting code, descriptive names are essential as variable names.

The following are the rules and naming conventions for variable names:

- They are case-sensitive.
- They consist of alphanumeric characters and underscore.
- They cannot start with a number.
- The naming convention is snake case.

You can declare a nonstatic local variable with the `let` statement. The type for the variable is set explicitly within the `let` statement or via type inference. Either way, the variable is statically typed. You can initialize the variable with the `let` statement or later. However, variables must be initialized before using them in some manner.

Here are different syntaxes for declaring an immutable variable:

```
let varname:type=value;
let varname=value;
let varname:type;
let varname;
```

Listing 3.1 provides examples of various declarations.

Code Listing 3.1. Example variable declarations

```
let var1: i8 = 10;   //  full declaration
let var2 = 11;       //  type inference
let var3: i8;        //  uninitialized variable
let var4;            //  type inference and uninitialized
var3 = 12;           //  delayed initialization
var4 = 13;           //  delayed initialization
```

Primitives

Primitives are the basic types and the building blocks of Rust. You can combine primitives to create more complex types, such as structs and enums. Primitives are intrinsic and implemented by the Rust compiler. Functions and attributes of the primitives are implemented in Rust libraries. For example, i32::MAX is an associated constant implemented for the i32 primitive.

Rust has both scalar and nonscalar primitives. Scalar primitives include the following types:

- signed integer
- unsigned integer
- float
- bool
- reference

Nonscalar primitives include the following:

- array
- tuple
- slice
- String
- str

Other primitive types include these:

- (): unit type
- fn: function pointer types
- raw pointer

In this chapter, we will review scalar primitive types. Other primitives, such as strings and arrays, are reviewed in later chapters.

Integer Types

Except for isize and usize, integer types are fixed sized, where the suffix of the type name defines the bit size. For example, i64 is a signed 64-bit integer.

The following are the signed integer types:

- isize
- i8
- i16
- i32
- i64
- i128

These are the unsigned integer types:

- usize
- u8
- u16
- u32
- u64
- u128

The size of the isize and usize types depends on the operating environment. It is the size of a pointer. If curious, you can confirm the size of any type with the `size_of` method function, as shown in Listing 3.2. This method is found in the `std::mem` module.

Code Listing 3.2.   Confirming the size of isize

```
let size = mem::size_of::<isize>();
println!("Size of isize: {}", size);
```

If inferred, the default type of signed integers is i32. For unsigned integers, the default type is u32. Listing 3.3 displays the default type of an inferred integer value. This code introduces several new topics, including generics, introspection, and the any type. All of this explained in more detail in later chapters.

Code Listing 3.3.   The `print_type_of` function displays the type of parameter.

```
fn print_type_of<T>(_: &T) {
    println!("{}", std::any::type_name::<T>())      // i32
}

fn main() {
    let value=1;                      // inferred typed
    print_type_of(&value);
}
```

For increased readability, underscores can be inserted as separators within numeric literals, for both integer and floating point values. Typically, underscores demarcate 10^3 segments. However, Rust is not the underscore police. You can place the underscore anywhere within a number, as demonstrated in Listing 3.4.

Code Listing 3.4.   Adding underscores to numbers as separators

```
let typical1=123_456_678;
let typical2=123_456.67;
let interesting=12_3_456;
```

Overflow

An integer overflow or underflow occurs when the minimum or maximum value of an integral type is exceeded. Generally speaking, both are considered overflows. When an overflow occurs, the result is dependent upon whether the binary is a debug or release build. If it's a debug build, a panic will occur when there is an overflow. Panics are exceptional events that can interrupt an application if unhandled. However, a panic does not occur when an overflow occurs within a release build. The overflow rotates the number from the maximum value to the minimum, or vice versa. In Listing 3.5, the number rotates from a maximum i8 value, 127, to a minimum i8 value, −128, when there is an overflow.

Code Listing 3.5.   Causing an overflow

```
let mut number = i8::MAX;
    number = number + 1;        // overflow  result=-128
```

An underflow is similar, except it rotates in the other direction, from −128 to 127, as shown in Listing 3.6.

Code Listing 3.6.   Causing an underflow

```
    let mut number = i8::MIN;
    number = number - 1;        // underflow result=127
```

The inconsistent results of an overflow, build versus release, can cause problems. The overflowing_add function provides an alternative with consistent results. With this function, the result is the same regardless of the build target. The overflowing_add function performs addition and returns a tuple as the result, which contains the result and the overflow status. If an overflow occurs, the overflow status is set to true. Listing 3.7 provides an example of using the overflowing_add function.

Code Listing 3.7.   Checking for an overflow with the overflowing_add function

```
let value = i8::MAX;
let result = value.overflowing_add(1); // (127, true)
```

The overflowing_sub function detects underflows. There are also other variations, such as overflowing_mul, overflowing_div, and overflowing_pow—each appropriately named.

Notations

Base 10 is the default base for integer values. You can change the base with the proper notation:

- 0b for binary
- 0o for octal
- 0x for hexadecimal

Listing 3.8 provides some sample code.

Code Listing 3.8.   Various base notations

```
println!("{}", 10);          // 10
println!("{:04b}", 0b10);    // 0010
println!("{}", 0o12);        // 10
println!("{}", 0xA);         // 10
```

Floating Point Types

For real numbers, Rust has single- and double-precision primitive types that adhere to the IEEE 754 specification. Each type consists of a sign, exponent, and mantissa component. The f32 type is for single-precision numbers that are 32 bits wide. The f64 type represents double-precision numbers that are 64 bits wide. For type inference, the default floating point type is f64.

Unlike integral types, floating point types, or floats, are always signed. Listing 3.9 is a floating point example.

Code Listing 3.9.   Floating point example

```
use std::f64::consts;

fn main() {
    let radius=4.234;
    let diameter=2.0*radius;
    let area=consts::PI*radius;

    println!("{} {} {}", radius, diameter, area);
}
```

Neither float types, f32 or f64, are ideal for fixed-point numbers. This is especially true for currency values where exact precision is important. Lost dollars and pennies can add up! The Decimal type, found in the rust_decimal crate, is a great type for fixed-point floating point numbers. You can find the rust_decimal crate in the crates.io repository. Create a Decimal number with the from_str constructor or the dec! macro, as shown in Listing 3.10.

Code Listing 3.10.   Creating a decimal

```
use rust_decimal::prelude::*;
use rust_decimal_macros::dec;

fn main() {
    let mut number1 = Decimal::from_str("-1.23656").unwrap();
    let mut number2 = dec!(-1.23656);     // alternative

    // round up value to 2 decimal places
    number = number1.round_dp(2);
    println!("{}", number);
}
```

Floating Point Constants

Well-known floating point constants are available for your convenience. The constants are implemented as f64 primitives in the std::f64::consts module. Table 3.1 is a list of some f64 constants.

Table 3.1. List of some f64 Constants

Name	Description	Value
E	Euler's number	2.7182818284590451f64
FRAC_1_PI	1/π	0.31830988618379069f64
FRAC_1_SQRT_2	1/sqrt(2)	0.70710678118654757f64
FRAC_2_PI	2/π	0.70710678118654757f64
FRAC_2_SQRT_2	2/sqrt(2)	1.1283791670955126f64
LN_10	ln(10)	2.3025850929940459f64
LOG10_2	Log10(2)	0.30102999566398127f64
PI	π	3.1415926535897931f64
SQRT_2	sqrt(2)	1.4142135623730951f64
TUA	2π	6.2831853071795862f64

Infinity

Rust supports 32-bit and 64-bit versions of infinity and negative infinity. INFINITY and NEG_INFINITY are const values found in either the `std::f32` or `std::f64` module. Here are two examples:

```
let space:f32=f32::INFINITY;
let stars:f64=f64::INFINITY;
```

Listing 3.11 shows sample code that leverages the INFINITY constant.

Code Listing 3.11.   Example of the INFINITY const

```
let circle_radius=10.0;
let pointw=0.0;
let number_of_points=circle_radius/pointw;
if number_of_points==f64::INFINITY {
    // Do something
} else {
    // Do something else
}
```

NaN

Not a Number (`NaN`) represents a numerically undefined or unknown result. This is sometimes the result of formulas that involve an INFINITY value. The square root of a negative number can also result in `NaN`, as shown in Listing 3.12.

Code Listing 3.12.   Using the NaN const

```
let n=0.0;
let result=f64::sqrt(n);
if f64::NAN!=result {
    // handle proper result
} else {
    // handle NAN
}
```

Numeric Ranges

Type sizes in Rust are more discrete than in some other languages. This enables developers to craft applications that are more efficient and specific to their requirements. Table 3.2 shows the minimum and maximum boundaries for signed integer types.

Table 3.2.   Range of Values for Signed Integer Types

Type	Size	Range
i8	8-bit	–128 to 127
i16	16-bit	–32768 to 32767
i32	32-bit	–2147483648 to 2147483647
i64	64-bit	–9223372036854775808 to 9223372036854775807
i128	128-bit	–170141183460469231731687303715884105728 to 170141183460469231731687303715884105727
isize	Pointer sized	Architecture dependent

Table 3.3 presents the range of values for unsigned integer types.

Table 3.3.   Range of Values for Unsigned Integer Types

Type	Size	Range
u8	8-bit	0 to 255
u16	16-bit	0 to 65535
u32	32-bit	0 to 4294967295
u64	64-bit	0 to 18446744073709551615
u128	128-bit	0 to 340282366920938463463374607431768211455
Usize	Pointer sized	Architecture dependent

Table 3.4 lists the range of values for the float types.

Table 3.4.   Range of Values for Floating Point Types

Type	Size	Range (Approximate)
f32	32-bit	-3.4×10^{38} to 3.4×10^{38}
f64	64-bit	-1.8×10^{308} to 1.8×10^{308}

For bounds checking at runtime, MIN and MAX are associated constants that return the minimum and maximum values, respectively, of specific types. Listing 3.13 provides an example.

Code Listing 3.13.   Displaying the MIN and MAX const values

```
println!("{} {}", u32::MIN, u32::MAX);
println!("{} {}", f32::MIN, f32::MAX);
```

Casting

You can cast a value, variable or literal, from its current type to another type. Rust does not provide wide support for implicit casting. Many languages allow implicit casting when no precision is lost. However, Rust requires explicit casting even in this circumstance. Listing 3.14 provides an example of casting.

Code Listing 3.14.   Casting between types

```
let var1=1 as char;
let var2:f32=123.45;
let var3=var2 as f64;
let var4=1.23 as u8 as char;
```

The preceding code contains a double cast, which is allowed. Because you cannot cast a floating point value directly to a char value in the example, the floating point value is first cast to an unsigned integer. The unsigned integer is then cast to a char.

When casting from a floating point value to an integer, the decimal portion of the floating point number is truncated.

Numeric literals can be explicitly cast with type suffixes. The specification is *valueType*, where *value* is a numeric literal and *Type* is the full type name, such as i32, u32, f64, and so on, as shown next. Note that single-letter suffixes, common to other languages, are not supported in Rust. The approach in Rust is more descriptive.

```
let val1=10i8;
let val2=20f64;
```

Boolean Types

The Boolean type in Rust is bool and represents logical values. The acceptable values for a bool type are true and false. Here's an example:

```
let condition:bool=true;
```

Internally, bool values are bitwise values 0x01 for true and 0x00 for false. You can cast bool values to i8 types. True becomes 1, while false becomes 0.

Bool values are often used within if keyword, as shown in Listing 3.15.

Code Listing 3.15.   Control path set with a boolean value

```
let balance=20;
let overdrawn:bool=balance < 0;
if overdrawn {
    println!("Balance: Overdrawn {}", balance,);
} else {
    println!("Balance is {}", balance,);
}
```

Char

The char type is for individual characters. This is a Unicode character, Unicode Scalar Value (USV), with UTF-8 encoding. Furthermore, char values are 4 bytes in size and a code point in the Unicode table. This includes alphanumeric characters, escape characters, symbols, and even emojis. Yes, Unicode now has smiley faces! Unicode has a code point for each character in the various writing systems around the world, providing support for internationalization. ASCII is at the beginning of the Unicode table.

Listing 3.16 shows how to define a literal char value within apostrophes.

Code Listing 3.16.   Literal values

```
let var1='a';
let var2:char='b';
```

Assuming a proper Unicode value, you can cast between an integer and char type, as shown in Listing 3.17.

Code Listing 3.17.   Casting literal values

```
let var1=65 as char;      // 'A'
let var2='A' as i32;      // 65
```

Unicode supports various escape characters. Many of these are otherwise hidden characters, such as a newline or tab character. Table 3.5 presents each of the escape characters.

Table 3.5.   Escape Characters

Escape	Type	Description
\n	ASCII	Newline
\r	ASCII	Carriage return
\t	ASCII	Tab
\0	ASCII	Null
\\	ASCII	Backslash
\x{nn}	ASCII	7-bit character code
\x{nn}	ASCII	8-bit character code
\u{nnnnnn}	Unicode	24-bit Unicode character
\'	Quote	Single quote
\"	Quote	Double quote

Pointers

Rust has two categories of pointers: references and raw pointers. References are safe pointers. Conversely, raw pointers simply point to a value in memory. There is no implied behavior, such as releasing the memory when the pointer is no longer available. It is similar to a C-style pointer.

The value of a raw pointer is a memory address. This could be a memory address to a value on the stack, heap, or a static memory location. Raw pointers themselves reside in memory somewhere and are often found on the stack. But not always—a raw pointer stored in a node of a link list could be on the heap, for example. The size of the raw pointer (i.e., memory address) depends on the architecture of the host system.

It is important to recognize that raw pointers, references, and regular values are different types. This is a subtle but important distinction. For example, i32 and &i32 are different types. The i32 type refers to a 32-bit integer value. However, &i32 refers to a reference that has a safe pointer to an i32 value. In addition, &i32 is different from a *i32 type, which is a raw pointer type. If desired, you can always cast a reference to a raw pointer of a like type.

The example in Figure 3.1 demonstrates raw pointers.

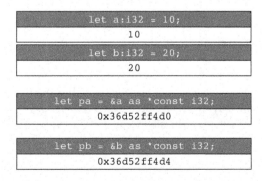

Figure 3.1.   "pa" and "pb" are raw pointers to a and b values.

Pointers are first-class citizens in the Rust language and have the same capabilities as any other type. Pointers can be used as variables, structure fields, function parameters, or return values.

References

References are safe pointers. Various rules apply to references, but not raw pointers, to ensure safeness. References *borrow* the value at the referenced memory location. Here are some other key points about references to keep in mind:

- References must be non-null.
- The underlying value must be a valid type.
- References have lifetimes.
- There is behavior associated with references, including ownership.

You declare a reference type with an ampersand, as shown previously. In addition, you can reference a value using the ampersand operator (&). In this context, you can interpret the ampersand as "get the reference of."

The dereference operator (*) dereferences a reference. You will receive the value at the memory address that is referenced. This is the underlying value of the reference. Listing 3.18 provides an example of dereferencing.

Code Listing 3.18.   Example of dereferencing

```
let aref:&i32=&5;
let value:i32=*aref;
```

Mathematical operators are implemented for both value and reference types, as shown in Listing 3.19. For a reference, the value is automatically deference before performing a mathematical calculation.

Code Listing 3.19.   References and math operators

```
let ref1=&15;
let ref2=&20;
let value1=ref1+10;
let value2=ref1*ref2;
println!("{} {}", value1, value2);  // 25  300
```

You can rewrite the preceding declarations for value1 and value2 differently, as shown in the next example. However, the result would be the same. But the following code is less readable. In fact, it is downright ugly! More importantly, the dereferencing is unnecessary. For the mathematical operations, it will automatically occur.

```
let value1=*ref1+10;
let value2=*ref1**ref2;
```

Listing 3.20 has examples of references, dereferencing, and mathematical operators.

Code Listing 3.20.   More examples of references

```
let fruit_grove=32;

// orange initialized with a reference to fruit_grove
let oranges:&i32=&fruit_grove;

// apples referenced with a reference to a literal value
let apples:&i32=&10;

// No need to deference the references
let basket=oranges+apples;

println!("{}", basket);
```

The == operator compares the value at a reference, not the memory location. If you want to compare the actual memory addresses, call the eq function, in the `std::ptr` module, as shown in Listing 3.21. The arguments for the eq function are the references to compare.

Code Listing 3.21.   Comparing pointers with eq function

```
let num_of_eggs=10;
let num_of_pizza=10;

let eggs=&num_of_eggs;
let pizza=&num_of_pizza;

eggs==pizza;                 // true
ptr::eq(eggs, pizza);        // false
```

Operators

The standard operators, listed next, define the core behavior of the scalar primitives:

- Mathematical operators
- Boolean operators
- Logical operators
- Bitwise operators

The mathematical operators, shown in Table 3.6, are primarily binary operators that perform various numerical calculations, such as addition and subtraction.

Table 3.6.   Mathematical Operators a = 25 | b = 10 | y = 25.0 | z = 10.0

Name	Operator	Example	Result
Addition	+	a + b	35
Subtraction	–	a – b	15
Multiplication	*	a * b	250
Division	/	a / b	2
Division	/	y / z	2.5
Modulus	%	a % b	5
Negation	–	–a	–25

Binary operations have a left value and a right value, representing either side of a binary operation. They are often referred to as l-value and r-value, respectively. You can use a compound operator when the l-value is also the variable to be assigned. The behavior of these two operations is the same.

```
value=value+5; // + operator
value+=5;      // compound + operator
```

Table 3.7 is a list of compound mathematical operators.

Table 3.7.   Mathematical Compound Operators a = 25 | b = 10 | y = 25.0 | z = 10.0

Name	Operator	Example	Result
Addition	+	a += b	a=35
Subtraction	–	a –= b	a=15
Multiplication	*	a *= b	a=250
Division	/	a =/ b	a=2
Division	/	y =/ z	2.5
Modulus	%	a %= b	5

Boolean operators are also mostly binary operations and return a true or false value. The success of the operation depends upon whether the values being compared, based on their types, are comparable.

Table 3.8 provides a list of Boolean operators.

Table 3.8.   Boolean Operators a = 25 | b = 10

Name	Operator	Example	Result
Equal	==	a == b	False
Less than	<	a < b	False
Greater than	>	a > b	True
Less than or equal	<=	a <= b	False

Name	Operator	Example	Result
Greater than or equal	>=	a >= b	True
Not equal	!=	a != b	False

Binary logical operators are lazy operators. With lazy operators, the r-value is evaluated only when necessary to resolve the overall expression. For example, the r-value of the && operator is evaluated only if the l-value is true. If the l-value of the && operator is false, the r-value would not be evaluated. This is called short-circuiting and can cause inadvertent software bugs. For Boolean operations, make sure that l-value do not cause necessary side effects. That side effect may not occur if there is short-circuiting. This can occur, for example, when you call a function as the r-value and it changes the state of your program, as required. If there is short-circuiting, the function is not called and a necessary change may not occur.

For the && and || operators, the & and | operators are companion operators that do not short-circuit. Listing 3.22 provides an example.

Code Listing 3.22.   Display message is an expression that does not short-circuit.

```
true  && {println!("does not short circuit"); false};   // displays message
false && {println!("short circuits"); false};           // does not display
false & {println!("does not short circuit"); false};    // displays message
```

Table 3.9 is a list of logical operators.

Table 3.9.   Logical Operators

Description	Operation	Example	Result	Short Circuit
Logical And	&&	false && true	True	Yes
Logical And	&&	true && false	False	No
Logical Or	||	true || false	True	Yes
Logical Or	||	false || true	False	No
Logical Not	|	true	N/A	No

The bitwise operators naturally perform bitwise operations. The input values for the bitwise operation must be integers.

Table 3.10 lists the bitwise operators.

Table 3.10.   Bitwise Operators a = 10 | b = 6

Name	Operator	Example	Result
Bitwise And	&	a & b	2 or 0010
Bitwise Or	|	a | b	14 or 9110
Bitwise Exclusive Or	^	a ^ b	12 or 1100

Name	Operator	Example	Result
Bitwise Shift-left	<<	a << 1	20 or 10100
Bitwise Shift-right	>>	a >> 1	5 or 0101

Compound operators are also available for bitwise operations and are listed in Table 3.11.

Table 3.11.   Compound Operators a = 10 | b = 6

Name	Operator	Example	Result
Bitwise And	&	a &= b	2 or 0010
Bitwise Or	|	a |= b	14 or 1110
Bitwise Exclusive Or	^	a ^= b	12 or 1100
Bitwise Shift-left	<<	a <<= 1	20 or 10100
Bitwise Shift-right	>>	a >>= 1	5 or 0101

Summary

In this chapter, you learned about an assortment of scalar types provided in the language. The scalar types include integers, floats, chars, and more.

Rust is a strongly typed language, which, when combined with ownership and lifetimes, presents an extraordinarily safe environment for application development, including the manipulation of scalar types.

Another safety feature of the language is limited casting. Implicit casting between different types is not allowed, even if theoretically safe. For example, you cannot cast from an i8 to an i32 value.

The normal assortment of built-in mathematical, logical, and Boolean operations is provided in Rust. The standard behavior, as related to primitives, was described in this chapter. Operators in Rust are consistent with operators in other languages.

Strings are probably the most well-known and utilized *non-scalar* types. You have used strings in the various Hello, World programs already! However, strings were not formally reviewed in this chapter, as this chapter is reserved for scalar types. But there is always the next chapter, which is dedicated to strings.

4

Strings

This chapter is dedicated entirely to strings. Strings are collections of printable and nonprintable characters. Rust strings adhere to the Unicode Standard with UTF-8 encoding. Unicode is a single codespace with code points for characters from around the world, including various languages and even emojis. Both active and inactive languages, such as hieroglyphics, are included in the standard. This provides support for internationalization, which makes it easier for your application to support users from around the world.

For example, the following is "hello" in hieroglyphics:

For your ancient Egyptian customers, this greeting is easier to provide because of Unicode.

Strings commonly appear in applications and are used in a variety of situations, including prompts, command-line information, user messages, file input, reporting, and more. Because of the ubiquity of strings in many applications, Rust offers safe strings and a wide variety of services for strings in the core language and other crates found at crates.io.

The primary string types in Rust are String and str, pronounced *stir*. We will discuss both.

Str

The str type is a primitive type and part of the core language. The str type has all the characteristics of a slice, including being unsized and read-only. Because str is a slice, you normally borrow a str, &str. A str consists of two fields: pointer to the string data and length.

String literals, defined within quotes ("..."), are str values that exist for the entirety of the program. As such, the lifetime of a string literal is static. The following is the notation for a string literal including the lifetime. You can find more about lifetimes in Chapter 9, "Lifetimes."

```
&'static str
```

Listing 4.1 is an example of declaring a str type.

Code Listing 4.1. Displaying a str

```
static STR_1:&str="Now is the time...";

fn main() {
    println!("{}", STR_1);
}
```

String

The String type, located in the Rust standard library (std), is implemented as a specialized vector that consists of character values. Strings can be mutable and are growable. Like a vector, the String type consists of three fields: pointer to a backing array, length, and capacity. The backing array contains char values included in the String. Length is the number of characters in the String, and capacity is the size of the backing array.

There are different approaches to creating new String types. Most often, String types are initialized using a string literal (i.e., str). Functions, such as `String::from` and `str::to_string`, convert a str to a String. In this book, we will use both functions for this conversion.

In Listing 4.2, we create two Strings from a string literal using both the `from` and `to_string` functions.

Code Listing 4.2. Converting strs to Strings

```
    let string_1=String::from("Alabama");
    let string_2="Alaska".to_string();
```

You can create an empty string for String with the new constructor. Typically, this is a mutable String where text can be added later.

In Listing 4.3, we create an empty String, which is mutable, and then append the string "Arizona" to it.

Code Listing 4.3. Appending to a String

```
    let mut string_1=String::new();
    string_1.push_str("Arizona");
```

As mentioned, Strings are a specialized vector—a collection of characters. You can even create a String directly from a vector. Create a vector of Unicode code points first, as integers. Each code point represents an individual character. The next step is to convert the vector to a string with the `from_utf8` function.

Listing 4.4 is an example of creating a String from Unicode characters.

Code Listing 4.4. Converting Unicode characters to a String

```
    let vec_1=vec![65, 114, 107, 97, 110, 115, 97, 115];
    let string_1=String::from_utf8(vec_1).unwrap();
```

In this example, the code points for "Arkansas" are included within a vector. The code point 65 is the 'A' character in the Unicode table, for example. The `from_utf` function then converts the vector into a String.

Length

What is the length of a specific Unicode string? This is a simple question with a complicated answer. First of all, it depends on whether you are referring to the number characters or bytes in the string. UTF characters can be described in 1 to 4 bytes. ASCII characters, at the beginning of the Unicode codespace, are 1 byte. However, the size of characters located elsewhere in the codespace may be multiple bytes.

Here are the byte sizes for various character sets:

- ASCII characters are a single byte in size.
- Greek characters are 2 bytes in size.
- Chinese characters are 3 bytes in size.
- Emojis are 4 bytes in size.

For ASCII, the length in bytes and the number of characters are identical. However, that may differ for other character sets. The `len` function returns the number of bytes in the string.

Here is how to get the number of characters within a String: You use the `chars` function to return an iterator to the characters of the String, and call the `count` function on the iterator to get the number of characters.

The example shown in Listing 4.5 displays both the number of bytes and characters in a string.

Code Listing 4.5.   Hello in different languages

```rust
let english="Hello".to_string();
let greek="γ ε ι α".to_string();
let chinese="你好".to_string();

// English Hello:  Bytes 5  Length 5
println!("English {}:  Bytes {}  Length {}",
    english, english.len(),
    english.chars().count());

// Greek    γ ε ι α:  Bytes 8  Length 4
println!("Greek    {}:  Bytes {}  Length {}",
    greek, greek.len(),
    greek.chars().count());

// Chinese 你好:  Bytes 6  Length 2
println!("Chinese {}:  Bytes {}  Length {}",
    chinese, chinese.len(),
    chinese.chars().count());
```

Extending a String

You can extend the value of a String, but not a str type. String has several functions for this purpose:

- push
- push_str
- insert
- insert_str

For a String, the push function appends a char value, while push_str appends a String. Listing 4.6 provides an example.

Code Listing 4.6.   Appending to a String

```
let mut alphabet="a".to_string();
alphabet.push('b');

let mut numbers="one".to_string();
numbers.push_str(" two");

// ab | one two
println!("{} | {}", alphabet, numbers);
```

The mathematical + operator is implemented for the String type. As an alternate to the push_str function, it is another way to concatenate strings. The advantage of using the + operator is convenience.

In Listing 4.7, we create a greeting using the + operator.

Code Listing 4.7.   Appending with + operator

```
let mut greeting="Hello".to_string();
let salutation=" Sir".to_string();
greeting=greeting+&salutation;

println!("{}", greeting);
```

You may not want to append text to a string but rather insert within it. For inserting text within a string, the insert function inserts a char value, while insert_str inserts a string. For the insert function, the first parameter is implicit and refers to the current String. The second parameter is the position where the character should be inserted. The final parameter is the character to insert. The insert_str function is identical to the insert function, except the final parameter inserts a String. Here is the function definition of each:

```
fn insert(&mut self, position: usize, ch: char)
fn insert_str(&mut self, position: usize, string: &str)
```

Listing 4.8 provides an example of inserting text within a string.

Code Listing 4.8.   Inserting within a string

```
let mut characters="ac".to_string();
characters.insert(1, 'b');
println!("{}", characters);    // abc

let mut numbers="one three".to_string();
numbers.insert_str(3, " two");
println!("{}", numbers);    // one two three
```

Capacity

As a specialized vector, Strings have a backing array and a capacity. The backing array is storage for the string's characters. Capacity is the size of the backing array, while length is the current size of the String. When the length exceeds the capacity, the backing array must be reallocated and expanded. There is a performance penalty when the backing array must be reallocated. Therefore, avoiding unnecessary reallocation can improve the performance of an application.

The String type has the same functions for managing the capacity as any vector.

Listing 4.9 provides an example of a mutable String that grows incrementally.

Code Listing 4.9.   Comparing capacity and length

```
let mut string_1='快'.to_string();  // a
println!("Capacity {} Length {}",
    string_1.capacity(), string_1.len());    // Capacity 3 Length 3

string_1.push('乐');    // b
println!("Capacity {} Length {}",
    string_1.capacity(), string_1.len());    // Capacity 8 Length 6

string_1.push_str("的");  // c
println!("Capacity {} Length {}",
    string_1.capacity(), string_1.len());    // Capacity 16 Length 9
```

The previous example created the word "happy" in Chinese (Mandarin), a character at a time. "Happy" in the Chinese language is "快乐的." Two reallocations occur during application execution. Here are the details of the example:

1. Declare a string with the first character of "快乐的." In Unicode, Chinese characters are 3 bytes wide. The initial capacity and length are 3.
2. Add the next character to the string. The length is now 6 and exceeds the capacity. This forces a reallocation.
3. Add the final character to complete the string. The length is 9, which exceeds the capacity again. This will force another reallocation.

Knowing the required capacity upfront enables a more efficient version of the previous application. The `with_capacity` function sets the capacity explicitly when you're declaring a String value. Here is the function definition.

```
fn with_capacity(capacity: usize) -> String
```

Listing 4.10 shows a better-performing version of the previous example.

Code Listing 4.10. Demonstrating the effectiveness of `with_capacity`

```
let mut string_1=String::with_capacity(9);

string_1.push('快');
println!("Capacity {} Length {}",
    string_1.capacity(), string_1.len());  // Capacity 9 Length 9

string_1.push('乐');
println!("Capacity {} Length {}",
    string_1.capacity(), string_1.len());  // Capacity 9 Length 9

string_1.push_str("的");
println!("Capacity {} Length {}",
    string_1.capacity(), string_1.len());  // Capacity 9 Length 9
```

The addition of the `with_capacity` function is impactful in this example. Initially, we set the capacity large enough to encompass three characters. This requires a capacity of 9 bytes. With the correct capacity, during execution, the backing array is not reallocated and performance is improved.

Accessing a String Value

Let's start with an example that demonstrates how to access elements of a String. The code in Listing 4.11 appears to access the second character of the String.

Code Listing 4.11. Attempting to display a character

```
    let string_1="hello".to_string();
    let character=string_1[1];
```

However, the preceding example causes a compiler error:

```
error[E0277]: the type `String` cannot be indexed by `{integer}`
 --> src\main.rs:3:19
  |
3 | let character=string_1[1];
  |     ^^^^^^^^^^^ `String` cannot be indexed by `{integer}`
```

The error message is accurate but does not completely explain the underlying problem. The concern is that trying to access a string with an index would be ambiguous. Does the index refer to the byte or character position? Without this knowledge, it is impossible, or at least unsafe, to resolve this expression. In Rust, accessing an individual character with an index is not allowed.

You *can* access characters in a String using a String slice, however. The starting index and ending index indicate byte position. The result of the slice notation is a str.

```
string[starting index..ending index]
```

The slice must align with the boundaries of a character. If not, a panic occurs at runtime. The example shown in Listing 4.12 runs successfully.

Code Listing 4.12.   **Displaying a Unicode character**

```
let string_1="快乐的".to_string();
let slice=&string_1[3..=5];
println!("{:?}", slice);  // 乐
```

Our diagram shows the byte position of each character in the "快乐的" string. The second character is from position 3 to 5, as shown in the example in Figure 4.1.

Byte	0	1	2	3	4	5	6	7	8
快乐的	快			乐			的		

Figure 4.1.   Byte diagram of the string "快乐的"

The following slice is an attempt to select the starting two characters of the "快乐的" string slice. However, the slice boundaries within the String are incorrect.

```
let slice=&string_1[0..=7];
```

When this is executed, the following panic occurs at runtime. It describes the problem in exceptional detail. The ending index is incorrect and does not align with the ending boundary of the second character. The message is helpful even identifying the correct boundary of the character you are within.

```
thread 'main' panicked at 'byte index 7 is not a char boundary;
it is inside '的' (bytes 6..9) of `快乐的`'
```

The is_char_boundary function of the str type confirms whether the indicated position aligns with the start of a char boundary. You can proactively call this function before creating a string slice, to determine the correct boundaries.

Listing 4.13 provides an example of the function is_char_boundary.

Code Listing 4.13.   Confirming character boundary alignment

```
let str_1="快乐的";
println!("{}", str_1.is_char_boundary(0) );   // true
println!("{}", str_1.is_char_boundary(1) );   // false
```

String Characters

Strings consist of characters. Iterating all the characters is sometimes useful. For example, you can apply some operation to each character, encode each character, count characters, or search and remove all words with the letter *e*, such as the book *Gadsby*. The chars function returns an iterator the characters of a str value.

There are plenty of exceptional ski resorts in the Czech Republic, including Špindlerův Mlýn, Keilberg, and Horní Domky. The word for skiing in the Czech language is "lyžování." The example shown in Listing 4.14 enumerates all the characters in that word.

Code Listing 4.14.   Displaying Czech characters

```
let czech_skiing="lyžování".to_string();

for character in czech_skiing.chars() {
    println!("{}", character);
}
```

You can display a character at a certain position using the nth function of the iterator. Here, we display the third character of the String:

```
println!("{}", czech_skiing.chars().nth(2).unwrap());
```

Deref Coercion

You can substitute a borrowed String, &String, anywhere &str is expected. At that time, the String inherits the methods of the str type. This is possible because the String type implements the deref trait for str. Appropriately, this conversion is called deref coercion. The reverse is not available—that is, converting from str to a String type.

Listing 4.15 shows an example of using deref coercion.

Code Listing 4.15.   Deref coercion from String to str reference

```
fn FuncA(str_1: &str) {
    println!("{}", str_1);
}

fn main() {
    let string_1="Hello".to_string();
    FuncA(&string_1);
}
```

For this example, the `FuncA` function has a `&str` parameter. In `main`, we declare a String for `"Hello"`. `FuncA` is then called successfully with `&String`.

Formatted String

For creating fancy strings, the `format!` macro is convenient. The `format!` macro is similar to the `print` family of macros, except it returns a formatted string. That includes identical parameters. The `format` specifiers are explained in detail in Chapter 5, "Console." Both the `print!` and `format!` macros rely on the `std::fmt` module.

Listing 4.16 is an example demonstrating the `format!` macro.

Code Listing 4.16. Creating formatted Strings with the `format!` macro

```
let left=5;
let right=10;
let result=format!("{left} + {right} = {result}", result=left+right);

println!("{}", result);    // 5 + 10 = 15
```

Helpful Functions

Rust has an impressive assortment of String functions that support string manipulation. Here are some of the more helpful functions for Strings.

- **clear**: Erases a String but does not reduce the current capacity. If desired, you can reduce the capacity with the `shrink_to_fit` function.

  ```
  fn clear(&mut self)
  ```

- **contains**: Searches for a pattern in a String and returns true if found.

  ```
  fn contains<'a, P>(&'a self, pat: P) -> bool
  ```

- **ends_with**: Returns true if the pattern is found as the String suffix.

  ```
  fn ends_with<'a, P>(&'a self, pat: P) -> bool
  ```

- **eq_ignore_ascii_case**: Returns true if the String matches a pattern. The comparison is case insensitive.

  ```
  fn eq_ignore_ascii_case(&self, other: &str) -> bool
  ```

- **replace**: Replaces a pattern found in a String. The modified String is returned.

  ```
  fn replace<'a, P>(&'a self, from: P, to: &str) -> String
  ```

- **split**: Splits a String into separate Strings at the specified delimiter. An iterator is returned to enumerate the split Strings.

  ```
  fn split<'a, P>(&'a self, pat: P) -> Split<'a, P>
  ```

- **starts_with**: Returns true if the String starts with this pattern.

  ```
  fn starts_with<'a, P>(&'a self, pat: P) -> bool
  ```

- **to_uppercase**: Converts the String to uppercase.

  ```
  fn to_uppercase(&self) -> String
  ```

Let's demonstrate each of these functions.

Listing 4.17 empties an existing String, after which the String does not contain any characters. The shrink_to_fit function then reduces the capacity accordingly. The is_empty function returns true if a String has no characters.

Code Listing 4.17.   Clearing the string and then shrinking to size

```
let mut string_1="something ".to_string();
string_1.clear();
string_1.shrink_to_fit();

// string_1 is empty: true
println!( "string_1 is empty: {}",
    string_1.is_empty());
```

In Listing 4.18, the contains function scans the String for the "fun" pattern and returns true. The println! macro displays the result. A raw string, "r#" prefix, is used within the macro because of the nested string within the format string.

Code Listing 4.18.   Finding a substring with the contains function

```
let string_2="this is fun.".to_string();
let result=string_2.contains("fun");

// "fun" is found in "this is fun.": true
println!(r#""fun" is found in "{string_2}": {result}"#);
```

In Listing 4.19, we look for "Topeka" as a suffix to the specified String. The result is true.

Code Listing 4.19.   Confirming a string suffix

```
let string_3="going to Topeka".to_string();
let result=string_3.ends_with("Topeka");

// "Topeka" suffix for "going to Topeka": true
println!(r#""Topeka" suffix for "{string_3}": {result}"#);
```

Non-case-sensitive comparisons are often useful. Listing 4.20 compares two Strings, using the eq_ignore_ascii_case function, that differ only in case. Notice that the second string is borrowed, using a reference (&). Moving the String would render the second String unavailable from that location forward. More about borrow versus move in Chapter 8, "Ownership." The function returns true in this example.

Code Listing 4.20.   **Case-insensitive comparison**

```
let string_4="ONE".to_string();
let string_5="One".to_string();
let result=string_4.eq_ignore_ascii_case(&string_5);

// "ONE" equals "One": true
println!(r#""{string_4}" equals "{string_5}": {result}"#);
```

In Listing 4.21, the `replace` function replaces the pattern "Bob" with "Alice". The result is the updated String.

Code Listing 4.21.   **Replacement within a string**

```
let string_6=
    "Bob went shopping; then Bob went home.".to_string();
let result_string=string_6.replace("Bob", "Alice");

// New string: Alice went shopping; then Alice went home.
println!("New string: {}", result_string);
```

The `split` function partitions a String at each instance of a delimiter. In Listing 4.22, the String is delimited at spaces, which is a common delimiter. The function returns an iterator to a collection of Strings created from the operation. You can then iterate them individually.

Code Listing 4.22.   **Splitting a String along spaces as delimiters**

```
let string_7="The magic of words.";
let iterator=string_7.split(" ");

// The magic of words.
for word in iterator {
    print!("{} ", word);
}
```

In Listing 4.23, since the String starts with "Sydney", the `starts_with` function returns true.

Code Listing 4.23.   **Confirming the String prefix**

```
let string_8="Sydney is scenic.".to_string();
let result=string_8.starts_with("Sydney");

// "Sydney" prefix for "Sydney is scenic.": true
println!(r#""Sydney" prefix for "{string_8}": {result}"#);
```

In Listing 4.24, the final example, the `to_uppercase` function converts "Cool!" to uppercase. Naturally, there is also a `to_lowercase` function.

Code Listing 4.24.   **Converting a String to uppercase**

```
    let string_9="Cool!";
    println!("{} : {}", string_9, string_9.to_uppercase());

    // Cool! : COOL!
```

Summary

Strings are a specialized vector where the elements must be Unicode characters. Rust does support other types of strings, such as OsString, CStr, CString, and ASCII string. Many of these strings types are discussed later in Chapter 22, "Interoperablity."

The standard Rust strings are the str and String types. The str type represents a string slice and is often used for string literals. Typically, strs are borrowed: &str. The String type is mutable, growable, and ownable. With deref coercion, you can freely substitute &string for &str.

Similar to a vector, a String type has three fields: pointer to the backing array, length, and capacity. You cannot access these fields directly except through functions of the String type.

You can access a string slice with slice notation. However, the slice must align on character boundaries. If not, a panic occurs at runtime. Scalar indexes are not allowed on strings.

We detailed some helpful functions for the String type. It may be worthwhile to explore the many other String functions found in the Rust documentation.

5

Console

Many applications choose to interact with the console. The command-line of the console is ideal for logging events, configuring applications, accepting user input, accessing developer tools, and more.

Console applications that rely entirely on a command-line interface (CLI) for interacting with users are not uncommon and are an acceptable alternative to a graphical user interface (GUI). Like GUI applications, command-line user interfaces can have a good or bad design. Note that the best practices for designing a CLI for a console application are different from those of a GUI. This chapter, however, focuses on the technical capabilities for reading and writing to a console, not design choices.

Several commands exist to read and write to the console. We will start with the `println!` and `println!` macros, which are the most common.

Print

The `print!` and `println!` macros are frequently used to display information on the console. Both macros insert a formatted string into the standard output stream (stdout). The `println!` macro appends a linefeed to the formatted output; the `print!` macro does not. The first parameter of each macro is a format string and a string literal. The format string may include placeholders, which are the {} characters. The remaining parameters of the `print!` macros are substitution arguments for the placeholders in the format string.

The `print!` and `println!` macros are variadic and can have a variable number of arguments. The `print!` macro must have at least one argument, the format string. The `println!` macro can have no arguments and simply display a linefeed.

The {} placeholders are reserved for public-facing types that implement the Display trait. Public-facing types typically have a well-known representation. Many of the primitive types in the standard library, such as integer and float, are considered public-facing types and implement the Display trait. Other types, such as structs, may not implement the Display trait. These types cannot be used within the {} placeholder.

The format string of the `println!` macro in Listing 5.1 has three placeholders. The placeholders are replaced with two variable values and a calculation.

Code Listing 5.1.   The `println!` macro and placeholders

```
let a = 1;
let b = 2;
println!("Total {} + {} = {}",
    a, b, a + b);  //   Total 1 + 2 = 3
```

The placeholders within the format string are replaced in order with the arguments a, b, and the result of (a + b). Each {} placeholder evaluates the next parameter in the sequence (see Figure 5.1).

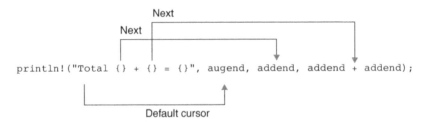

Figure 5.1.   `Println!` macro with a format string and placeholders

Positional Arguments

Format strings can have positional arguments as placeholders. You indicate the positional argument within the placeholder using an index: {index}. The index is zero-based and a usize type.

The main benefit of using positional arguments is to allow the unordered display of the parameters, as shown in Listing 5.2. The formatted string in this example displays the arguments in reverse order.

Code Listing 5.2.   Positional arguments in `println!` macro

```
let a = 1;
let b = 2;
println!("Total {1} + {0} = {2}",
    a, b, a+ b);  // Total 2 + 1 = 3
```

In a format string, you can mix types of placeholders: non-positional and positional. However, the non-positional arguments are evaluated first. The source code shown in Listing 5.3 uses both types of arguments.

Code Listing 5.3.   Mixing non-positional and positional arguments

```
let (first, second, third, fourth) = (1, 2, 3, 4);
let result = first + second + third + fourth;
println!(
```

```
    "{3} + {} + {} + {} = {4}",
    first, second, third,
        fourth, result);  // 4 + 1 + 2 +_3 = 10
```

Figure 5.2 diagrams how the format string is evaluated.

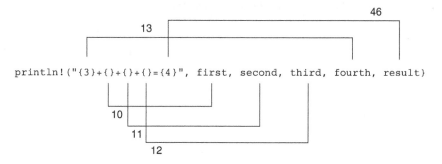

Figure 5.2. Depiction of normal and positional arguments in a format string

Variable Arguments

Placeholders in the format string can also reference variables. A variable argument is a type of positional argument. The referenced variable must be within scope and visible at the time. In Listing 5.4, the first, second, third, fourth, and result variables are referenced within placeholders in the format string.

Code Listing 5.4. A `println!` macro with variables as placeholders

```
let (first, second, third, fourth) = (1, 2, 3, 4);
let result = first + second + third + fourth;
println!("{first} + {second} + {third} + {fourth}
    = {result}");
```

Named Arguments

The `print!` macros can use named arguments. The syntax is *name=value*. These arguments can then be used within placeholders in the format string. In Listing 5.5, `result` is a named argument and referenced within the last placeholder of the format string.

Code Listing 5.5. Named arguments in `println`

```
let (first, second, third, fourth) = (1, 2, 3, 4);

println!(
    "{} + {} + {} + {} = {result}", first,
        second, third, fourth,
        result = first + second + third + fourth
);
```

Both named and positional arguments can appear within placeholders in the format string. However, positional arguments cannot follow the named arguments in the parameter list. In Listing 5.6, `prefix`, a named argument, precedes any positional arguments in the `println!` macro.

Code Listing 5.6. A `println!` macro with named and positional parameters

```
let (first, second, third, fourth) = (1, 2, 3, 4);
let result = first + second + third + fourth;

println!(
    "{prefix} {first} + {second} + {third} + {fourth}
        = {result}",
    prefix = "Average: ",
    result = result as f32 / 4.0
);
```

Padding, Alignment, and Precision

Within the format string, you can set the padding, alignment, or numeric precision of the placeholders. This is great for creating professional-looking displays and reports. You can fine-tune the format specification after a : (colon) character in the placeholder, `{:format}`.

You set the padding, or the column width, for a placeholder using the `{:width}` syntax. Within the column, the default alignment for numerical values is right alignment. Left alignment is the default for strings. You can override the default alignment with these characters:

>   Right alignment

<   Left alignment

^   Center alignment

The source code shown in Listing 5.7 demonstrates how to define the width and alignment of a placeholder.

Code Listing 5.7. Defining the width and alignment of a placeholder

```
let numbers = [("one", 10), ("two", 2000), ("three", 400)];
println!("{:7}{:10}", "Text", "Value");
println!("{:7}{:10}", "====", "=====");
for (name, value) in numbers {
    println!("{:7}{:<10}", name, value);
}
```

The result is a report consisting of two columns of data. The first column is seven characters wide and contains text that defaults to left alignment. The second column is ten characters and consists of numbers. However, alignment is explicitly set as left alignment.

Here is the report:

```
Text    Value
====    =====
one     10
two     2000
three   400
```

For floating point numbers, you can add precision within the placeholder. You can control the number of positions displayed after the decimal place. In the placeholder, stipulate floating point precision after the padding. The syntax is *padding.precision*. If padding is not present, the syntax is simply *.precision*. For integral types, precision in the placeholder is ignored.

In Listing 5.8, two floating point numbers are displayed. The first is displayed with the precision of two decimal places within a column ten characters wide. The second is shown with four decimal places and a default width.

Code Listing 5.8.   Setting decimal places in the `println!` macro

```
let (f1, f2) = (1.2, 3.45678);
println!("Result: {:<10.2} {:.4}",
     f1, f2);  // Result:  1.20 3.4568
```

You can parameterize either the precision or width with the $ character. In the format string, precede the $ with the position of the argument within the parameter list.

In Listing 5.9, the `println!` macro displays two floating point numbers. Notice the placement of the $ characters, each identifying the precision specification as an argument. The same argument, zero, is chosen to set the precision of both placeholders to three.

Code Listing 5.9.   Using the $ to select a replacement argument

```
let (f1, f2) = (1.2, 3.45678);
println!("Result: {1:<10.0$} {2:.0$}", 3, f1, f2);
```

Figure 5.3 is a diagram of the format string displaying floating point numbers.

```
println!("Result: {1:<10.0$} {2:.0$}", 3, f1, f2);
```

Figure 5.3.   Depiction of the $ substitution parameter in a format string

Here is the result. Both floating point numbers have the same precision.

```
Result: 1.200      3.457
```

You can also parameterize both the padding and precision in the format string, as shown next. This is similar to the preceding example, except the padding specified in the first place-holder is also parameterized.

```
println!("Result: {2:<0$.1$} {3:.1$}", 10, 2, f1, f2);
```

Figure 5.4 shows how the substitutions are applied to the format string at three locations.

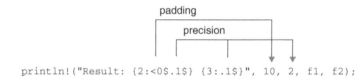

Figure 5.4. Parameterizing the padding and precision format specification

Here is the result of the preceding `println!` macro in the formatted string:

```
Result: 1.20      3.46
```

Base

For the `print!` macros, the default base for numbers is Base 10. However, you can specify a wide variety of other bases, including binary and hexadecimal. There is a letter designation for each supported base type. For hexadecimal, there are two designations: upper- and lowercase "x" for upper- and lowercase hexadecimal characters.

Description	Base	Format Specifier
Binary	Base 2	B
Octal	Base 8	O
Decimal (default)	Base 10	None
Hexadecimal	Base 16	X
Hexadecimal (uppercase)	Base 16	X

Listing 5.10 is an example demonstrating the various base types.

Code Listing 5.10.   Setting the base in the format specification

```
println!("Default    {}",   42);  // 42
println!("Binary     {:b}", 42);  // 101010
println!("Octal      {:o}", 42);  // 52
println!("Hexadecimal {:x}", 42);  // 2a
println!("HEXADECIMAL {:X}", 42);  // 2A
```

Developer Facing

For the print! macros, the public-facing types implement the Display trait for the {} place-holder. Other types are considered "developer facing" and use the {:?} placeholder. The {:?} placeholder requires an implementation of the Debug trait. Developer-facing format is from the developer perspective and is not necessarily user friendly. Some primitives and other types in the std library implement both the Display and Debug traits. Other types, such as arrays and vectors, implement the Debug trait but not the Display trait.

Listing 5.11 is an example of the {:?} placeholder.

Code Listing 5.11. Displaying a vector with the {:?} placeholder

```
let vec1=vec![1,2,3];
println!("{:?}", vec1);
```

Most notably, user-defined types do not implement either the Display or Debug trait. You can add a default implementation of the Debug trait with the following derive attribute:

```
#[derive(Debug)]
```

In Listing 5.12, the Planet struct is assigned a default implementation of the Debug trait using the derive attribute. Planet is then used later in the program in the println! macro with the {:?} placeholder.

Code Listing 5.12. Displaying struct in the println! macro

```
#[derive(Debug)]
struct Planet<'a> {
    name: &'a str,
    radius: f64,
}
fn main() {
    let earth = Planet {
        name: "Earth",
        radius: 3958.8,
    };
    // Planet { name: "Earth", radius: 3958.8 }
    println!("{:?}", earth); }
}
```

The developer-facing view may not be as "pretty" as the public-facing view. The emphasis of the developer-facing view is practicality, and it can be rather pedantic. There is an option with developer-facing types for pretty print using the {:#?} placeholder. This adds a linefeed between each element displayed. The following displays the earth value using pretty printing:

```
println!("{:#?}", earth);
```

Here is the result:

```
Planet {
    name: "Earth",
    radius: 3958.8222,
}
```

Write! Macro

The print! and println! macros display to standard output. The write! macro is more flexible and can forward formatted strings to different targets that implement either the fmt::Write or io::Write trait. The parameters for the macros are the target value, format string, and format parameters. The formatted string is written to the target. For that reason, the target should be mutable and a borrowed value.

The Vec type, for example, implements the std::io::Write trait and therefore can be used as a target within the write! macro, as shown in Listing 5.13.

Code Listing 5.13.   Displaying a vector using the write! and println! macros

```
let mut v1 = Vec::new();
write!(&mut v1, "{}", 10);
println!("{:?}", v1);   // [49, 48]
```

The write! macro converts the value 10 into a string. The implementation of the macro for Vec converts each character within the string into a Unicode character that is stored as separate elements in the vector.

Standard output is also a possible target for the write! macro. With Stdout as the target, the write! macro behavior is similar to the print! macro. In Rust, Stdout represents the standard output stream. It is found in the std::io module. Call the **stdout** function to obtain the Stdout. The code in Listing 5.14 displays a format string to the console, like the print! macro.

Code Listing 5.14.   Displaying the result of the write! macro to stdout

```
let res = write!(
    &mut std::io::stdout(),
        "The radius of {} is {} {}", "the Earth",
            3958.8, "miles")
        .unwrap();
```

Display Trait

The {} placeholder of a format string accepts arguments that implement the Display trait for a public-facing view. You may want to implement the Display trait for your types.

Found in the std::fmt module, the Display trait consists of the fmt function:

```
pub trait Display {
    fn fmt(&self, f: &mut Formatter<'_>) -> Result<(), Error>;
}
```

The fmt function creates the public-facing representation of the type. This is an instance method. For that reason, the first parameter is self. The second parameter of the fmt function, Formatter, is an out parameter containing the public-facing rendering of the type. The function returns a Result type to indicate whether the function succeeded.

Exponent is a user-defined type that consists of a base and pow fields, which are inputs for evaluating an exponent. By default, structs do not implement the Display trait and therefore are not available to use with the {} placeholder.

```
struct Exponent {
    base: i32,
    pow: u32,
}
```

Let's implement the Display trait for Exponent, which requires the fmt function. The public-facing view of the Exponent structure is naturally the result of the exponentiation calculation. Listing 5.15 is the implementation of the Display trait for the Exponent structure.

Code Listing 5.15. Implementing the Display trait for Exponent

```
impl fmt::Display for Exponent {
    fn fmt(&self, formatter: &mut fmt::Formatter)
                                    -> fmt::Result {
        write!(formatter, "{}",
            i32::pow(self.base, self.pow))
    }
}
```

In the function, the write! macro calculates the exponent value and places the formatted string into the formatter argument.

With the implementation shown in Listing 5.16, the Exponent structure can now be used with the {} placeholder.

Code Listing 5.16. Using the Exponent type in the println! macro

```
let value = Exponent { base: 2, pow: 4 };
println!("{}", value);    // 16
```

Debug Trait

The {:?} placeholder renders the developer-facing view of a value. Values used with the {:?} placeholder must implement the Debug trait found in the std::fmt module. Similar to the Display trait, the Debug trait consists of a fmt method:

```
pub trait Debug {
    fn fmt(&self, f: &mut Formatter<'_>)
        -> Result<(), Error>;
}
```

By default, Rectangle structure does not have a developer-facing view. For debugging, we decide to implement the Debug trait for the type:

```
struct Rectangle {
    top_left: (isize, isize),
    bottom_right: (isize, isize),
}
```

Listing 5.17 shows the implementation of the Debug trait. In the fmt function, the write! macro renders the developer-facing view to the formatter. For the Rectangle type, the developer-facing view shows the top-left and bottom-right corners.

Code Listing 5.17.   Implementing the Debug trait for the Rectangle type

```
use std::fmt;
impl fmt::Debug for Rectangle {
    fn fmt(&self, formatter: &mut fmt::Formatter)
                                        -> fmt::Result {
        write!(formatter, "({} {}) ({} {})",
            self.top_left.0, self.top_left.1,
            self.bottom_right.0, self.bottom_right.1)
    }
}}
```

A rectangle value can now be used within the {:?} placeholder, as shown in Listing 5.18.

Code Listing 5.18.   Using the Rectangle type in the println! macro

```
let value = Rectangle {
    top_left: (10, 10),
    bottom_right: (40, 25),
};
println!("{:?}", value);   // (10 10) (40 25)
```

Format! Macro

Until now, we have mainly focused on the print macros, print! and println!, which send formatted strings to standard output. However, there are several other related macros that create formatted strings:

- print! sends a formatted string to standard output
- println! sends a formatted string with an appended linefeed to standard output
- eprint! sends a formatted string to standard error
- eprintf! sends a formatted string with an appended linefeed to standard error
- format! creates a formatted string
- lazy_format! creates a formatted string with delayed rendering

Console Read and Write

You may want to create a fully interactive console application for the user. This, of course, would include exchanging information with the user via the console. The std::io module provides these helpful functions to access the console:

- stdout: Returns a handle to the standard output stream as a Stdout type
- stdin: Returns a handle to the standard input stream as a Stdin type
- stderr: Returns a handle to the standard error stream as a Stderr type

For reading input from the console, Stdin implements the BufRead and Read traits. These traits provide several functions for reading from the console. Here is the shortlist:

- read: Reads input into a byte buffer
- read_line: Reads a line of input into a String buffer
- read_to_string: Reads input to EOF into a String buffer

In Listing 5.19, the user is first presented a prompt using the println! macro. The user is prompted to enter their name. The read_line function reads the response and saves to an out argument. Afterwards, the String::trim_end function removes extraneous non-printable characters that can appear at the end of an input buffer. That can include a return and linefeed that was received with the user input. At the end, the program displays a hello message using the user's name.

Code Listing 5.19.   This application is interactive.

```
use std::io;
fn main() {
    println!("What is your name? ");
    let mut name = String::new();

    io::stdin().read_line(&mut name).unwrap_or_default();
    if name != "" {
        print!("Hello, {}!", name.trim_end());
    } else {
```

```
        print!("No name entered.");
    }
}
```

Instead of using print macros, you can display directly to the console using the standard output handle. First, get the handle to the standard output stream with the `stdout` function, which implements various functions that can display information in the console window. The `write_all` function is one of them and displays bytes, as shown here:

```
io::stdout().write_all(b"Hello, world!")
```

Summary

The console can be an effective tool for communicating with users for a variety of reasons. The simplicity and straightforwardness of the console are sometimes preferred to a traditional graphical user interface.

You have learned how to read and write to the console using various instructions. This includes macros that write to the standard output. The `print!` and `println!` macros are the most common. These macros display formatted strings to the console. The formatted string is derived from the format string, placeholders, and substitution values, which are input parameters.

Console applications are becoming more mainstream. Text web browsers, games that interact from the command-line, and developer tools are examples of this growing genre of applications.

6

Control Flow

Control flow is the path of execution through your source code. Execution could start at `main` and execute source statements in order until the end of the function. This approach works for only the simplest of programs, such as a hello, world application. Even the most mundane application requires some level of variability in code execution, such as arcs and various branches. Transfer of control is the most common method for nonconsecutive execution and the focus of this chapter.

Rust has the usual suspects of keywords determining the control path and causing a transfer of control within an application. This includes the following expressions:

- `if`
- `loop`
- `while`
- `for`
- `match`

Of course, Rust applies its own viewpoint to these familiar constructs. Most notably, these are *expressions,* not statements, as in many other languages. Like other Rust features, this can have a significant impact on the *look and feel* of Rust code. In addition, certain programming artifacts are not included for safeness, such as the ternary operator or "goto" statement.

Although the `match` expression is included in the preceding list, it is primarily discussed in Chapter 15, "Patterns."

The `if` Expression

The most common transfer of control is the `if` expression. The `if` evaluates a conditional expression as true or false to determine the control flow.

If the conditional expression evaluates to true, the if block is executed. Otherwise, the block is skipped.

Syntax for the `if` is as follows:

```
if condition {
    // true block
}
```

You can combine the if with an else block. This provides both a true and false block for the if. The if block is executed when the conditional expression evaluates as true. Otherwise, the else block is executed.

Here is the syntax for the combined if else:

```
if condition {
        // true block
} else {
        // false block
}
```

Listing 6.1 provides an example of an if else.

Code Listing 6.1.   An if else example

```
let city="Honolulu";
let is_new_york="New York City"==city;
if is_new_york{
    println!("Welcome to NYC");
} else {
    println!("Not NYC");
}
```

We declare city as a string literal that is compared to "New York City". The result is used as the conditional expression for the if. If true, the Welcome to New York greeting is displayed.

Optionally, you can have one or more else if after the if. The else if is essentially a nested if. If more than one else if is present, they are evaluated in order until a conditional expression evaluates as true. At that time, the else if block is executed. The else, if present, must follow all else if blocks. In this context, consider the else block the default behavior.

Here is the syntax for the else if:

```
if boolean condition {
        // true block
} else if condition  {
        // nested true block
} else {
        // false block
}
```

Listing 6.2 shows the sample code.

Code Listing 6.2.   An if else example

```
let city="Bangalore";
if city == "New York City" {
    println!("Welcome to NYC");
} else if city == "Paris" {
    println!("Welcome to Paris");
```

```
} else if city == "Bangalore" {
    println!("Welcome to Bangalore");
} else {
    println!("City not known")
}
```

Similar to the previous example, we declare a variable, city, as a string literal. The variable is then compared to a series of cities. If there is a match, the related block is executed.

The if let expression is a variation to the if. Instead of using a conditional expression, pattern matching will determine the control path. If the pattern matches, the related block is executed. Otherwise, the block is skipped. In addition, else and else if can be used with the if let. Pattern matching is discussed further in Chapter 15, "Patterns."

Here is the syntax of the if let expression with optional else if and else blocks:

```
if let pattern = expression {
        // pattern matches
} else if pattern = expression {
        // pattern matches
} else {
        // pattern does not match
}
```

Listing 6.3 provides an example of the if let.

Code Listing 6.3.   Creating an assignment with an if let

```
enum Font {
    Name(String),
    Default,
}

let font=Font::Name("Arial".to_string());
if let Font::Name(chosen) = font {
        println!("{} font selected", chosen);
} else {
        println!("Use default font");
}
```

This example creates a Font enum. The enum has two variants: the Name, for a specific, and Default. Afterwards, we create a font for Arial. The if let will match the Font::Name pattern. If the pattern is found, the underlying font is assigned to chosen, which is then displayed.

For an if, the if block can return a value. The default return is the empty tuple (). All the blocks within an if, including else and else if, must return a consistent type. The return value can be used to initialize a new variable, an assignment, or be part of a larger expression.

In Listing 6.4, the if returns either 1 or 2, based on the Boolean flag.

Code Listing 6.4. Assigning a value using an `if` expression

```
let flag=true;

let value=if flag {
    1
} else  {
    2
};

println!("{}", value);
```

The flag is hardcoded as true. For that reason, 1 is assigned to `value`, which is then displayed.

The `while` Expression

The `while` expression is a predicate loop. The `while` block is repeated while the conditional expression is true. When the conditional expression is false, execution continues after the `while` block. If the conditional expression is initially false, the `while` block is never executed. For this reason, the `while` block is iterated zero or more times.

To avoid an infinite loop, the conditional expression for the `while` should eventually evaluate to false. There are legitimate reasons, however, for an infinite `while` loop, such as a message pump.

Here is the syntax for a simple `while` loop:

```
while condition {
        // while block
}
```

The `while` expression in Listing 6.5 calculates a factorial result.

Code Listing 6.5. A `while` loop example

```
let mut count=5;
let mut result=1;

while count > 1{
    result=result*count;
    count=count-1;
}
```

`while let` is a variation of `while`. It will iterate the `while` block while the pattern matches. This is similar to the `if let`, except with a loop.

Listing 6.6 calculates a factorial using the `while let` expression.

Code Listing 6.6.   A while let example

```
let mut count=Some(5);
let mut result:i32=1;
while let Some(value)=count {
    if value == 1 {
        count=None
    } else {
        result=result*value;
        count=Some(value-1);
    }
}
```

The while let iterates the while block while the pattern matches Some(value). The value is decremented within each iteration and multiplied against the previous product, result. When the underlying value becomes 1, the pattern is set to None, which means the pattern no longer matches. At that time, result will have the final factorial value.

The break and continue Keywords

The break and continue keywords can alter the execution of a while. The continue statement continues execution at the next conditional expression. This skips the remainder of the current block.

Listing 6.7 only displays odd numbers. If an even number is encountered, the continue statement skips the remainder of the block, and the number is not displayed.

Code Listing 6.7.   Continue at the next iteration

```
let mut i=0;
while i < 10 {
    i=i+1;
    if i % 2 == 0 {
        continue;
    }
    println!("{}", i);
}
```

The while expression in Listing 6.8 iterates until a prime number is found, between 100,000 and 200,000. This example uses the Primes crate located in the crates.io repository. The while loop breaks when a prime number is found, skipping the remainder of the block and exiting the while.

Code Listing 6.8.   Break when a prime number is found.

```
let mut i=100_000;
while i < 200_000 {
    if is_prime(i) {
        println!("Prime # found {}", i);
```

```
        break;
    }
    i=i+1;
}
```

The for Expression

The for expression is an iterator loop. Iterators implement the Iterator trait and can be used directly with the for in syntax. However, collections, such as arrays and vectors, are not iterators but implement the IntoIterator trait. The IntoIterator trait describes the conversion from *some type* to an Iterator. Fortunately, this trait supports for also.

Here is the syntax for the for:

```
for value in iterator {
    //
}
```

Listing 6.9 is an example that tests a for using a range literal. A range literal defines a sequence of values. It is an instance of the Range type, with a start and end field, which is exclusive. The result of a range literal is an iterator.

Code Listing 6.9.   A for loop that iterates a Range

```
use std::ops::Range;

fn main() {
    let r=Range {start: 0, end: 3};
    for value in r {
        println!("{}", value);
    }
}
```

The for will display the numbers 0, 1, and 2 on separate lines.

The shorthand syntax for a range literal is start..end or start..=end. Note that the .. operator is exclusive of the ending value, while the ..= operator is inclusive.

In Listing 6.10, for in iterates a range literal.

Code Listing 6.10.   A for that iterates a range literal

```
for value in 1..=5 {
    println!("{}", value);
}
```

This displays 1, 2, 3, 4, and 5 on separate lines.

Iterators have an enumerate function that returns a tuple with two fields for the index and value of the current item.

Listing 6.11 provides an example.

Code Listing 6.11.   A for that uses the enumerate function

```
for value in (1..=10).enumerate() {
    println!("{:?}", value);
}
```

Here is the result of the application, where the first field of the tuple is the index and the second field is the value:

```
(0, 1)
(1, 2)
(2, 3)
(3, 4)
(4, 5)
```

Arrays and vectors are popular collections but, as already mentioned, are not iterators. They are converted to iterators with their implementation of the IntoIterator trait.

In Listing 6.12, we enumerate the elements of a vector within a for in expression.

Code Listing 6.12.   Iterating a vector in a for loop

```
let values=vec![1,2,3];
for item in values {
    println!("{}", item);
}
```

In the previous code, we could attempt to use the enumerate function with the vector. However, this would not work. The implementation of the IntoIterator trait does not provide an implementation of this function. First, you must convert the collection explicitly to an iterator with one of these functions: iter, iter_mut, or into_iter. After the conversion, the enumerate function can be called.

Here is how the iter, iter_mut, and into_iter functions are different:

- The iter function yields immutable references (&T).
- The iter_mut function yields mutable references (&mut T).
- The into_iter function yields either a T, &T, or &mut T, depending on the use case.

In Listing 6.13, we declare a vector containing integer values. Within the for, the vector is converted to an iterator and then the enumerate method is called. This returns an iterator where each element is a (index, value) tuple. Within the for loop, the tuple is displayed.

Code Listing 6.13.   A for that displays indexes and values of vector elements

```
let values=vec![1,2,3];
for item in values.iter().enumerate() {
    println!("{:?}", item);
}
```

In the next example, Listing 6.14, we iterate just the values in the vector. Within the for block, the items are displayed. We also attempt to modify the item. However, that will not compile.

Code Listing 6.14.   A for loop that modifies values in a vector

```
let mut values=vec![1,2,3];
for item in values {
    println!("{}", item);
    item=item*2;
}
```

Here is the error message:

```
3 |      for item in values {
  |          ----
  |          |
  |          first assignment to `item`
  |          help: consider making this binding mutable: `mut item`
4 |          println!("{}", item);
5 |          item=item*2;
  |          ^^^^^^^^^^^ cannot assign twice to immutable variable
```

Examining an error message always makes for interesting reading. In this example, the error message does clarify the problem. We require mutable references! This is necessary to update the original vector. By default, for in returns a simple T for value, which is immutable. This invalidates our attempt to update the value. The iter_mut function provides a &mut T, making the value mutable. The version, Listing 6.15, works because of the iter_mut function.

Code Listing 6.15.   A for loop with a mutable iterator

```
let mut values=vec![1,2,3];

for item in values.iter_mut() {
    println!("{}", item);
    *item=*item*2;
}
```

The version in Listing 6.16 also does not work. Since the default iterator yields T, the string values are moved with the for in. The reason is that strings have move semantics. When the

Strings are iterator, ownership is transferred to the value within the loop. This causes the final println! macro, after the for block, to generate a compiler error from the borrow checker.

Code Listing 6.16.   A for loop that moves String values

```
let values=["a".to_string(), "b".to_string(),
    "c".to_string() ];
for item in values {
    println!("{}", item);
}
println!("{}", values[1]);   // borrow checker error
```

This can also be fixed with the correct iterator for the circumstances, not the default iterator. Call the iter function instead to obtain an iterator that returns &T, a reference. For our latest example, this means the Strings are borrowed, not moved, within the for block. This allows the Strings to be used later after the for block, as shown in Listing 6.17.

Code Listing 6.17.   A for loop iterates values as &T.

```
let values=["a".to_string(), "b".to_string(),
    "c".to_string() ];

for item in values.iter() {
    println!("{}", item);
}

println!("{}", values[1]);
```

The loop Expression

The loop expression is an infinite loop by design. There are various use cases for an infinite loop, including a message pump. However, you can always interrupt a loop with a break.

The loop is more than a "while true" loop. There are additional features that make the loop unique and preferred to the while true loop, in some circumstances.

Listing 6.18 is a template for a basic message pump using a loop. The loop receives a stream of messages. When the APPLICATION_EXIT message is received, the match arm ends the application, which of course exits the loop also.

Code Listing 6.18.   A loop expression example

```
loop {
    match msgid {
        APPLICATION_EXIT=>return,
```

```
        // handle other messages

        _=>write!(
            &mut std::io::stderr(),
              "Invalid message").unwrap(),
    }
};
```

The `loop` break Expression

We have used a break to interrupt a loop. However, the break can also return the loop result, but only for loop. This feature is not available for either while or for. The default return type of the break expression is the ! type, the never type. The never type means *no value*.

Listing 6.19 uses a loop to iterate an array until an even number is found.

Code Listing 6.19.   A `loop` that returns the first even number

```
let values=[1,5,6,4,5];
let mut iterator=values.iter();
let mut value;

let even=loop {
    value=iterator.next().unwrap();
    if value%2 == 0 {
        break value;
    }
};
```

In this example, we declare an integer array, iterator, and an integer value at the beginning. In the loop, the next function is called with the iterator to get successive array values. Each value is checked. If the value is even, the break interrupts the loop and returns the value as the result.

The `loop` Label

The loop label provides flexibility and extends the scope of the break and continue keywords. This feature is not supported in many other languages.

With nested loops, you are typically limited to breaking or continuing within the context of the current loop, whether a for, while, or loop expression. With labels, however, Rust can continue or break in an outer loop. This avoids layers of break or continue keywords to achieve the same result. Nothing is more inelegant than a series of break or continue keywords to unwind a nested loop. Labels are a more direct solution.

As an annotation, you can add a label to a while, for, or loop expression. Here is the syntax of a label:

```
'label:loop
'label:while
'label:for
```

Labels adhere to the naming convention of lifetimes. In addition, labels can be nested and even shadow other labels. You can transfer control to a label using a break or continue expression.

Here is the syntax:

```
break 'label;
continue 'label;
```

In Listing 6.20, a loop label is used to continue to an outer for.

Code Listing 6.20. A loop label example

```
let values=[[1,2,4,3], [5,6,7,8],
    [10,9,11,12]];
'newrow:for row in values {
    let mut prior=0;
    for element in row {
        if prior > element {
            continue 'newrow;
        }
        prior=element;
    }
    println!("{:?} in order", row);
}
```

In this example, we create a multidimensional array consisting of three rows. The goal of the application is to iterate each row and display its values. However, the values must be in ascending order. If the values are out of order, work on the current row should stop and start on the next. The outer for loop iterates the rows, while the inner for loop iterates the row values. In the inner loop, if a row value is out of order, the break returns control to the outer for loop and the next row is iterated.

Listing 6.21 is another example of using label. This example has an outer while and a nested loop. The outer loop is annotated with the thewhile label. There are also outer and inner counters. Both are incremented within their respective loops. When the inner counter is greater than or equal to the outer counter, the continue transfers control back to the outer while. The outer counter will then be incremented and the nested loop restarted. This continues while the outer counter is less than 10. The application will display a triangle of values.

Code Listing 6.21. **A `loop` label used within an inner loop**

```
let mut outercount: i8 = 0;
'thewhile: while outercount < 10 {
    outercount += 1;
    let mut innercount: i8 = 1;
    println!();
    loop {
        print!("{} ", innercount);
        if innercount >= outercount {
            continue 'thewhile;
        }
        innercount += 1;
    }
}
```

This is the result of running the application:

```
1
1 2
1 2 3
1 2 3 4
1 2 3 4 5
1 2 3 4 5 6
1 2 3 4 5 6 7
1 2 3 4 5 6 7 8
1 2 3 4 5 6 7 8 9
1 2 3 4 5 6 7 8 9 10
```

The Iterator Trait

Iterators have an important role in most languages, including Rust. Iterators iterate over a sequence of items, from beginning to end. For a collection, such as a link list, an iterator could iterate the nodes. With a sequence, such as the Fibonacci series, an iterator iterates the values in the sequence. Types that expose iterators are more flexible and convenient. For example, iterators are conveniently used with the `for`, `while`, and `loop`.

There are different types of iterators. Forward and reverse iterators are examples. As shown earlier, you can also have iterators that return a normal, mutable, reference, or mut reference item.

Iterators implement the Iterator trait. Types that implement an iterator often maintain a cursor, referred to as the `item`. The `item` is the current location in the collection or sequence. For the iterator trait, next is the only function that must be implemented. The next function returns each item, as a Result in order, as Some<T> or None when all items have been iterated.

The next function of an iterator is called implicitly with `for in` syntax. With a `while` or `loop`, you call the next function explicitly.

As an example, we will implement an iterator for the triangular sequence. The triangular sequence counts the number of points within an equilateral triangle. The formula is as follows:

$$\frac{n(n+1)}{2}$$

Figure 6.1 shows the result of equilateral triangles when the sides consist of 2, 3, or 4 points.

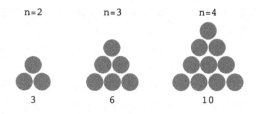

Figure 6.1   Showing equilateral triangles of different sizes

Listing 6.22 is the implementation of an iterator that iterates the triangular sequence.

Code Listing 6.22.   Implementation of an iterator for the triangular sequence

```
// state machine
struct Triangular(u32);
impl Iterator for Triangular {
    type Item = u32;
    fn next(&mut self) -> Option<Self::Item> {
            self.0+=1;
            // calculate triangular value
            Some((self.0*(self.0+1))/2)
    }
}

fn main() {
    let tri=Triangular(0);
    for count in tri.take(6) {
        println!("{}", count);
    }
}
```

Triangular is a tuple struct that implements the triangular sequence as an iterator. For that reason, the struct implements the Iterator trait; each item is a u32 type. The self.0 field represents the number of points per side of the triangle. The next function increments the number of sides and then calculates the next value in the triangular sequence. The result is returned as Some(*n*).

It's important to note that the triangular sequence is endless. The next function never returns None! For that reason, using the `next` function in the for could lead to an infinite loop. Instead, we used the `take` function to return just the next six items of the sequence.

Summary

It's hard to create a meaningful application that just marches in a straight line. Transfer of control statements is integral to controlling the program path during execution. Rust supports many language components for managing the control path, including the following:

- `if` expression
- `for` expression
- `while` expression
- `loop` expression

Each is an expression with an associated block. The control flow is based on their conditional expression.

The `if` can be combined with an `if else` and `else`. The conditional expression determines whether the `if` block is executed. The `if let` expression is similar but relies on pattern matching, not a conditional expression, to determine whether the `if` block is executed.

The `for`, `while`, and `loop` execute a block repeatedly based on a conditional expression. The block can execute 0..n times. You can use the `continue` and `break` keywords to either continue to the next iteration or interrupt the loop entirely.

You can create iterative types with the implementation of the Iterator trait. Iterators are helpful with the collections and sequences. The next function is responsible for returning the next item in the sequence using the iterator.

The `match` expression, function calls, and others means of transfer of control are discussed in later chapters.

7

Collections

Scalar types are often not convenient or practical for holding multiple values. In this chapter, we expand the conversation to include collection types, which are ideal for holding values. Imagine creating a financial application that tracks sales for 20 regions. You could create and manage 20 separate scalar variables, one for each region. It is more convenient to create a single variable—a collection of 20 elements. The collection would also be better at managing multiple elements, including sorting, creating reports, and displaying values.

The core collection types in Rust are similar to those in other languages: array, vector, and hash map.

- **Array type**: Array is a fixed-sized collection of values. The values of the array must be the same type.
- **Vector type**: Vector is an expandable collection of values that are the same type.
- **HashMap type**: A hash map is a lookup table that consists of entries. Each entry consists of a unique key and value.

These collections are comparable to similar types in other languages, but with the unique protection of the Rust environment. Most importantly, the semantics of ownership and lifetimes apply to collections.

Arrays

An array consists of a fixed number of elements of the same type. The array type and size must be established at compile time. Arrays would be a bad choice for keeping track of transactions, for example. The number of transactions will increase throughout the year, and arrays are not growable. However, arrays are perfect for keeping track of monthly values. There are 12 months a year, and that is not likely to change.

An array is a primitive type and found in the standard prelude in the Rust environment. You declare an array with a variable name and square brackets. Within the square brackets stipulate the array type and number of elements. The size of the array must be known at compile time, which limits the length to a literal or constant value. Here is the notation:

```
array_name[type; length]
```

Array literals are also described with square brackets. There are two notations. You can simply list the values, of the same type, within the square brackets, as shown here:

```
[value, value2, ..]
```

Alternatively, array literals can be described as a repeat expression, which includes a value and a repeat count. The repeat count is the size of the array. Each element will be set to the value. Here's the notation:

```
[value; repeat]
```

Listing 7.1 shows various declarations of arrays.

Code Listing 7.1. **Declaring various arrays**

```
let array_1:[i32; 4]=[1,2,3,4];  // a
let array_2=[1,2,3,4];  // b
let array_3=[10;5];  // c

println!("{:?}", array_1);  // 1, 2, 3, 4  - d
println!("{:?}", array_2);  // 1, 2, 3, 4
println!("{:?}", array_3);  // 10, 10, 10, 10, 10
```

In the example, we declare and initialize three arrays.

a. `array_1` is an array with four i32 values. It's initialized with [1,2,3,4].
b. `array_2` array is declared using type inference. It's also initialized with [1,2,3,4].
c. With the repeat expression, `array_3` array is composed of five values, each initialized to 10.
d. Display each array with the `println!` macro. Arrays implement the Debug trait. For that reason, an array can be displayed with the {:?} placeholder in the format string.

Array values are stored in contiguous memory. If declared as a local variable, the values are placed on the stack. Arrays can also be boxed where the values are copied to the heap, as discussed in Chapter 20, "Memory."

In Listing 7.2, various local variables are declared.

Code Listing 7.2. **Explicitly declared local arrays**

```
let array_1:[i32;1]=[1];          // 0x6f612ff7e8
let array_2:[i32;2]=[1,2];        // 0x6f612ff7ec
let array_3:[i32;3]=[1,2,3];      // 0x6f612ff7f4

println!("a {:p}\nb {:p}\nc {:p}", &array_1, &array_2, &array_3);
```

The arrays in this example reside on the stack and are progressively larger. Based on their addresses, as shown in Figure 7.1, the arrays are in contiguous memory. The actual memory addresses may vary based on the platform architecture. Figure 7.1 depicts the array in memory, where the diff (difference) column is the distance, in bytes, from the prior array.

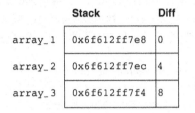

	Stack	Diff
array_1	0x6f612ff7e8	0
array_2	0x6f612ff7ec	4
array_3	0x6f612ff7f4	8

Figure 7.1. Memory layout of arrays on the stack

The len function returns the length of an array, which can be helpful at times. In Listing 7.3, we display the length of two arrays.

Code Listing 7.3. Displaying the length of two arrays

```
let array_1=[1.23, 4.56];
let array_2=[1.23, 4.56, 7.89];

println!("len 1: {} | len 2: {}", array_1.len(),
    array_2.len());    //  len 1: 2 len 2: 3
```

Multidimensional Arrays

Most arrays are single dimensional. However, multidimensional arrays can be useful also. Two-dimensional arrays consist of rows and columns, while three-dimensional arrays consist of rows, columns, and depth. And so on. There is no limit to the number of dimensions except your ability to comprehend the resulting code and readability.

Figure 7.2 shows the syntax for declaring a multidimensional array with square brackets.

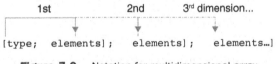

Figure 7.2. Notation for multidimensional array

Listing 7.4 shows how to declare a two-dimensional array.

Code Listing 7.4. Declaring a two-dimensional array

```
let array_1=[[1,2,3],[4,5,6]];
println!("{}", array_1.len());    // 2
```

We also display the length of `array_1`, which is 2 elements. By default, the len function applies to the first dimension of the array.

As an example, we can model a sports league as a three-dimensional array (see Listing 7.5). The dimensions would consist of divisions, teams, and then players. You have multiple divisions. Each division would have multiple teams, while each team has three players.

Code Listing 7.5. Initializing a three-dimensional array

```
let teams:[[[&str;3];4]; 2]=
    [[["Bob","Sam","Julie"],["Rich","Donis","Bob"],
        ["Hope","Al","Fred"],["Olive","Wanda","Herb"]],
    [["Alice","Sarah","Adam"],["Jeff","Jason","Eric"],
        ["Cal","Sal","Edith"],["Alice","Ted","Duane"]]];
```

The dimensions are described in order: the first dimension has three elements, second dimension has four elements, and the third dimension has two elements. In the array, the teams and divisions are anonymous. It would be nice to map each team to a unique team and division name. A lookup table would be perfect for this. Later in this chapter, we will present lookup tables in Rust, which is the HashMap type.

Accessing Array Values

You can access individual elements of an array using an index. Indexes are an offset from the beginning of the array. For that reason, arrays are zero-based, with the first element at position zero. Indexes are the usize type and appear within square brackets.

Listing 7.6 is an array of users. We access and display the second element.

Code Listing 7.6. Displaying an array element with `index`

```
let index:usize=1;


let users=["bob".to_string(), "alice".to_string(),
    "sarah".to_string(), "fred".to_string()];
println!("{}", users[index]);    // alice
```

What occurs if we attempt to move a String value from the array instead of borrowing it?

```
let users=users[1];
```

This would cause unpredictable behavior, where portions of the array are not owned. For this reason, this is not allowed and the following error occurs:

```
cannot move out of here
move occurs because `users[_]` has type `String`, which does not
implement the `Copy` trait
help: consider borrowing here: `&users[1]`
```

You can access an element in a multidimensional array with additional brackets. Each dimension requires separate brackets.

In Listing 7.7, we have a two-dimensional array. There are two rows of three users. This requires double brackets, one for each dimension, to access a specific value.

Code Listing 7.7.   Displaying an element in a two-dimensional array with an index

```
let users=
    [["bob".to_string(), "alice".to_string(), "adam".to_string()],
     ["sarah".to_string(), "fred".to_string(), "susan".to_string()]];
let user=&users[1][0];  // sarah
println!("{}", user);
```

Slices

A slice is a partial array that references a contiguous sequence of elements. A slice consists of two fields: a starting location and length. Define a slice with starting and ending indexes, with ellipses as a delimiter. Here is the notation:

```
arrayname[starting_index..ending_index]
```

The starting index is inclusive, while the ending index is exclusive. Listing 7.8 provides an example.

Code Listing 7.8.   Displaying a slice

```
let array_1=[2, 4, 6, 8];
println!("{:?}", &array_1[1..3]);  // [4, 6]
```

Figure 7.3 highlights the slice relative to the input array.

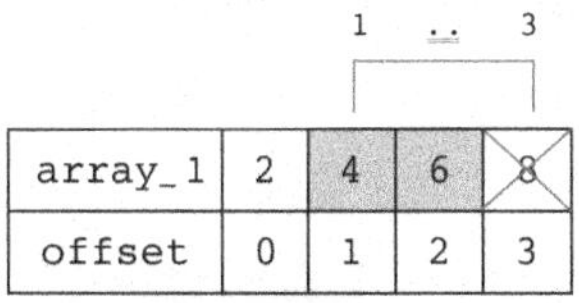

Figure 7.3. Memory layout of arrays on the stack

When defining a slice, precede the ending index with an equal sign to make it inclusive. Listing 7.9 is the same example as before, except the ending index is inclusive.

Code Listing 7.9.   Displaying a slice using an inclusive range

```
let array_1=[2,4,6,8];
println!("{:?}", &array_1[1..=3]);  // [4, 6, 8]
```

Within the slice notation, the starting and ending indexes can be omitted. When they are omitted, the default is the extents of the array. Here are the possibilities:

- The starting index defaults to the beginning of the array.
- The ending index defaults to the end of the array.
- Without either, the default is the entire array.

Listing 7.10 demonstrates using defaults within the slice notation.

Code Listing 7.10.   Showing various slice ranges

```
let array_1=[0,1,2,3,4,5];
println!("{:?}", &array_1[..]);    // [0, 1, 2, 3, 4, 5]
println!("{:?}", &array_1[2..]);   // [2, 3, 4, 5]
println!("{:?}", &array_1[..3]);   // [0, 1, 2]
println!("{:?}", &array_1[..=4]);  // [0, 1, 2, 3, 4]
println!("{:?}", &array_1[4..]);   // [4, 5]
```

Comparing Arrays

Arrays implement the PartialEq trait for comparisons. The equal (!) and not equal (!=) operators are the only logical operators that are available for array comparisons. The type of comparison is based on the array type. Valid comparisons for arrays adhere to these rules:

- Both arrays must be the same type.
- Both arrays have the same number of elements.
- The array type supports logical comparisons.

The example in Listing 7.11 confirms the equality of various arrays.

Code Listing 7.11.   Comparing arrays for equality

```
let array_1=[1,2,3,4];   // a
let array_2=[1,2,3,4];
let array_3=[1,2,5,4];
let array_4=[1,2,3];

let result=if array_1==array_2 {true}else{false};    // b
println!("array_1 == array_2: {}", result);

let result=if array_1==array_3 {true}else{false};    // c
println!("array_1 == array_3: {}", result);

let result=if array_1==array_4 {true}else{false};    // d
println!("array_1 == array_4 {}", result);
```

Here is the explanation of the comparisons:

a. Four integer arrays are declared.

b. The `array_1` and `array_2` arrays have the same number of elements and values. Therefore, the arrays are equal.

c. The `array_1` and `array_3` arrays have the same number of elements but different values. They are not equal.

d. The `array_1` and `array_4` arrays are different lengths. This disqualifies the comparison, and a compile error will occur.

Iteration

Rust provides various methods to iterate an array. The most straightforward method is a simple for loop. Arrays implement the IntoIterator trait to support this behavior. The for loop shown in Listing 7.12 returns each value of the array, in order.

Code Listing 7.12.   Iterating an array in a for loop

```
let array_1=[1,2,3,4];
for value in array_1 {
    println!("{}", value);
}
```

The previous example listed the values of the array. You can also iterate both the value and associated index. The `iter` function returns an iterator for the array. The enumerate function for the iterator then returns the current index and value, as a tuple.

Listing 7.13 shows an example.

Code Listing 7.13.   Iterating an array with the enumerate function

```
let array_1=[1,2,3,4];

let e=array_1.iter();
for element in e.enumerate() {
    println!("{:?}", element);   // (0, 1) (1, 2) (2, 3) (3, 4)
}
```

Coercion

It is sometimes necessary to convert an array to a slice or to convert a slice to an array. Fortunately, converting from an array to a slice happens implicitly in Rust. However, converting from a slice to an array is not implicit. You can call the try_into function on a slice to create an array. The array and slice must be the same length. The try_into function returns Result<T, E>. If successful, the function returns the array within the Ok<T> variant. Otherwise, an error is returned, as Err(E).

Listing 7.14 converts a slice to an array.

Code Listing 7.14.   Converting between slices and arrays

```
let slice_1=&[1,2,3,4][1..3];
let array_1:[i32; 2]=slice_1.try_into().unwrap();
```

In the example, slice_1 is created from an array and has two elements, 2 and 3. Next, the slice is converted to an array using the try_into function. If successful, the result is assigned to array_1, which also has two elements.

Vectors

Vectors are dynamic arrays. In Rust, Vec is the vector type and found in the standard prelude. Vectors are an excellent counterpoint to arrays. Often, a collection may need to grow and even shrink. This is allowed with vectors, but not arrays.

Since a vector is dynamically sized, it is unsized at compile time. For that reason, the vector itself cannot reside on the stack. Vectors have an underlying array, the backing array, where the element values are stored. This backing array is allocated on the heap.

The binding for a vector has three fields:

- The current size of the vector
- A pointer to the backing array on the heap
- The capacity (size) of the backing array

These fields are not directly available but accessed through functions, such as the capacity and len functions.

The backing array is allocated when the vector is created. It is dropped when the binding is removed from memory. *Capacity* refers to the size of the backing array. *Length* refers to the actual number of values in the vector. This is always equal to or less than the capacity. When the length exceeds the capacity, the backing array is reallocated, copied, and capacity increased. Here is an overview of what occurs when this happens:

1. Capacity is increased.
2. A larger backing array is allocated.
3. Values are copied to the new backing array.
4. The original backing array is dropped.
5. The pointer and capacity of the vector are updated.

Figure 7.4 depicts the memory for a typical vector.

Vec is a generic type. Generics are discussed in Chapter 14, "Generics." You can declare an empty vector with the constructor function, new, as shown in Listing 7.15.

Code Listing 7.15.   Declaring a vector and adding an element

```
let mut vec_1:Vec<i32>=Vec::new();
let mut vec_2=Vec::new();
vec_2.push('a');
println!("{:?}", vec_2);
```

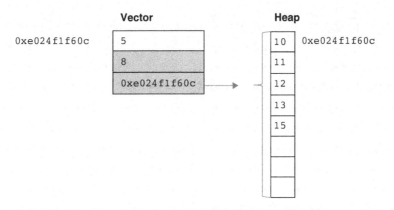

Figure 7.4. For this vector, the underlying array has five elements with a capacity of eight.

In this example, two vectors are declared. The first vector is empty but can contain i32 values. It is mutable to add values in the future. The second vector is also mutable and empty, but the type is determined with type inference. The subsequent push adds a character to the vector. This also establishes the vector as a vector of characters. The println! macro displays the second vector.

You can also initialize binding for a vector with the vec! macro, as shown in Listing 7.16. You can use either array notation or a repeat expression.

Code Listing 7.16.   A vec! macro example

```
let vec_1=vec![1,2,3,4];
println!("{:?}", vec_1);    // 1,2,3,4
```

The len and capacity functions return the length and capacity of a vector, respectively, as shown in Listing 7.17.

Code Listing 7.17.   For a vector, the length and capacity are functions.

```
let vec_1=vec![1,2,3,4];
let length=vec_1.len();        // 4
let capacity=vec_1.capacity(); // 4
println!("Length {} Capacity {}", length, capacity)
```

In this example, both the length and capacity are 4. However, the length and capacity of a vector can be, and often are, different. This is further explained later in this chapter.

Multidimensional

Declare a multidimensional vector with the same notation of a multidimensional array. Listing 7.18 is an example using the vec! macro.

Code Listing 7.18.   Declaration of two-dimensional vectors

```
let vec_1=vec![[1,2,3,4],[ 5, 6, 7, 8]];
let vec_2=vec![[1,2],[5, 6], [7, 8]];
```

This example declares a vector with two rows and four columns and a second vector with three rows and two columns.

Access

Individual values in a vector are accessible with indexes. Listing 7.19 is an example of returning an element from a vector.

Code Listing 7.19.   Accessing elements of a vector

```
let vec_1=vec![1,2,3];
let vec_2=vec![[1,2,3],[4,5,6]];
let var_1=&vec_1[2];        // 3
let var_2=&vec_2[1][1];     // 5
```

As a slice, you can return multiple values from a vector. Remember, slices are partial arrays, not a vector. The to_vec function is handy for converting a slice to a vector, as shown in Listing 7.20.

Code Listing 7.20.   Creating slices from vectors

```
let vec_1=vec![1,2,3];                 // a
let vec_2=vec![[1,2,3],[4,5,6]];       // b

let slice_1=&vec_1[0..2];              // c
let slice_2=&vec_2[0][..];             // d
let vec_3=&vec_1[..=1].to_vec();       // e
```

Here is an explanation of the example:

a. Declare vec_1 as a vector of three integers.
b. Declare vec_2 as a two-dimensional vector of integer values. The vector has two rows and three columns.
c. Create a slice from the first two values in vec_1.
d. Create a slice from the first row of values in vec_2.
e. Create a slice from the first two values in vec_1. Convert back to a vector.

When you access a vector, an invalid index can cause a panic at runtime. For example, mistreating a vector as one-based is a common problem, which can lead to this sort of error (see Listing 7.21).

Code Listing 7.21.   Invalid access to a vector

```
let vec_1=vec![1,2,3];
let var_2=vec_1[3];      // panic occurs
```

The following panic occurs when this code is executed:

```
thread 'main' panicked at 'index out of bounds: the len is 3
but the index is 3', src\main.rs:3:15
```

For accessing elements, the get function is a robust solution for getting a specific value. The get function accepts the index as a parameter and returns an Option<T> enum. If successful, Some<T> is returned where T is the vector value. Otherwise, None is returned.

The get function is used in Listing 7.22 to safely access an individual value in a vector.

Code Listing 7.22.   Getting an element with the get function

```
let vec_1=vec![1,2,3];
if let Some(var_1)=vec_1.get(3) {
      println!("{}", var_1);
} else {
      println!("Not found");
}
```

Let's examine the example. A vector with three integer values is declared. Within an if let expression, the get function is called to request the fourth value of the vector. If this is successful, var_1 is initialized with the underlying value and displayed. Otherwise, an error message is displayed.

Iteration

You can iterate a vector in the same manner as an array. Listing 7.23 provides an example.

Code Listing 7.23.   Iterating a vector with a for loop

```
let vec_1=vec![1,2,3,4];

for value in vec_1 {
    println!("{}", value);
}
```

Resizing

You can add or remove values from a mutable vec. The push and pop functions treat the vector as a stack. The push function adds an element to the end of vec, with no return value. The pop function removes the last element and returns Option<T>. If successful, the pop function returns the removed value as Some<T>. Otherwise, None is returned.

Listing 7.24 provides an example of pushing and popping values of a vec.

Code Listing 7.24.   Resizing a vector with the push and pop functions

```
let mut vec_1=Vec::new();

vec_1.push(5);
vec_1.push(10);
vec_1.push(15);
vec_1.pop();

println!("{:?}", vec_1);    // [5, 10]
```

You can also insert elements anywhere within a vector. The insert function adds a value before the position indicated. It has two parameters: the position and the value to insert. There is no return value. Listing 7.25 is an example of the insert function.

Code Listing 7.25.   Inserting new elements in a vector

```
let mut vec_1=vec![1,2,3];
vec_1.insert(1, 4);        // 1, 4, 2, 3
```

Capacity

For a vector, *capacity* refers to the size of the backing array. Managing the capacity can improve the performance of vectors.

The reallocation of the backing array occurs whenever the capacity is exceeded. Writing your code to reduce the number of reallocations can improve performance.

Listing 7.26 highlights the potential impact of capacity.

Code Listing 7.26.   Displaying the capacity of a vector

```
let mut vec_1=vec![1,2,3];

// Length 3 Capacity 3
println!("Length {} Capacity {}",
    vec_1.len(), vec_1.capacity());

vec_1.push(4);

// Length 4 Capacity 6
println!("Length {} Capacity {}",
    vec_1.len(), vec_1.capacity());
```

In this example, length and capacity for vec_1 are initially 3. The push function adds a value to the vector. The length of the vec_1 will now exceed the capacity and a reallocation of the backing array occurs. Boom—performance hit! The length is updated to 4, while the new capacity is 6. When a reallocation occurs, the capacity is doubled.

We can use our insight of the application to avoid the performance hit. In the version shown in Listing 7.27, the capacity of the vector is set to 4 initially.

Code Listing 7.27. Preset capacity with the `with_capacity` function

```
let mut vec_1=Vec::with_capacity(4);
let mut vec_2=vec![1, 2, 3];
vec_1.append(&mut vec_2);

// Length 3 Capacity 4

vec_1.push(4);

// Length 4 Capacity 4
println!("Length {} Capacity {}",
vec_1.len(), vec_1.capacity());
```

In this version, the with_capacity function sets the initial capacity to 4. We initialize the vec_1 with a second vector that has three elements. A fourth element is then added to vec_1 without a performance hit, unlike the prior example.

In addition to `with_capacity`, there are two other functions helpful for managing capacity. The `reserve` function increases the capacity of an existing vector. The `shrink_to_fit` function reduces capacity, mainly to conserve unused memory, as shown in Listing 7.28.

Code Listing 7.28. Managing a vector with `reserve` and `shrink_to_fit` functions

```
let mut vec_1=vec![2,4,6];        // length = 3 capacity = 3
vec_1.reserve(7);                 // length = 3 capacity = 10
vec_1.push(8);                    // length = 4 capacity = 10
vec_1.shrink_to_fit();            // length = 4 capacity = 4
```

HashMap

A hash map is a lookup table where entries consist of both a key and value. It is a growable collection where entries can be inserted and removed at runtime. The hash map in Rust is similar to a dictionary or map in other languages. The key must be unique within the hash map. You cannot have duplicate keys. However, values can be nonunique. You look up a specific value in the hash map using the associated key. The key is equivalent to an index for an array, but it's more versatile. You are not limited to a usize type. Keys can be virtually any type, including integers, floats, strings, structures, arrays, and even other hash maps.

The HashMap<K, V> type is the implementation of a hash map in Rust. It is a generic type with K and V as the type parameters. K is the key type, while V is the value type. Both the key and value types are homogenous. All keys in the hash map are the same type (K).

Separately, all values are the same type (V). The key type is flexible but must implement the Eq and Hash traits, as shown next. You can also add the implementation of these traits to a type with this attribute.

```
#[derive(PartialEq, Eq, Hash)]
```

For the HashMap type, the default hashing function is implemented with quadratic probing and SIMD lookup. In addition, the default hasher provides reasonable protection against hash DoS attacks. For additional security, the hashing function has a random key based on available entropy. You can substitute custom hashers that implement the BuildHasher trait. Also, alternative hashers are available in crates.io.

Hash maps are not a fixed size. For that reason, the entries for the hash map are placed on the heap. If desired, similar to a vector, you can also set the capacity of the hash map.

Creating a HashMap

The HashMap type is not included in the standard prelude. It is used less frequently than arrays or vectors. HashMap is found in the std::collections::HashMap module.

Create a HashMap with the new constructor function. This will create an empty HashMap. You can then populate the hash map using the insert function. In Listing 7.29, we create two HashMaps.

Code Listing 7.29. Declaring and initializing two hash maps

```
let mut map_1:HashMap<char, f64>=HashMap::new();
let mut map_2=HashMap::new();
map_2.insert("English".to_string(),
    "Hello".to_string());
println!("{:?}", map_2);
```

We create an empty HashMap, map_1 with the new constructor function. It is mutable to allow for additional entries later. Next a second HashMap, with the type inferred as HashMap<String, String>, is created, also mutable. It is named map_2. The insert function is then called to add an entry. map_2 is then displayed

We can also remove entries from a HashMap with the remove function. Here, we remove an entry from the HashMap in the previous example:

```
map_2.remove(&"English".to_string());
```

We can also create a HashMap from an array of tuples. field.0 of the tuple is the key, while field.1 is the value. The from function creates a HashMap from the array with the tuples as entries. Listing 7.30 shows an example.

Code Listing 7.30. Initializing a HashMap with an array

```
let famous_numbers=HashMap::from([
    ("Archimedes' Constant", 3.1415),
    ("Euler's Number", 2.7182),
    ("The Golden Ratio", 1.6180),
    ("Archimedes' Constant", 6.0221515*((10^23)as f64)),
]);
```

This example creates a HashMap<&str, f64>. The HashMap is initialized with four entries, each a famous number.

Accessing the HashMap

With the key, the `get` function looks up a value in the HashMap. The function returns an `Option` enum. If the key exists, the value is returned as `Some(value)`. Otherwise, `None` is returned.

A HashMap with two entries is created in Listing 7.31. We then request a value for a specific key, "Spanish." If successful, the value for the selected key is displayed.

Code Listing 7.31. Getting the value of a hash map entry

```
let mut map_1=HashMap::new();
map_1.insert("English", "Hello");
map_1.insert("Spanish", "Hola");

let result=map_1.get(&"Spanish");

match result {
    Some(value)=> println!("Found {}", value),
    None=>println!("Not found")
}
```

Updating an Entry

You can update an entry in the hash map simply by reinserting a value at an existing key, as shown in Listing 7.32.

Code Listing 7.32. Updating a hash map

```
let mut map_1=HashMap::new();
map_1.insert("English", "Hello");
map_1.insert("Spanish", "Hola");
map_1.insert("English", "Howdy");
```

In this example, we create a hash map with multiple entries. Each entry maps a language to a flavor of "Hello." The "English" key is seemingly added twice to the hash map. However, the second insert simply replaces the value. Therefore, the final value for the "English" key is "Howdy."

At times, it is helpful to know whether the insert function is inserting or updating a hash map entry. The return value provides this information as an Option<T> enum. When a new entry is inserted, None is returned. However, if the entry exists, the value is updated and Some<T> is returned, where T is the previous value.

Listing 7.33 is an updated version of the previous example. It is modified to confirm the result of the insert function.

Code Listing 7.33.   Confirming insertion in a hash map

```
let map_1:HashMap<bool, isize>=HashMap::new();

let mut map_2=HashMap::new();
map_2.insert("English", "Hello");
map_2.insert("Spanish", "Hola");
let result=map_2.insert("English", "Howdy");

match result {
    Some(previous)=>println!("Previous: {}", previous),
    None=>println!("New entry")
}
```

In this example, the result of the final insert function is checked. The match displays whether the entry has been inserted or replaced.

The entry function is another way to access a HashMap value. The only parameter is the HashMap key. It is a convenient way to modify a value. The entry function returns an Entry<K,V> enum, which indicates whether the entry is occupied or vacant. Here is the type.

```
pub enum Entry<'a, K: 'a, V: 'a> {
    Occupied(OccupiedEntry<'a, K, V>),
    Vacant(VacantEntry<'a, K, V>),
}
```

Occupied means the requested entry is found. *Vacant* means the entry does not exist. If the entry is occupied, the or_insert function returns a mutable reference to the value. You can dereference to change the value in place. If the entry is vacant, the or_insert function sets a default value.

Let's create an aquarium as a hash map to demonstrate the Entry<K, V> type (see Listing 7.34). Of course, the aquarium is replete with fish.

Code Listing 7.34.   Updating an entry in the hash map table

```
let mut aquarium=HashMap::from([("DottyBack", 10),
    ("Hawkfish", 5), ("Angelfish", 7)]);
let mut count=aquarium.entry("Hawkfish").or_insert(0);
*count=*count+1;

// {"DottyBack": 10, "Hawkfish": 6, "Angelfish": 7}
println!("{:?}", aquarium);
```

We created an aquarium using a mutable HashMap. Each entry is a type of fish with the quantity in the tank. The entry function is then called for "Hawkfish," as the key. The or_insert function is called on the result. This function returns a mutable reference to the value. The reference is dereferenced to increment the count of Hawkfish.

Iteration

There are a variety of methods for iterating the contents of a HashMap. The for loop returns each entry, as a tuple, from the hash map. You can accept the tuple or decompose it into separate key and value variables, as shown in Listing 7.35.

Code Listing 7.35.   Iterating a hash map to display the keys and values

```
let map_1=HashMap::from([('a',2), ('b',3)]);

for (key, value) in map_1 {
    println!("{} {}", key, value);
}
```

Summary

This chapter reviewed the primary collections in Rust: Array, Vector, and HashMap. They are invaluable for creating solutions that model real-world problem domains. Here are the unique characteristics of each:

- Array is fixed sized and created in contiguous memory.
- Vector is a dynamic array and unsized. The backing store is allocated on the heap.
- HashMap is a dynamic key / value table and unsized. The entries are allocated on the heap.

Arrays should be the preferred collection. They are simpler and better performing.

Each collection has many helpful and fun functions. Only the core functions are discussed in this chapter. Review the Rust documents to uncover other capabilities. In addition, you can customize the standard collections through the implementation of the necessary traits. This could include a trailblazing sort routine, implementing a highly performant hasher, updating the meaning of equality, and more.

8
Ownership

Ownership is part of the memory strategy in Rust that encourages safe memory management. For developers, memory management has been a consistent reason of application instability. Memory violations, freeing the same memory twice, race conditions, and various security vulnerabilities are some of the problems that can occur. Worst of all, these problems may be inconsistent and often occur intermittently. Developers sometimes spend long hours, if not days, debugging memory issues. Ownership addresses many of these issues, making the resulting code more robust and reliable, giving developers confidence in their own code.

The term "borrow checker" appears frequently in this chapter. In Rust, ownership sets the rules for memory safeness. The borrow checker is the component that enforces those rules at compile time. You need to make the borrow checker your friend. The role of the borrow checker is the same as yours—quality, safe, and secure code.

Ownership is a unique feature of Rust. For this reason, you may be unfamiliar with the concepts introduced in this chapter. However, you will soon embrace ownership as an "old friend."

Historically, native and managed languages have different memory models (and neither is similar to ownership in Rust):

- For native languages, developers typically have the primary responsibility for managing memory, especially for dynamic memory: allocating and deallocating memory, managing pointers, and making sure data is in the correct memory location. The essential benefits of this approach are transparency, flexibility, and deterministic memory management. However, making developers responsible for the nuts and bolts of memory management poses risk in the form of human error. Unfortunately, these types of problems are often uncovered at runtime, where they pose the most risk.
- Managed languages frequently have a component that manages memory, usually called garbage collection (GC). GC is a major reason that managed languages are considered *managed*. Developers largely delegate responsibility for memory management to the GC. This limits human error. However, the GC may adversely impact performance. Other shortcomings include nondeterministic memory management and some level of inflexibility based on the GC algorithm.

Ownership in Rust encompasses some of the best features of both the native and managed memory models, without the drawbacks. Memory management with ownership is deterministic, flexible, and doesn't have the performance overhead of garbage collection.

Stack and Heap Memory

Distinguishing between the stack and heap is helpful when discussing ownership.

The stack is the private memory given each thread. When a function is run, a stack frame is added to the stack and consists of the function state, such as the local variables and parameters. The size of a stack frame is determined at compile time. When a function exits, the associated stack frame is removed from memory—the stack shrinks. At that time, the function state, including local variables, is automatically removed from memory.

Heap memory provides storage for dynamic memory allocation at runtime. The heap belongs to the application and is accessible from any thread. Various languages have different keywords, such as new and delete, for managing memory allocations on the heap. When allocated, a pointer is returned to the location on the heap where the memory resides.

A stack-based replace may contain a reference to heap memory. This is common with the resource acquisition is initialization (RAII) paradigm. When the stack-based value is dropped (removed from memory), the related heap memory must also be freed. This is typically done with a destructor function or something similar.

Shallow versus Deep Copy

Shallow copy and deep copy are common techniques for transferring data between values.

A shallow copy is a bitwise copy, which is trivial and efficient. Shallow copy is appropriate for most types, except pointers. Figure 8.1 demonstrates the problem with pointers. The Complex type includes an integer and a pointer to an integer that resides on the heap. Both variablea and variableb are Complex types, where variableb is assigned variablea. A shallow copy is performed for this operation. This creates a dependency where both variables point to the same integer on the heap. Let's assume that variablea is removed from memory first and deallocates its pointer. At that time, the variableb now owns an invalid pointer, which could lead to errors at runtime.

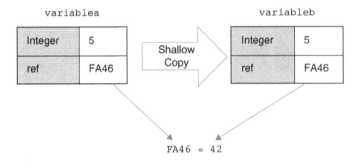

Figure 8.1. Showing the result of a shallow copy when pointers are included

A deep copy implements additional logic to handle pointers safely. When copying variablea to variableb, new memory is allocated for variableb's pointer. The value at the integer pointer for variablea is then copied to the new memory. This removes the dependency between the variables. Figure 8.2 shows the result.

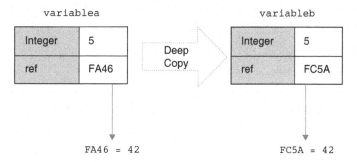

Figure 8.2. Showing the result of a deep copy when pointers are included

For deep copies, the additional logic for safe pointers makes the deep copy more expensive and less transparent. Regardless, deep copies are sometimes required for appropriate memory management, especially when you're implementing the "resource acquisition is initialization" (RAII) pattern.

Car Analogy

In this section, we will use the purchase of an automobile to describe ownership in Rust. For this comparison, a car is allowed a single owner and, of course, that person is recorded on the car's title. Limiting ownership to a single person prevents a variety of abuses, such as two people selling the same vehicle.

Let's assume you purchase a car. Several months later, someone wants to use that vehicle. Based on the single ownership principle, you have two options: sell or lend the vehicle to the other person. If selling, the title for the vehicle is transferred to the buyer. The new owner has permanent possession of the car. Of course, you have lost any claim to the car and no longer have access to the vehicle. This is called "move semantics" in Rust.

If you lend the vehicle to someone else, the borrower has temporary possession. When they are finished with the vehicle, possession of the vehicle returns to you. However, you never lost ownership. These are the principles of "copy semantics" in Rust.

Move Semantics

Rust supports both move and copy semantics, where the default is move semantics. With move semantics, ownership of a value is transferred during an assignment. This is the behavior regardless of the type of assignment: declaration, function argument, or function return. After the assignment, the original binding no longer has access to the moved value.

In Listing 8.1, the owner variable is initialized with the "automobile" String. Ownership of the String is then transferred to the new_owner variable. Afterward, new_owner has sole possession of the "automobile" String. For this reason, you can only display the new_owner variable, not the owner variable.

Code Listing 8.1.   Moving ownership of a String

```
let owner = String::from("automobile");
let new_owner = owner;
println!("{}", new_owner);
```

In Listing 8.2, a String is assigned as a function argument. This transfers ownership into the buy_car function. The owner variable in main will then lose ownership. For that reason, you cannot display owner in the println! macro afterward.

Code Listing 8.2.   Moving ownership of a String from main to buy_car

```
fn buy_car(new_owner: String) {
    println!("{}", new_owner);
}

fn main() {
    let owner = String::from("automobile");
    buy_car(owner);
    println!("{}", owner); // compile error
}
```

In Listing 8.3, the buy_car function returns a string. This returns ownership to main and reestablishes the original ownership for owner. The println! macro now successfully displays owner.

Code Listing 8.3.   Returning ownership from a function

```
fn buy_car(new_owner: String) -> String {
    println!("{}", new_owner);
    new_owner
}

fn main() {
    let mut owner = String::from("automobile");
    owner = buy_car(owner); // reestablish ownership
    println!("{}", owner);
}
```

Borrow

Ownership can be borrowed instead of moved. For borrowing, you assign a reference (&) instead of the value. In Listing 8.4, the `borrow_car` function has a reference parameter. The `borrower` parameter borrows the String. In `main`, `owner` retains ownership. The values of both `borrower` and `owner` can be displayed.

Code Listing 8.4.   String value borrowed by `borrow_car`

```
fn borrow_car(borrower: &String) {
    println!("{}", borrower);
}

fn main() {
    let owner = String::from("automobile");
    borrow_car(&owner);
    println!("{}", owner);   // works
}
```

You can borrow with either a mutable or mutable reference. However, you are limited to a single mutable reference at a time. This prevents potential concurrency issues. In Listing 8.5, multiple mutable references to the same value cause a compile error.

Code Listing 8.5.   Using two mutable references to the same value is not allowed.

```
let mut owner = String::from("automobile");
let borrower = &mut owner;
let borrower2 = &mut owner;     // compile error
println!("{} {}", borrower, borrower2);
```

Copy Semantics

Types with the Copy trait have copy semantics. When copied, a bitwise copy is performed. Types that reference external resources or memory, such as Strings, do not support copy semantics.

The Copy trait is a marker trait found in the `std::marker` module, with other marker traits. Other marker traits include Send, Size, Sync, and Unpin. Types with this trait implicitly support copy semantics. You simply perform an assignment.

In Rust, all scalar types have the copy trait. In Listing 8.6, both `width` and `height` are integers, which is a scalar type. During the assignment, the `width` value is copied to `height`. The result is that `width` and `height` own separate values.

Code Listing 8.6. An example of copy semantics

```
let width = 10;
let height = width;
println!("W {} : H {}", width, height);
```

Clone Trait

Implement the Clone trait when a deep copy is required.

The String type, for example, implements the Clone trait. Why? Strings include a pointer to the underlying string, which is on the heap. For this reason, the String type does not support copy semantics. If allowed, this would create problematic dependencies. Instead, the String type implements a deep copy using the Clone trait. Here are the general steps for cloning Strings:

1. For the target String, allocate memory on the heap for the String buffer.
2. Copy the buffer from the originating String into the new buffer.
3. Update the target String to reference this memory.

The result of this are Strings with the same value, `stringa` and `stringb`, at different locations in memory (see Figure 8.3).

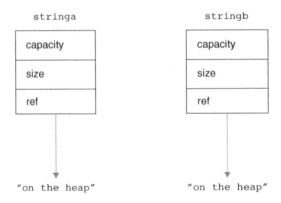

Figure 8.3. Showing result of cloning stringb from stringa

Cloning must be invoked explicitly with the `clone` function, which is a member of the Clone trait. In Listing 8.7, the `stringa` variable is cloned to initialize `stringb`.

Code Listing 8.7. Cloning a String

```
let stringa = String::from("data");
let stringb = stringa.clone();
println!("{} {}", stringa, stringb)
```

Copy Trait

You can assign the Copy trait to types that support a shallow copy.

Here is the Copy trait:

```
pub trait Copy: Clone { }
```

Notice that the Clone trait is a supertrait of the Copy trait.

Structs support move semantics by default. An assignment transfers ownership. See Listing 8.8.

Code Listing 8.8.   When assigned, structs are moved by default.

```
struct Transaction {
    debit: bool,
    amount: f32,
}

fn main() {
    let t1=Transaction{debit: true, amount: 32.12};
    let t2=t1;  // moved
}
```

The Copy trait can be applied to structs if each field supports copy semantics. This is a trivial implementation and can be done with the #[derive] attribute, as shown in Listing 8.9.

Code Listing 8.9.   Applying the Copy trait using the derive attribute

```
#[derive(Copy, Clone)]
struct Transaction {
    debit: bool,
    amount: f32,
}

let t2 = t1;  // copied
```

Let's add a description field, as a String type, to Transaction, as shown next. This would appear to be a reasonable addition to our structure. However, this means the struct no longer supports copy semantics. This is because the added String field does not support copy semantics.

```
struct Transaction {
    description: String,
    debit: bool,
    amount: f32,
}
```

However, references support copy semantics. In Listing 8.10, we have modified the structure to change the String to &String. The struct now supports copy semantics, which is provided with the #[derive] attribute.

Code Listing 8.10.   This is a struct that supports copy semantics.

```
#[derive(Copy, Clone)]
struct Transaction<'a> {
    description: &'a String,
    debit: bool,
    amount: f32,
}
    . . .
let t2 = t1; // copied
```

You can implement the Copy trait manually, not using the #[derive] attribute. As a marker trait, there is no implementation for the Copy trait. The existence of the Copy trait instructs Rust to perform a bitwise copy. However, the Clone trait must be implemented as the super-trait. This means implementing the clone function. The function should return the current object by value, which is consistent with a bitwise copy. See Listing 8.11 for the implementation of the Copy trait for Transaction.

Code Listing 8.11. Explicit implementation of the Copy trait

```
impl Copy for Transaction {}

impl Clone for Transaction {
    fn clone(&self) -> Transaction {
        *self  // return current object by value
    }
}

struct Transaction {
    debit: bool,
    amount: f32,
}
```

Clone Trait

The Clone trait implements a deep copy for types that do not support a bitwise copy.

For the Clone trait, you must implement the clone function, which returns the cloned value. The implementation must also remove any dependencies caused by pointers.

For struct, assuming all the fields are cloneable, you can simply add the #[derive] attribute for the Clone trait. This attribute calls the clone method on each field.

Every member of the Transaction type is cloneable. This means you can apply the #[derive(Clone)] attribute. See Listing 8.12.

Code Listing 8.12.   Applying the Clone trait to Transaction

```
#[derive(Clone)]
    struct Transaction {
        description: String,
        debit: bool,
        amount: f32,
    }

...

    let t1 = Transaction {
        description: String::from("ATM"),
        debit: true,
        amount: 32.12,
    };
```

If desired, you can explicitly implement the Clone trait for Transaction. In our imple-mentation, the description field is reset when cloning a Transaction. The other fields are just copied for cloning. See Listing 8.13 for the implementation of the trait.

Code Listing 8.13.   Explicit implementation of the Clone trait

```
struct Transaction {
    description: String,
    debit: bool,
    amount: f32,
}

impl Clone for Transaction {
    fn clone(&self) -> Transaction {
        let temp = Transaction {
            description: String::new(),
            debit: self.debit,
            amount: self.amount,
        };
        return temp;
    }
}
```

Summary

Ownership is a seminal feature of Rust programming and enforces safe and secure programming techniques for memory management. This prevents many of the common memory-related problems that occur in other languages.

The borrow checker enforces the rules of ownership at compile time, preventing memory errors from seeping into binaries and occurring at runtime.

Move semantics is the default behavior. When you assign a value, ownership is moved. If a reference is assigned, a borrow occurs and ownership is not transferred.

Alternatively, types that have the Copy trait support copy semantics. Copy semantics is implicit and performs a bitwise copy, which is a shallow copy. This is appropriate for scalar types.

You can apply the Copy trait with the `#[derive(Copy, Clone]` attribute. However, you can manually implement either trait. It is more common to implement the Clone trait.

You implement the Clone trait for types that require a deep copy. The actual implementation of the trait depends on the type.

Lifetimes also provide memory safeness. Ownership and lifetimes together provide a complete solution for memory management in Rust. The conversation on lifetimes is next.

9

Lifetimes

An important promise from Rust to developers is memory safeness, which is enforced within the ownership model. Ownership and borrowing are two of the three pillars in the ownership model. Lifetimes is the final pillar to complete our conversation about the subject. Despite this laudable goal, there is a general misunderstanding of lifetimes within the Rust community. Most Rust developers are satisfied knowing just enough about lifetimes to prevent the borrow checker from complaining. The objective of this chapter is to provide clarity on this important topic. Lifetimes should be a benefit, not something to ignore.

Lifetimes is another unique feature within the Rust language. Other languages, such as C, C++, and Java, do not have a lifetime feature, or something similar. For most developers, this means a lack of familiar context as a starting point to understanding lifetimes. No worries. You will learn both the context and syntax of lifetimes in this chapter.

The principal objective of lifetimes is to prevent dangling references. *That's it!* Keep this in mind especially when you're deep in the vagaries of lifetimes. What is a dangling reference? A dangling reference occurs when a reference outlives a borrowed value. At that time, the reference points to invalid memory.

Listing 9.1 shows an example of a dangling reference.

Code Listing 9.1. `ref1` **becomes a dangling reference**

```
fn main() {
    let ref1;
    { // -------------------- inner block (start)
        let num1=1;
        ref1=&num1;
    } // -------------------- inner block (end)
    println!("{}", ref1);  // dangling reference
}
```

Here, `ref1` is a reference and it borrows `num1`, which is then dropped at the end of the inner block. Therefore, the reference to `num1` in the `println!` macro outlives the borrowed value—the very definition of a dangling reference. If allowed to continue, the program is no longer memory safe.

It is hard to discuss lifetimes without including the borrow checker in the conversation. The borrow checker relies on lifetimes to determine when a reference outlives the borrowed value. Developers frequently *fight with the borrow checker*. A goal of the last chapter was to make the borrow checker your friend. We continue that goal in this chapter.

Lifetimes is another Rust feature included in zero-cost abstraction. The idioms of lifetimes are enforced at compile time. You receive the full benefits of memory safeness without any performance penalty.

We will start with the building blocks of lifetimes. After that, more complex concepts are introduced, including lifetimes subtyping.

Introduction to Lifetimes

A lifetime spans the *lifetime* of a value. The interrelationship of various lifetimes can expose dangling references. A lifetime starts at the binding and continues until the variable is dropped.

Listing 9.2 is a trivial example of lifetimes.

Code Listing 9.2.   Lifetimes of num1 and num2

```
fn main() {
    let num1=1; // <----- lifetime for num1 starts
    let num2=2; // <----- lifetime for num2 starts
}  // lifetime for num1 and num2 ends
```

In the previous example, the lifetimes are described but not named. It is more concise to show a lifetime name instead of a wordy description. Lifetimes are named with an apostrophe and a variable name. By convention, lifetime names are alphabetic letters, starting with 'a. Subsequent lifetimes would be 'b, 'c, 'd, and so on. If desired, lifetimes can have nonconventional names, such as "moon" and "stars." For convenience, choosing an enumerable value for a lifetime name is preferred, however.

Here is an example with references, values, and lifetimes. The lifetimes shown here are inferred, similar to type inference:

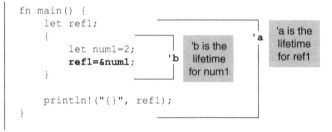

Here, ref1 is a reference and it borrows num1. However, the lifetime for ref1 outlives the lifetime for num1, as shown. Because of this, at the end of lifetime 'b, num1 is dropped. At that time, ref1 becomes a dangling reference. Therefore, ref1 in the subsequent println! macro is invalid. Fortunately, the borrow checker detects this problem at compile time and displays the following message:

```
5 |             ref1=&num1;
  |                  ^^^^^ borrowed value does not live long enough
6 |     }
  |     - `num1` dropped here while still borrowed
```

The "does not live long enough" message is probably the most dreaded compiler message in Rust. Developers new to Rust may receive this message frequently. It is an indication of a dangling reference. Nonetheless, the message is informative, correctly identifying that the borrowed value, num1, has not lived long enough, thus leaving ref1 as a dangling reference.

Function Headers and Lifetimes

Functions can create unsafe memory access. Functions that accept references as arguments and return values require special consideration.

Function headers with references have three classifications of a lifetime: input lifetime, output lifetime, and target lifetime.

Input lifetime is the lifetime of a function argument as a reference. You can have multiple input lifetimes. Listing 9.3 is an example of an input lifetime.

Code Listing 9.3.   An input lifetime for do_something is lifetime 'a

```
fn do_something(ref1:&i32){
      // doing something
}
fn main() {
    let num1=1;
    do_something(&num1);        'a    'a is the
}                                      lifetime
                                       for num1
```

Here, the function is called with &num1 as the argument. This sets the input lifetime for ref1 to lifetime 'a. This is the lifetime received from the num1 function argument. This indicates how long the value you are borrowing lives.

Output lifetime is the lifetime for the return value of the function. The output lifetime is typically selected from one of the input lifetimes. There are a couple of reasons for this. A reference to a local value cannot be returned from a function since the borrowed value is immediately dropped. You can return a reference to a static value, but that is less common. Therefore, an input lifetime is more often returned as the output lifetime.

In Listing 9.4, the do_something function accepts and returns a reference. For the output lifetime, there is one input lifetime to select from. Therefore, the input and output lifetimes are lifetime 'a.

Code Listing 9.4. Output lifetime for `do_something` is lifetime `'a`.

```
// lifetime:         'a              'a
fn do_something(ref1:&i32)->&i32{
    ref1  // lifetime 'a returned
}

fn main() {
    let num1=1;
    let result=do_something(&num1);
}
```

'a 'a is the
    lifetime
    for num1

Lastly, the target lifetime is the lifetime of the reference that is bound to the function result. Listing 9.5 illustrates the three lifetimes: input, output, and target.

Code Listing 9.5. This example highlights various lifetimes.

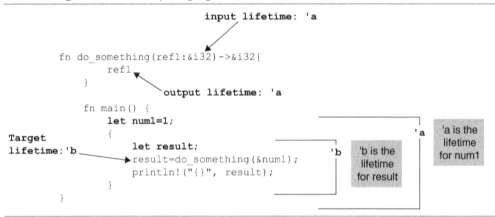

Will this example compile? Specifically, whenever the target lifetime outlives the output lifetime, there is the potential of a dangling reference. Let's break down this explanation. Ultimately, the output lifetime is the lifetime of a borrowed value. The borrowed value cannot be bound to a reference with a longer lifetime. If a reference outlives the borrowed value, it becomes a dangling reference.

In the preceding example, the target lifetime (`'b`) is fully contained within the output lifetime (`'a`). Therefore, the `result` variable is always valid. The compiler will compile the program successfully.

Listing 9.6 is another example to consider with a different outcome.

Code Listing 9.6.   Target lifetime outlives the output lifetime.

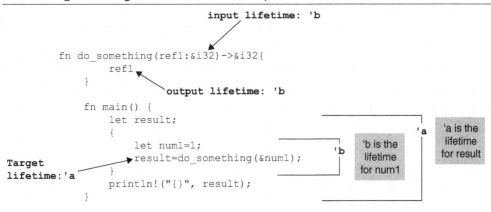

This version of the example does not compile. Why? The output lifetime for the function return is lifetime `'b`. This is the lifetime for num1. However, the target lifetime for result is lifetime `'a`. Regrettably, the target lifetime outlives the output lifetime (i.e., result outlives num1). When this occurs, there is a potential for a dangling reference. The borrow checker will highlight the problem in an error message.

A lifetime table is often helpful when we're analyzing the various lifetimes. Table 9.1 is the lifetime table for the previous example.

Table 9.1.   Target lifetime greater than output lifetime

Type	Entity	Borrow	Lifetime
input	ref1	num1	`'b`
output	ref1	num1	`'b`
Target	result	num1	`'a`

Lifetime Annotation

Until now, lifetimes have been inferred. We have not explicitly named lifetimes. With lifetime annotations, you can formally name lifetimes. A lifetime annotation only *labels* a lifetime. It does not modify a lifetime in any manner. However, as you will see, just labeling a lifetime can be helpful. It allows you to instruct the borrow checker on your intention.

Lifetime annotation requires declaring lifetime parameters. This is done using the same syntax for declaring generic parameters, which are reviewed in Chapter 14, "Generics." Instead, you include lifetimes.

Listing 9.7 is an example of declaring a lifetime parameter with lifetime annotation.

Code Listing 9.7.   Formally naming a lifetime as lifetime 'a

```
fn do_something<'a>(ref1:&'a i32)->&'a i32{
    ref1
}

fn main() {
    let num1=1;
    let result=do_something(&num1);
    println!("{}", result);
}
```

'b lifetime 'b is inferred   'a lifetime 'a is named

In this example, the input lifetime is formally named lifetime 'a. This labels the lifetime for num1. The lifetime for num1 is unchanged; it's simply formally named. The target lifetime is inferred as lifetime 'b.

Table 9.2 is the lifetime table for this example.

Table 9.2.   Output lifetime greater than target (Example is memory safe)

Type	Entity	Borrow	Lifetime
input	ref1	num1	'a
output	ref1	num1	'a
target	result	num1	'b

Lifetime Elision

Within certain guidelines, the compiler is allowed to infer lifetimes, such as the input and output lifetimes. This is called lifetime elision. Eliding lifetimes can make code easier to read and more concise.

Here is an example of lifetime elision where the lifetimes are elided (notice the absence of lifetime annotations):

```
fn do_something(ref1:&i32)->&i32{
    ref1
}
```

The following is the desugared version of the function header without elision:

```
fn do_something<'a>(ref1:&'a i32)->&'a i32{
    ref1
}
```

Certain rules apply to lifetime elision:

- Each input lifetime that is elided is assigned a separate lifetime.
- When there is a single input lifetime, it is elided to the output lifetime.
- For methods, if self is a reference, the lifetime for self is elided to the output lifetimes.

In general, lifetime elision cannot occur when the output lifetime is ambiguous. The compiler will not guess the output lifetime. It is easier not to compile and ask you to resolve the ambiguity with explicit lifetime annotation.

Lifetime elision is always optional. If desired, you can always explicitly name lifetimes.

Complex Lifetimes

Some functions accept multiple parameters as references. Each reference may have the same or a different input lifetime. This also means multiple candidates for the output lifetime. This creates ambiguity for the borrow checker. Which input lifetime should be assigned to the return value as the output lifetime? As mentioned, the compiler will not guess the proper output lifetime. With lifetime annotation, you can state your intention to the compiler.

The function in Listing 9.8 accepts two references. With lifetime annotation, we indicate that the return value should be lifetime 'a.

Code Listing 9.8. Named ('a) and inferred lifetimes ('b and 'c)

```
fn do_something<'a>(ref1:&'a i32, ref2:&i32)->&'a i32{
    ref1
}

fn main() {
    let num1=1;
    let num2=2;
    let result;
    result=do_something(
        &num1, &num2);
    println!("{}", result)
}
```

This example has three lifetimes. Lifetime 'a is formally named, while lifetimes 'b and 'c are inferred. The do_something function returns lifetime 'a. This is a constraint preventing the return of any other lifetime. For this reason, you can only return the first parameter.

Table 9.3 describes the various lifetimes in this example.

Table 9.3. Output lifetime greater than target (Example is memory safe)

Type	Value	Borrow	Lifetime
input	ref1	num1	'a
input	ref2	num2	'b
output	ref1	num1	'a
target	result	num1	'c

Listing 9.9 shows a different version of the previous example. The do_something function still has two references and returns a reference. However, both input lifetimes are named in this example, as lifetime 'a and 'b. As the output lifetime, the function can only return lifetime 'b.

In addition, we have moved the code around in `main`. Consequently, some of the lifetimes have also been moved.

Code Listing 9.9.   Example of overlapping lifetimes

```
fn do_something<'a, 'b>(ref1:&'a i32, ref2:&'b i32)->&'b i32{
    ref2
}

fn main() {
    let result;
    let num1=1;
    {
        let num2=2;
        result=do_something(&num1, &num2);
    }
    println!("{}", result)
}
```

Examine Table 9.4, the lifetime table for this example, to identify any problems. Most importantly, is there a potential for a dangling reference?

Table 9.4.   Target lifetime outlives the output lifetime

Type	Value	Borrow	Lifetime
input	ref1	num1	'a
input	ref2	num2	'b
output	ref2	num2	'b
target	result	num2	'c

In this example, the output lifetime does not live long enough. This means num2 will be dropped from memory while `result` is borrowing the value. This creates a dangling reference. This is another example where the source code will not compile.

Sharing a Lifetime

You can share an input lifetime across multiple parameters. Recall that an input lifetime represents the lifetime of a borrowed value. When you share a lifetime, the scope of the lifetime is the intersection of lifetimes of two borrowed values.

In Listing 9.10, the `do_something` function has two parameters. Both references are assigned the same lifetime, `'a`.

Code Listing 9.10. Another example of overlapping lifetimes

```
fn do_something<'a>(ref1:&'a i32, ref2:&'a i32)->&'a i32{
    ref1
}

fn main() {
    let result;
    let num1=1;
    {
        let num2=2;
        result=do_something(&num1, &num2);
    }
    println!("{}", result)
}
```

```
                                            'num1


                                            'num2    'a
```

As function arguments, ref1 borrows num1 and ref2 borrows num2. Lifetime 'a labels the intersection of the lifetimes of num1 and num2. This will become the input lifetime for both references. Eventually, this will also become the output lifetime for this function, as this is the only input lifetime to select from.

In this example, the intersection of the lifetimes for num1 and num2, lifetime 'a, does not live long enough. For this reason, the program does not compile. This is despite the fact the lifetime for num1 does live long enough.

Table 9.5 is the lifetime table for this example.

Table 9.5. Another example of the output lifetime not living long enough

Type	Value	Borrow	Lifetime
input	ref1	num1	'a='num1 ∩ 'num2
input	ref2	num2	'a='num1 ∩ 'num2
output	ref1	num1	'a='num1 ∩ 'num2
target	Result		'b

When a lifetime is shared, the borrow checker adopts a conservative approach. It will assume the *intersection* of the combined lifetimes, which is the smaller lifetime, versus a *union*.

Static Lifetimes

A static lifetime, 'static, spans the entire application. For example, globals have a static lifetime. By definition, other lifetimes, shorter than the entire application, cannot outlive the static lifetime.

For Rust, string literals have a static lifetime. The task function returns a string literal as an error message. String literals are &str values, which are always static, as shown in Listing 9.11.

Code Listing 9.11.   The str type must be static.

```
fn task1(ref1:&i32)->Result<i32, &'static str>{
    Err("error found")
}
```

Structs and Lifetimes

Lifetimes for structs have the same role as lifetimes elsewhere—preventing dangling references. This may occur because structs can have fields that are references. A dangling reference can occur if the field references a value that does not live long enough. Fields of a struct must have a lifetime as long as the struct itself.

For lifetime annotation, declare lifetime parameters after the struct name. You can then assign named lifetimes to fields, which are references. There is no lifetime elision for structs. Structs with references as fields require lifetimes.

Listing 9.12 is an example of a struct containing a reference.

Code Listing 9.12.   Struct lifetime applied to a field

```
struct Data<'a>{
    field1:&'a i32
}

fn main() {
    let num1=1;
    let obj=Data{field1:&num1};
    println!("{}", obj.field1)
}
```

'b is the lifetime for obj

'a is the lifetime for num1

In this example, a `Data` struct borrows `num1` as field1. In this case, the struct will not outlive the borrowed value. For that reason, there is no opportunity for a dangling reference.

Methods and Lifetimes

Functions implemented for structs, methods, can also accept and return references. This creates the same potential for dangling references, which can be identified with lifetimes. Methods can share the lifetime parameters of the struct or declare free lifetimes, which are specific to the method.

Lifetime annotations are considered part of the struct type. When we're implementing methods, the `impl` block must reference the lifetime parameters, as part of the struct's name. The lifetime parameters of the struct are both included after the `impl` keyword and the struct name.

Case in point, a structure with lifetimes `'a` and `'b` would have the `impl` block shown in Listing 9.13.

Code Listing 9.13.   The `impl` block for a struct with lifetimes

```
struct Data<'a, 'b>{
    field1:&'a mut i32,
    field2:&'b mut i32,
}

impl<'a, 'b> Data<'a, 'b> {
}
```

When implementing methods, do not redeclare the lifetimes of the struct. You can simply apply the lifetimes to references within the function header. Remember, this is the same lifetime that can be applied to fields. When the same lifetime is applied to multiple items, the compiler takes a conservative approach. The named lifetime will be the intersection of the various items.

Listing 9.14 demonstrates the possible dual role of lifetimes within structs and methods. Lifetime `'a` is used for both a field and method parameter.

Code Listing 9.14.   Lifetime `'a` applied to the `Data` struct and `do_something` method

```
struct Data<'a>
    field1:&'a i32,
}

impl<'a> Data<'a> {
    fn do_something(self:&Self, ref1:&'a i32)->&'a i32 {
        ref1
    }
}

fn main(){
    let num1=1;
    let obj=Data{field1:&num1};        'num1
    let result;
    {
        let num2=2;
        result=obj.do_something(&num2);    'num2    'a
    }
    println!("{}", result);
}
```

Will this example compile? Lifetime `'a`, intersection of the lifetimes for num1 and num2, is less than the lifetime of obj, which is the related struct. Therefore, the example will not compile. The reason is that lifetime `'a` does not outlive the struct instance, obj.

Methods can also declare free lifetimes. Free lifetimes are declared in the method definition, not the struct. They are called free lifetimes because they are free of the lifetime requirements of the struct.

The struct in Listing 9.15 has two methods. Both use free lifetimes.

Code Listing 9.15. Combining lifetimes from struct and free methods

```
struct Data<'a>{
    field1:&'a i32,
}

impl<'a> Data<'a> {
    fn do_something1<'b>(self: &Self,
                ref1:&'b i32)->&'b i32 {
        ref1
    }

    fn do_something2<'b>(self: &Self, ref1:&'a i32,
            ref2:&'b i32)->&'a i32 {
        ref1
    }
}
```

In the preceding example, lifetime `'a` is declared with the struct. The `Data` struct has `do_something1` and `do_something2` methods. The `do_something1` method declares lifetime `'b`, which is a free lifetime. It is assigned to the input lifetime of `ref1`. For the `do_something2` method, `'b` is declared again as a free lifetime. However, lifetime `'a` from the struct is also used as the input lifetime for the other parameter. You can use both struct lifetimes and free lifetimes within the same method.

Free lifetimes, even the same lifetime, are not shared across methods. Lifetime `'b` in the previous example was not shared across both methods. Each has their own lifetime `'b`. However, lifetimes declared in a struct are shareable across the methods of the struct.

Subtyping Lifetimes

Subtyping lifetimes creates an extensible relationship between two lifetimes. This relates to concepts established in object-oriented programming.

In object-oriented programming, subtyping typically refers to interfaces. A subtype is the interface that extends the behavior of a super interface. The principle of substitutability then applies, where the subtype can be substituted for the super interface, at all times.

For lifetimes, a subtype lifetime extends another lifetime. You can then substitute a base lifetime with a subtype lifetime.

Enough of the theoretical! Let's look at a practical example, including where subtype lifetimes are helpful. The example in Listing 9.16 does not compile.

Code Listing 9.16.   Normal lifetimes, no subtyping

```
fn either_one<'a, 'b>(ref1:&'a i32,
                ref2:&'b i32, flag:bool)->&'b i32 {
      if flag {
          ref1
      } else {
          ref2
      }
  }

  fn main() {
      let num1=1;
      {
          let num2=2;
          let result=either_one(&num1,
              &num2, true);
      }
  }
```

'a is the lifetime for result

'b is the lifetime for num1

The output lifetime for the either_one function is lifetime **'b**. Therefore, we cannot return lifetime **'a**. Nonetheless, we attempt to return ref1, with a lifetime **'a**. Kaboom! However, that is silly! Close examination of main shows that lifetime **'a** extends lifetime **'b**. Stated otherwise, lifetime **'a** is the subtype of lifetime **'b**. This means the principle of substitutability should apply and can solve our problem.

Here is the syntax for declaring a lifetime parameter as a subtype:

'subtype:'basetype

The version shown in Listing 9.17 will compile correctly. The changes are limited to the function header. In the lifetime declaration, lifetime **'a** is defined as the subtype for lifetime **'b**. This means lifetime **'a** can substitute for lifetime **'b**. That is the solution required for this application to work.

Code Listing 9.17.   Lifetime 'a subtypes 'b.

```
Fn either_one<'a:'b>(ref1:&'a i32,
              ref2:&'b i32, flag:bool)->&'b i32 {
      if flag {
          ref1
      } else {
          ref2
      }
  }

  fn main() {
      let num1=1;
      {
```

```
        let num2=2;
        let result=either_one(&num1, &num2, true);
    }
}
```

Anonymous Lifetimes

Lifetime elision is based on three specific rules, as established earlier. However, lifetime elision is not perfect. There may be situations where a lifetime is apparent but eliding does not apply. Also, lifetime annotation can be overly ornate, as you have probably noticed! This can result in dense code. For these scenarios, you may want to use anonymous lifetime, which is '_.

Listing 9.18 is an example where an anonymous lifetime could be useful. For structs with lifetimes, the syntax of the impl block is somewhat dense, as mentioned.

Code Listing 9.18.   Lifetime 'a explicitly applied to struct and impl block

```
struct Data<'a>{
    field1:&'a i32,
}

impl<'a> Data<'a> {
    fn do_something<'b>(&self, ref1:&'b i32)->&'b i32 {
        ref1
    }
}
```

Since there is no variability in the syntax, you might want to elide lifetimes in the impl block. This is outside the rules of lifetime elision. The anonymous lifetime, however, allows you to explicitly elide the lifetime, as demonstrated in Listing 9.19.

Code Listing 9.19.   Demonstrating how to apply anonymous lifetimes

```
impl Data<'_> {
    fn do_something<'b>(&self, ref1:&'b i32)->&'b i32 {
        ref1
    }
}
```

Generics and Lifetimes

Generic and lifetime parameters are declared within angle brackets after a function or struct. You have seen generic and lifetime parameters implemented separately. Lifetime and generic parameters can also be combined in the same declarations.

When we are declaring both, lifetime parameters should precede the generic type parameters in the declaration. Otherwise, lifetimes and generics will behave as expected.

Listing 9.20 is an example function with both lifetime and generic parameters.

Code Listing 9.20.   Combining lifetime and generic parameters

```
fn do_something<'a, T>(ref1:&'a T, ref2:&T)->&'a T{
    ref1
}
```

Summary

The lifetimes feature is a difficult subject that cannot be ignored. It is a component of the ownership model that ensures memory safeness. Specifically, lifetimes remove the possibility of dangling references, which are the leading cause of vulnerable memory in non-Rust programming languages.

A dangling reference occurs when a borrowed value does not live long enough making the memory unsafe. Luckily, however, the borrow checker is tasked with preventing dangling references. This is done at compile time as part of zero-cost abstraction.

Function headers with references have lifetimes, either explicit or elided. There are three types of lifetimes:

- The input lifetime is the lifetime of a borrowed value.
- The output lifetime is the lifetime returned from the function.
- The target lifetime is the lifetime of the binding from the function return.

You have learned that when the output lifetime is less than the target lifetime, a dangling reference can occur. The lifetime table is a helpful tool in understanding the relationship between lifetimes and uncover problems before the borrow checker.

Lifetime elision elides the lifetimes, which makes the syntax more concise and readable. In some circumstances, when this is not available, anonymous lifetimes can help.

With lifetime annotation, you can formally name lifetimes. Lifetime parameters are declared using the syntax of generics.

Structs with references also have lifetimes. The goal is to ensure that references live as long as the struct. Lifetimes in a structure cannot be elided. Methods can use lifetimes declared in the struct or free lifetimes.

Hopefully, after the last two chapters, you have become *close* friends with the borrow checker.

10

References

References, `&T`, are primitives and the preferred pointer type in Rust.

A reference is a safe pointer to a value located somewhere in memory, whether the stack, heap, or static data area. You can access the value through the reference.

References are values themself. For that reason, references can even reference other references, as a value.

Actually, Rust has two types of pointers: safe pointers (references) and raw pointers, which are inherently unsafe. The safeness of a reference is enforced at compile time with the borrow checker, as part of the ownership model. However, raw pointers are outside the scope of the borrow checker. For this reason, references are preferred in Rust. Raw pointers are primarily used with interoperability and reviewed in Chapter 22, "Interoperability."

Pointers, including references, are first-class citizens in the Rust language and have the same capabilities as any other primitive type. Pointers can be used as variables, fields in a structure, function parameters, or even function return values.

References, `&T` and `&mut T`, are dissimilar to non-pointer types. This is a subtle but important distinction. For example, `i32` and `&i32` are different types. The `i32` type refers to a 32-bit integer value, whereas `&i32` is a reference to a i32 value. In addition, a reference is a fixed size, where the size is dependent on the platform architecture.

Assume there are two local variables on the stack. The variable `val_a` is 10, and `ref_a` is a reference to `val_a`. The size of `val_a` is 4 bytes, while `ref_a` is 8 bytes, assuming a 64-bit architecture. Figure 10.1 provides a view of the stack in memory.

Figure 10.1. Depiction of val_a and ref_a

Declaration

As with other types, you create a normal variable binding for a reference with the let state-ment. However, an ampersand (&) should precede the type to define a reference. Within an expression, however, the & operator has a different meaning. It is used to "get the memory address" of a value.

References are also strongly typed and should be initialized with references of the same type. In the following example, ref_a is a &i32 reference and initialized with the &10, also a &i32 reference:

```
let ref_a:&i32=&10;
```

You can also infer the reference type, as shown here:

```
let ref_a=&10;
```

In Listing 10.1, we show various methods for declaring references.

Code Listing 10.1.   Declaring references

```
let val_a=10;
let ref_a: &i32=&val_a;
let ref_b=ref_a;
```

We declare the ref_a variable as &i32 initialized &10, which is a reference to 10 as a literal. The ref_b variable is initialized with ref_a. The result is two references to the same value, 10. This is safe because both references are immutable.

Borrowing

References borrow values. This means ownership remains with the original binding. In Listing 10.2, the reference is the borrower.

Code Listing 10.2.   Using a reference to borrow a value

```
let val_a=10;  // owner of 10
ref_a=&val_a;  // borrow of 10
```

The lifetime of the owner must outlive the borrower (i.e., the reference). When the owner no longer exists, the referenced value is no longer available, as discussed in the previous chapter. The borrower cannot continue to use the value.

In Listing 10.3, the owner outlives the borrower.

Code Listing 10.3.   The value outlives its reference.

```
let val_a=10;              // owner

    {
        let ref_a=&val_a;     // borrower
    }

    println!("{}", val_a);
```

The `val_a` variable is declared first in the outer block. It is the owner of the 10 value. In the inner block, `ref_a` references `val_a`. Now `ref_a` is the borrower of the 10 value. After the inner block closes, ref_a is dropped but val_a remains available. Therefore, the owner outlives the borrower—and life is good!

Let's switch this around in Listing 10.4.

Code Listing 10.4.   The reference outlives the value.

```
let ref_a: &i32;         // borrower
    {
        let val_a=10;
        ref_a=&val_a;        // owner
    }

    println!("{}", ref_a);  // darn!
```

In this version, the reference, `ref_a`, is declared in the outer block. The variable `val_a` is declared within the inner block and as the owner of the 10 value. Next, `ref_a` references `val_a`. It becomes a borrower of the 10 value. After the inner block ends, `val_a` no longer exists. In the outer block, `ref_a` continues to borrow the value, however. The borrow checker will complain since the lifetime of the borrower exceeds that of the owner. The following message is displayed.

```
ref_a=&val_a;
      ^^^^^^ borrowed value does not live long enough
```

Dereferencing

For references, the ★ (asterisk) operator provides access to the referenced value. This is called dereferencing.

We dereference `ref_a` and `ref_b` in Listing 10.5.

Code Listing 10.5.   Dereferencing a reference to access the indirect value

```
let ref_a=&10;
let ref_b=&20;
let result=*ref_a + *ref_b;
```

Two references are declared, `ref_a` and `ref_b`, at the start. Both references are then dereferenced (using the * operator) to access the indirect values of 10 and 20. The values, not the references, are then totaled.

The built-in mathematical operators implement the Deref and DerefMut traits to implicitly dereference a reference. When performing mathematical operations, it is assumed that the values at the memory address are the target, not the pointers themselves.

In the previous example, wasn't the intention obvious? Adding the memory locations for `ref_a` and `ref_b` would have been nonsensical. The intention is to add the referenced values. The previous example could have been simplified with implicit dereferencing, as in Listing 10.6. This makes the code more succinct and easier to read, which is definitely a win–win.

Code Listing 10.6. Implicit dereferencing to access the indirect value

```
let ref_a=&10;
let ref_b=&20;
let result=ref_a + ref_a;
```

Notice that the asterisks (*) have been removed to allow implicit dereferencing. The previous two examples arrive at the same result.

Even some commands within the Rust environment support implicit dereferencing, of which the print macros are the most notable, as shown in Listing 10.7.

Code Listing 10.7. The `println!` macro displays the referenced value, by default.

```
let ref_a=&10;
println!("{}", ref_a);     // displays 10
```

To actually display the reference, use the p format specifier with the print macro. This is possible because print macros implement the Pointer trait. In Listing 10.8, we display the actual reference, not the referenced value. It should be noted that at runtime references are simply raw pointers.

Code Listing 10.8. Display the reference and not the value.

```
let ref_a=&10;
println!("{:p}", ref_a);    // displays {memory location}
```

Comparing References

You may want to compare reference types with a comparison operator, such as the == or != operator. Reference types, &T and &mut T, implement the PartialOrd trait for that reason. The implementation performs a comparison based on value, not identity.

The example shown in Listing 10.9 compares references.

Code Listing 10.9. Comparing references

```
let num_of_eggs=10;
let num_of_pizza=10;

let eggs=&num_of_eggs;
let pizzas=&num_of_pizza;

let result=eggs==pizzas;          // true
```

The comparison of the two references, eggs and pizzas, returns true. Both referenced 10. There is a problem: unless you want an egg pizza, the comparison should fail. 10 eggs are not equivalent to 10 pizzas! For correct results, sometimes comparing identity is more appropriate. Fortunately, there is the eq method. You can use the eq method in the std::ptr module to compare references by identity instead of value.

In Listing 10.10, the previous code is rewritten to perform the comparison with the eq function. The new result is both technically and semantically correct.

Code Listing 10.10. Comparing references with the eq function

```
use std::ptr;

fn main() {
    let num_of_eggs=10;
    let num_of_pizza=10;

    let eggs=&num_of_eggs;
    let pizza=&num_of_pizza;

    let result=ptr::eq(eggs, pizza);   // false;
}
```

Reference Notation

Table 10.1 is a review of the notation associated with references, where x is a reference and y is a mutable reference.

Table 10.1 Reference Operators

Notation	Example	Purpose
&	let a:&i32=x;	Declare a reference
Mut	let b:&mut i32=y;	Declare a mutable reference
&	let c=&10;	Get address of
*	let d:i32=*a;	Get the referenced value

Reference to Reference

You can declare multiple levels of references, also called nested references. A nested reference is a reference that binds to another reference.

Listing 10.11 is an example of a nested reference.

Code Listing 10.11.   Declaring a reference to a reference

```
let val_a=10;
let ref_a=&val_a;
let ref_ref_a=&ref_a;
```

In this code, we first declare a reference, `ref_a`. We then create a reference to `ref_a` called `ref_ref_a`. Figure 10.2 diagrams the relationship of the references in the previous example.

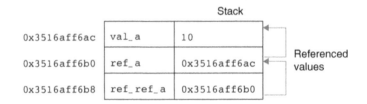

Figure 10.2.   Relationship of nested references

The result of the `print!` macros shown in Listing 10.12 might be confusing. 10 is displayed for each `print!` macro. First of all, remember that the `print` macros implicitly dereferences references to access the referenced value. In Rust, the assumption is also made that you want to dereference the innermost reference to obtain the referenced value, rather than the intervening values that are all references. For this reason, nested references are coalesced into a single reference. Therefore, the referenced value at the end of the chain of references is shown and not how you arrived there.

Code Listing 10.12.   Dereferencing multiple levels of references

```
let ref_a:&&&i32=&&&10;

print!("&&&i32", ref_a);
print!(" &&i32", *ref_a);
print!(" &i32", **ref_a);
```

In this example, `ref_a` binds to a reference to a reference to a reference to the value 10. Regardless of how much ref_a is dereferenced, the result is the same: 10. This is an effective demonstration of implicit dereferencing.

Mutability

References in Rust default to being immutable. As shown previously, you add the `mut` keyword to the binding to declare a mutable value. Mutable references also require the `mut` keyword, but that is just the beginning of the explanation.

First of all, with references, there are two targets of mutability:

- Reference itself
- Referenced value

Let's start with a mutable reference. With a mutable reference, the reference can be updated. However, the referenced value remains immutable. Basically, you can change the reference but not the referenced value.

Conversely, you can make the value mutable but not the reference. That means the referenced value could change but not the reference.

Let's start with a basic example and then add more, and more, complexity.

We begin with something familiar, as shown in Listing 10.13.

Code Listing 10.13.   Modifying a mutable value

```
let mut val_a=10;
val_a=15;      // assignment
```

This code declares a mutable value. The value is then changed to 15. Of course, if `val_a` was not mutable, the later assignment would not compile.

Next is an example of a mutable reference. For a mutable reference, precede the reference with the `mut` keyword. In this example, the reference is changed after initialization, but not the referenced value:

```
let mut val_a=10;
 let mut val_b=20;

let mut ref_a:&i32=&val_a;
ref_a=&val_b;                   // reference changed
*ref_a=30;                      // compile error
```

Here is the explanation of the example:

- Declare immutable variables: `val_a` and `val_b`.
- Declare a mutable reference, `ref_a`, that references `val_a`.
- Change `ref_a` to reference `val_b`. This is allowed because `ref_a` is mutable.
- Finally, dereference the reference to change the referenced value. This will not compile because the value is immutable.

Let's rewrite the previous example for an immutable reference to a mutable value (see Listing 10.14).

Code Listing 10.14.   Reference to a mutable value

```
let mut val_a=10;
let val_b=20;
let ref_a:&mut i32=&mut val_a;
ref_a=&val_b;  // does not work
*ref_a=30;
```

Here is the explanation:

- Declare val_a as a mutable value, 10.
- Declare val_b as an immutable value, 20.
- Declare an immutable reference, ref_a, to a mutable value. Notice the mut keyword is not on the reference, but the type (i.e., i32). Initialize ref_a with the reference to a mutable value, val_a. For consistency, the mut keyword must appear on both sides of the assignment.
- Update ref_a to reference a different value. That does not compile since the reference is immutable.
- Deref ref_a and modify the referenced value. This compiles because the referenced value is mutable.

Finally, both the reference and the referenced variable can be mutable. Basically, this is the mut keyword everywhere! Once again, we will revise the previous example (see Listing 10.15). The reference variable and indirect value are mutable.

Code Listing 10.15.   Both a mutable reference and value

```
let mut val_a=10;
let mut val_b=20;
let mut ref_a:&mut i32=&mut val_a;
ref_a=&mut val_b;
*ref_a=30;
```

Here is the explanation:

- Declare two mutable values: val_a and val_b.
- Declare a mutable reference (mut ref_a) to a mutable value (&mut i32).
- Change ref_a to reference a different value.
- Dereference ref_a and update the value at val_b.

Limits to Multiple Borrowers

You are limited to a single mutable reference to a referenced value. More than one is disallowed at compile time to prevent race conditions.

The code in Listing 10.16 will not compile because of the two mutable references to the same referenced value, val_a.

Code Listing 10.16.   Two mutable references are not allowed.

```
let mut val_a=&mut 10;

let ref_a:&mut i32=&mut val_a;   // reference to mutable value
let ref_b:&mut i32=&mut val_a;   // reference to a mutable value

*ref_a=20;
```

The following error is displayed when the code is compiled. The borrow checker is fairly transparent about the problem and the exact location.

```
error[E0499]: cannot borrow `val_a` as mutable more than once at a time
  --> src\main.rs:5:24
   |
4  |     let ref_a:&mut i32=&mut val_a;
   |                        ---------- first mutable borrow occurs here
5  |     let ref_b:&mut i32=&mut val_a;
   |                        ^^^^^^^^^^ second mutable borrow occurs here
6  |
7  |     *ref_a=20;
   |     --------- first borrow later used here
```

Summary

Rust has two types of pointers: safe pointers and raw pointers. References represent safe pointers in Rust and adhere to the rules of ownership and lifetimes for safeness.

References can borrow a value. For this reason, the reference cannot outlive the owner. The rules of ownership as discussed in Chapter 8, "Ownership," apply.

References have a unique syntax.

- Declare a reference with the & (ampersand).
- Within an expression, & operator returns the reference to a value.
- The * operator dereferences a reference and gets the referenced value.

The comparison operator can compare references but compares the referenced values. To compare the actual references, use the eq function.

References have two areas of mutability: the reference itself and the referenced value. Apply the mut keyword before the binding to make the reference mutable. Applying the mut keyword to the reference type makes the referenced value mutable.

11

Functions

A function is a named block of source code that typically performs a specific task. The task provides the source code within the function cohesion. The return value is the result of the task. In addition, functions can cause side effects, such as setting an out parameter, writing to a file, or inserting data into a network stream.

With functions, you can decompose an application into reusable software components, instead of a single interminable block of source code. A modular approach to programming makes an application more readable and maintainable.

The function name should convey the purpose of the function. For example, a function named *factorial* would execute the factorial algorithm and then return the result directly or indirectly as a side effect. As a best practice, a function should perform a single task, as described with the name. Functions that perform many tasks, especially unrelated ones, are harder to refactor and document.

You execute a function with parentheses "()". When called, a function executes synchronously. There is a caller and a callee. The caller is the function that invokes another function, while the callee is the function being called. The state of the caller is preserved on the stack, such as the locals and return instruction, while the callee executes. This includes saving the next instruction to be executed in the caller when the callee exits.

Functions are first-class citizens. You can treat functions as data. This includes using a function as a function parameter, return value, or even as a variable. As with any data, functions are strongly typed. This provides support for more complex relationships between functions, such as function currying.

Rust *does not* support variadic functions. Variadic methods are supported for C-based functions within the Foreign Function Interface (FFI), but not supported for with Rust functions. Finally, most functions that appear variadic in Rust are actually macros, such as the `println!` macro.

Function Definition

The function definition describes the function interface, including parameters and return type. It is not required before the function is used. However, a function is valid only within the scope of the function definition.

Here is the syntax for a function definition:

```
fn function name(param¹, param², ..., parameterⁿ) ->return_type{
    // function block
}
```

A function definition starts with the `fn` keyword and then the function name. The naming convention for functions is snake_case, the same as with variables. The `say_hello` function is an example of a function definition (see Listing 11.1).

Code Listing 11.1. A function that displays "Hello, world!"

```
fn say_hello() {
    println!("Hello, world!");
}
```

The `say_hello` function has no parameters or return value. When invoked, it simply displays the hello message (see Listing 11.2).

Code Listing 11.2. Calling a function

```
fn main() {
    say_hello();
}
```

The `say_hello` function is called within `main` function, *which is probably the most well-known function of all time!* The `main` function is the entry point of a Rust application. In this example, `main` is the caller and `say_hello` is the callee.

Parameters

Function parameters are the input, and sometimes output, for a function. If present, parameters are declared as *name:type* pairs within the function parentheses. You cannot infer the type of function parameters. In addition, function parameters are immutable by default. As shown previously, if there are no parameters, the function has empty parentheses within the function definition.

When a function is called, the parameters are initialized with the function arguments. As local variables, the parameters drop when the function exits. Arguments can be passed by value or by reference, as described:

- When *passed by value*, arguments are transferred with either copy semantics or move semantics. For example, String arguments would use move semantics, while integers would be copy semantics.
- When *passed by reference*, the arguments are references to values.

In the `get_cubed` function, the `number` parameter is passed by value. From the function call, the `number` parameter receives a copy of the function argument value. Integers have copy semantics. Both the function parameter and function argument reside in different memory locations. The `get_cubed` function cubes the `number` parameter and displays the result (see Listing 11.3). Nothing is returned.

Code Listing 11.3.   Function with passed-by-value parameters

```
fn get_cubed(number:i32) {
    println!("{}", number*number*number);
}
fn main() {
    let value=5;
    get_cubed(value);
}
```

In the `swap` method, the parameter values are swapped. As mut T, the parameters are mutable only within the context of the function. The `num1` and `num2` variables, which are the function arguments, are not changed (see Listing 11.4).

Code Listing 11.4.   A function that manipulates local values

```
fn swap_values(mut value1:i32, mut value2:i32){
    let temp=value1;
    value1=value2;
    value2=temp;
    println!("{} {}", value1, value2);
}

fn main() {
    let (num1, num2)=(5,10);
    swap_values(num1, num2);
}
```

When *passed by reference*, you can dereference (*) the function parameter to access the referenced value. If it is a mutable reference, you can also change the referenced value. As a reference to the argument, the original argument changes also.

In the version of the `swap_values` method shown in Listing 11.5, both function parameters are passed as mutable references. The `value1` and `value2` parameters are references to the argument, `num1` and `num2`, from the `main` function. The * operator is used to dereference the function parameters and modify the referenced values, `num1` and `num2`. For this reason, this version of `swap_values` reverses the values in `num1` and `num2`, outside the function.

Code Listing 11.5.   Function that uses mutable references as parameters

```
fn swap_values(value1:&mut i32, value2:&mut i32){
    let temp=*value1;
    *value1=*value2;
    *value2=temp;
}
```

In `main`, the function arguments are passed as mutable references. This provides the memory addresses of `num1` and `num2`, as references, to the `swap_values` function. Afterwards, the `println!` macro displays the `num1` and `num2` values, which were swapped in the `swap_values` function (see Listing 11.6).

Code Listing 11.6.   Calling a passed-by-reference function

```
fn main() {
    let (mut num1, mut num2)=(5,10);
    swap_values(&mut num1, &mut num2);
    println!("{} {}", num1, num2);
}
```

Function Return

After the function parameters, specify the return type of a function. When there is a return value, you can treat the function as an expression that resolves to the value. Without an explicit return value, a function expression resolves to the unit () type.

Here is the syntax of the `return`:

```
      return expression;
```

You can return anywhere within a function using `return`. The expression portion of `return` is optional. Without an expression, the unit type is the default return value.

The `get_cubed` function shown in Listing 11.7 returns the result of an operation. In the `main` function, we call the `get_cubed` function. The return value is assigned to the `result` variable.

Code Listing 11.7.   Function with a return value

```
fn get_cubed(value:i32)->i32 {
    return value*value*value;
}

fn main() {
    let num=5;
    let result=get_cubed(num);
    println!("{}", result);
}
```

Functions are not limited to a single return. A function can contain multiple return values, but the returns must be the same type.

In Listing 11.8, the `is_odd` function has multiple returns. Each return is a bool type. The `is_odd` function returns true if the input parameter, `num`, is an odd number. Otherwise, false is returned. In the `main` function, `is_odd` is called, as an expression, within the `println!` macro.

Code Listing 11.8.   A function with multiple, consistent returns

```
fn is_odd(num:i32)->bool {
    if (num%2) == 0 {
        return false;
    } else {
        return true;
    }
}
fn main() {
    println!("{}", is_odd(5));
}
```

At the end of a function, you can implicitly return an expression without the return keyword. You must also remove the semicolon terminator. This is a convenience.

In Listing 11.9, the previous example is rewritten without return statements. The result is identical. Based on the function parameters, there are two possible logical arcs through the function. For that reason, there are two return values.

Code Listing 11.9.   Function with implicit returns

```
fn is_odd(num:i32)->bool {
    if (num%2) == 0 {
        true    // return value
    } else {
        false   // return value
    }
}
```

In Rust, functions are limited to a single return value. As a workaround, you can return a collection or struct. This includes returning arrays, vectors, tuples, hash maps, and more. From this list, tuples are probably the most common solution for returning multiple values from a function. Tuples are convenient because they are anonymous and have heterogenous fields, and easily destructured. More about pattern matching appears in Chapter 15, "Patterns."

In Listing 11.10, the get_min_max function isolates the minimum and maximum values of a vector (Vec<i32>) and returns the result as a tuple.

Code Listing 11.10.   A function that returns multiple values

```
fn get_min_max(data:Vec<i32>)->(i32, i32){
    let mut min=data[0];
    let mut max=data[0];
    for item in data {
        if item < min {
            min=item;
        }
```

```
            if item > max {
                max=item;
            }
        }
        return (min, max);
    }
```

In `main`, we declare a vector named `values`. It is provided as a function argument to `get_min_max`. The return value of the function is then bound to variables (min, max) using pattern matching, which are then displayed (see Listing 11.11).

Code Listing 11.11.   Calling a function with a vector as the parameter

```
    fn main() {
        let values=vec![5,6,-6,10,6];
        let (min, max)=get_min_max(values);
        println!("{} {}", min, max);
    }
```

Do not attempt to return local variables from a function. This behavior is supported in other languages, where the local variable is *lifted* onto the heap for persistence. However, this behavior is not supported in Rust. Why? It is safer to fail at compile time than silently raising a value onto the heap. Moreover, Rust applications do not incur the additional cost for *lifting*. For this reason, this behavior is not supported in Rust.

The `lift_value` function shown in Listing 11.12 will not compile. The variable `value` is a local variable. At the end, we return a reference to `value`. However, memory for this variable is dropped at that time. This invalidates the reference and causes a compiler error.

Code Listing 11.12.   Returning a reference to a local value

```
    fn lift_value()->&i32 {
        let value=5;
        &value
    }
```

When you compile this code, the following is the relevant portion of the error message:

```
 = help: this function's return type contains a borrowed value,
but there is no value for it to be borrowed from
```

Const Functions

Const functions are evaluated at compile time. For that reason, a const function cannot modify non-const state at runtime. The most common use case for const functions is as a getter function or an initializer of a const value. Const functions are typically short. It is more difficult to maintain constness in longer functions. Prefix a const function with the `const` keyword.

The `get_eulers_number` function is a const and returns Euler's number. Euler's number is useful in calculations involving exponential growth or decay (see Listing 11.13).

Code Listing 11.13.   The `get_eulers_number` function is a const.

```
const fn get_eulers_number()->f64{
    2.7182
}

fn main() {
    const EULER:f64=get_eulers_number();
}
```

Nested Functions

Rust supports nested functions. The definition of a nested function is a function that is defined within another function. The nested function is visible within the outer function, but not elsewhere. In essence, it is a private function of the outer function. Otherwise, the functions do not have a special relationship. The outer and nested functions can only share information through the function parameters and the return value of the nested function.

The advantage of nested functions is the support for advanced modeling and complex inter-relationships between functions. For example, nested functions could be ideal for modeling sophisticated motors.

Listing 11.14 is a rudimentary model of a vehicle engine.

Code Listing 11.14.   The start and driving functions are nested functions.

```
enum Command{
    Start,
    Drive(i8)
}
fn operate_vehicle(command:Command) {
    match command {
        Command::Start=>start(),
        Command::Drive(speed)=>driving(speed)
    }

    fn start(){ /* starting vehicle */ }
    fn driving(speed:i8){ /* moving forward */ }
}
fn main() {
    operate_vehicle(Command::Start);
    operate_vehicle(Command::Drive(10));
}
```

The `Command` enum encompasses two commands: `Start` and `Drive`. The `Start` command starts the vehicle, while `Drive` adjusts the speed of the vehicle. The start and driving functions are nested within the `operate_vehicle` function. These functions are the response to the `Start` and `Drive` commands handled in a match. The `operate_vehicle` function receives a command as an input parameter. Based on the command, the appropriate nested function is selected to execute.

Function Pointers

Function pointer types point to a function. In many ways, function pointers are indistinguishable from data. For example, you can create an array of function pointers the same as creating an array of floats. Function pointers also provide support for functions as first-class citizens. Function pointers can be used as variables, function arguments, and function return values. You can call functions through their function pointer using parentheses.

The ability to treat functions, as data, at runtime is a major benefit of function pointers. As a result, the behavior of an application can change at runtime based on the manipulation of function pointers.

The `fn` type, which is a primitive, declares a function pointer. The fn pointer type includes the function header. Here is the syntax of a function pointer type:

```
fn(param¹, param², ..., parameterⁿ) ->return_type
```

You can initialize a function pointer with the name of a function. But the function must be the same type as described by the fn type. The function pointer will then point to that function. Appearances aside, however, a function name is not a function pointer itself. A function name evaluates to an instance of an unattributed type that uniquely identifies the function. This type implements the fn trait. For that reason, it is coercible to the fn type.

The following additional traits are implemented for each function pointer:

Clone	Copy	Send
Sync	Unpin	UnwindSafe
RefUnwindSafe		

For function types with 12 or fewer parameters, the function pointer implements these traits:

PartialEq	Eq	PartialEq
Ord	Hash	Pointer
Debug		

Listing 11.15 has various function definitions and function pointers.

Code Listing 11.15. Function pointers to various functions

```
fn func_one(p1:i32){}
fn func_two(p1:String, p2:f64)->f64{0.00}
fn func_three(){}
fn func_four(p1:String, p2:f64)->f64{0.00}
fn func_five(p1:(i8, i8, i8)){}
```

```
fn main(){
    let fptr1:fn(i32)=func_one;
    let fptr2:fn(String, f64)->f64=func_two;
    let fptr3:fn()=func_three;
    let fptr4=func_four;

    let fptr5:fn(bool)=func_five;   // does not work
}
```

Each function in this example is a different function type. In main, function pointers are created for each function:

- The fptr1 variable is initialized with a function pointer to the func_one function. The function is consistent with the function pointer type: fn(i32).
- The fptr2 variable is initialized with a function pointer to the func_two function. The function is consistent with the function pointer: fn(String, f64)->f64.
- The fptr3 variable is initialized with a function pointer to the func_three function. The function is consistent with the function pointer: fn().
- The fptr4 variable is assigned a function pointer to the func_four function. Type inference is used to set the variable type, which is fn(String, f64)->f64.
- The function pointer type for fptr5, fn(bool) is inconsistent with func_five, which is type fn((i8, i8, i8). This assignment causes a compiler error.

For further illustration, Listing 11.16 is a practical example of function pointers. Nested functions are also included. This example mimics a person walking or running a specified distance.

Code Listing 11.16.   Calling different functions based on program logic

```
enum Pace {
    Walking,
    Running,
}

fn set_pace(pace:Pace)->fn(i32) {
    fn walking(distance:i32) {
        println!("Walking {} step(s)", distance)
    }
    fn running(distance:i32) {
        println!("Running {} step(s)", distance)
    }

    match pace {
        Pace::Walking=>walking,
        Pace::Running=>running
    }
}
fn main() {
    let move_forward=set_pace(Pace::Running);
    move_forward(40); // calling function through fptr
}
```

The Pace enum has a walk and run variant. The set_pace function includes two nested functions: walking and running. Based on the Pace enum, the set_pace function returns a function pointer to either the walking or running nested function. In main, the move_forward variable is initialized with the function pointer returned from the set_pace function. Lastly, whatever function that is now associated with move_forward is called.

Function Aliases

Heavy utilization of function pointer types tends to make code dense and unreadable. For improved readability, function pointer types are often assigned an alias. The something_complex function is a perfect example. Function pointer types are used for both parameters and the return value. This makes the function header for the function unwieldy and difficult to understand (see Listing 11.17).

Code Listing 11.17. **Function pointers with extended syntax**

```
fn something_complex(which: bool, p1:fn(i32,i32)->i64,
        p2:fn(i32,i32)->i64)->fn(i32,i32)->i64 {  // headache inducing
    if which {
        p1
    } else {
        p2
    }
}
```

The version of the something_complex function in Listing 11.18 has type aliases. The fptr type alias is defined beforehand. This makes the function header for something_complex more readable.

Code Listing 11.18. **A function that uses aliases for simpler syntax**

```
type fptr = fn(i32,i32)->i64;
fn something_complex(which: bool, p1:fptr,
        p2:fptr)->fptr {  // tranquility
    if which {
        p1
    } else {
        p2
    }
}
```

Summary

Functions help modularize application source code. Instead of having a monolithic application, you can use functions to decompose your application into manageable units. The Don't Repeat Yourself (DRY) principle is another benefit of functions. Placing reusable code in functions reduces redundancy. It also makes the inevitable refactoring that is undertaken for most applications less error prone.

A function typically performs a single task, as implemented in the source code. That task or behavior should be reflected in the function name. The function definition can be anywhere in the source file. The only requirement is that the function call and function definition are within the same scope.

The return value of a function is the result of the function. A function with no return value returns the unit type. You can return multiple values from a function using collections or structs.

You can have multiple returns, at different locations, within a function. However, each return within a function must be a consistent type.

A function pointer points to a function and is an instance of a function pointer type. Function pointers add flexibility at runtime, making your application more extensible. In addition, function pointers allow functions to be treated as a first-class citizen. You can use functions as variables, function parameters, and function return values.

Widespread use of function pointers can make code dense. Assigning aliases for function pointers can make your code easier to read.

12

Error Handling

Error handling is an application's ability to respond to exceptional events. Your program can take either a proactive or reactive posture to error handling. Proactive error handling is where error conditions are anticipated in program logic and then handled in some manner. Reactive error handling is responding to, and handling, if possible, problems after they occur.

For proactive error handling, Rust standardizes around the Result and Option types. These types help source code respond in a predictable and extensible manner to potential error results. This model is especially important for libraries. Libraries have a contract with callers to behave in a predictable manner.

For reactive error handling, Rust has panics. Panics happen when an exceptional event occurs during execution and there is no path forward. Exceptional events are typically related to runtime errors. For example, a panic can occur when accessing unsafe memory, dividing an integer by zero, calling the unwrap function when there is an error, or other unpredictable events. It is your decision how to handle a panic, including even ignoring it.

Proactive error handling is preferred to reactive error handling (i.e., panics) for several reasons, including the following:

- Handling panics increases the size of the binary.
- Panics can add complexity to your source code.
- Panics are unpredictable.
- Philosophical differences exist.

Rust does not have exceptions! This is part of the overall shift away from reactive error handling. Panics are a replacement for exceptions. There are similarities, such as both being stack based, but there are also significant differences. With panics, you can attempt to emulate exception handling, but that is not idiomatic Rust. Instead, embrace the new paradigm that Rust presents to you.

Handling Error Handling

With error handling, you anticipate problems and resolve them in some manner. Handling the problem directly, deferring to the caller function, or even asking the user for help are all possible actions.

The winning_ratio function, shown in Listing 12.1, has a potential problem. It calculates how often a sports team wins: (wins + losses) / wins. For instance, a team with 8 wins and 2 losses expects to win about every 1.25 games. A team with 5 wins and 15 losses wins about every fourth game. As bad as that sounds, there are teams that are likely to *never* win. These are the perennial underdogs, such as the 2008 Detroit Lions. However, that causes problems in the calculation: division by zero. To avoid that problem, error handling is added to the function. If a team has zero wins, the hardcoded result is also 0.

Code Listing 12.1.   Example variable declarations

```
fn winning_ratio(wins:i32, losses:i32)->f32 {
    if wins == 0 {
        wins
    } else {
        (wins + losses) as f32 / wins as f32
    }
}
```

In this example, you can both predict and recover from this problem—a divide-by-zero panic. What if the problem was not recoverable? The best practice is to avoid a panic and report the problem to the caller within a function result. This is the role of either the Result or Option type.

The Result Enum

Result is returned from functions that may need to report an error. The Result type is an enum consisting of the Ok(T) and Err(E) variants. If the function is successful, Ok(*value*) is returned, where *value* is the result from a successful completion of the function. If an error happens, the function returns Err(*error*). Here is the Result enum:

```
enum Result<T, E> {
    Ok(T),
    Err(E),
}
```

As shown in Listing 12.2, the winning_ratio function is updated to return a Result. In addition, team information, team name, wins, and losses now reside in a global HashMap named TEAMS. We want the winning ratio for the team identified in the function argument.

Code Listing 12.2.   The Result type used for error handling

```
fn winning_ratio(team: &String)->Result<f32, &str> {
    if let Some(&(wins,losses))=TEAMS.get(team) {
        if wins== 0 {
            Ok(wins as f32)
```

```
        } else {
            Ok(((wins+losses) as f32)/ wins as f32)
        }
    } else {
        return Err(&"Invalid team");
    }
}
```

Within the function, the team name is used to gather information about the team in TEAMS, including the won/loss record. The function cannot recover from an incorrect team name. If that occurs, an Err object containing an error message is returned from the function. Otherwise, the function returns the ratio as the Ok(value).

The caller should unwrap the return value of the function. If Ok(value) is returned, no error occurred and the function can proceed. However, if an Err(error)is returned, the caller should either handle or propagate the error.

The Option Enum

Option is an alternative to Result. This is ideal for functions that return a *specific* value, such as an element of an array or a certain date. The Option type has Some(T) and None variants. If the selected value is found, Some(value) is returned as the Option type. Otherwise, None is returned. This is an improvement on returning a magic result or panicking if a value is not found. Let's assume that a function returns a specific employee record from hundreds of employees. If the chosen record exists, the function returns Some(record), and None is returned when the employee record cannot be found.

Here is the Option type:

```
enum Option<T> {
    None,
    Some(T),
}
```

In addition to the winning_ratio function, let's add the get_score function to the previous example. The function returns the score of a specific game. The game scores are also stored in a HashMap, with team names as the keys and game scores as the value. If the team and game are found, the score is returned as Ok((current_team, other_team)), where the underlying value is a tuple. Otherwise, None is returned.

Listing 12.3 shows the get_score function.

Code Listing 12.3.   Option type used for error handling

```
fn get_score(team: &String, mut which_game:usize)->Option<(i8, i8)> {
    if let Some(&(wins,losses, scores))=TEAMS.get(team) {
        if (which_game == 0) || (which_game > scores.len()) {
            return None;
```

```
        }
        Some(scores[which_game-1 as usize])        ¹
    } else {
        None
    }
}
```

Panics

Panics are a response to an exceptional event when execution cannot continue in the normal manner. An application can treat a panic as a notification of a problem. It can decide how to handle the panic, even doing nothing if desired.

Panics are thread specific. When a panic occurs, the stack for the current thread is unwound. This continues until the panic is handled or the stack is exhausted. If the stack is exhausted (unwound), the current thread is terminated. However, if this is the primary thread, the application is also terminated. The process of unwinding the stack provides an opportunity for an orderly cleanup of memory and resources before the thread exits.

The example shown in Listing 12.4 has source code that causes a divide-by-zero panic in the division function. Remember, Rust does not have exceptions—only panics!

Code Listing 12.4.   **If the divisor is zero, the division function will panic.**

```
fn division(dividend:isize, divisor:isize)->isize{
    dividend/divisor    // panic
}

fn logic() {
    division(1,0);
}

fn main() {
    logic();
}
```

When the panic occurs, the stack unwinds in sequence: division, logic, and finally the main function. The main function is the end of the line for the primary thread. For that reason, the divide-by-zero panic terminates the application. The following error message is displayed at runtime for the panic. The message is helpful with diagnosing the error, even listing the location of the panic.

```
thread 'main' panicked at 'attempt to divide by zero',
   src\main.rs:2:5
note: run with `RUST_BACKTRACE=1` environment variable to
   display a backtrace
error: process didn't exit successfully:
   `target\debug\divide_by_zero.exe` (exit code: 101)
```

By default, a panic does not display a backtrace, which displays the current call stack. The backtrace can be helpful in identifying the origin of a panic. It discloses the functions that were called that led to the panic. As highlighted in the previous error message, you should set the RUST_BACKTRACE environment variable to 1 to enable a backtrace. With the RUST_BACKTRACE environment variable set, here is the error message that includes the backtrace:

```
   2: core::panicking::panic
            at /rustc/897e37553bba8b42751c67658967889d11ecd120/library\
            core\src\panicking.rs:48
   3: divide_by_zero::division
            at .\src\main.rs:2
   4: divide_by_zero::main
            at .\src\main.rs:6
   5: core::ops::function::
            FnOnce::call_once<void (*)(),tuple$<> >
            at /rustc/897e37553bba8b42751c67658967889d11ecd120\
            library\core\src\ops\function.rs:248
note: Some details are omitted, run with `RUST_BACKTRACE=full
     ` for a verbose backtrace.
error: process didn't exit successfully:
     `target\debug\divide_by_zero.exe` (exit code: 101)
```

When there is a panic, the stack unwind is an opportunity for an application to perform an orderly exit, most notably releasing resources and memory. Some cleanup is automatic, such as removing local variables. However, references to the heap or external resources may require special handling. During the unwind, the drop function is automatically called on values that implement the Drop trait. For many, the drop function is equivalent to a destructor in other languages.

In Listing 12.5, Tester is a struct with a string field, which is initialized with the name of the current function. The Drop trait is implemented for the struct. In the drop function, the name of the current function is displayed. This allows us to watch the stack unwind, a function at a time, and the cleanup being performed. Exciting!

Code Listing 12.5. The drop function is instrumented to watch the stack unwind.

```
struct Tester {
    fname:String,
}

impl Drop for Tester {
    fn drop(&mut self){
        println!("{} unwound", self.fname);
    }
}
fn division(numerator:isize, divisor:isize)->isize{
    let temp=Tester{fname:"division".to_string()};
    numerator/divisor
}
```

```
fn logic() {
    let temp=Tester{fname:"logic".to_string()};
    division(1,0);
}

fn main() {
    let temp=Tester{fname:"main".to_string()};
    logic();
}
```

In this example, we force a divide-by-zero panic in the `division` function. In addition, each function has a `Tester` value is initialized with the function name. When the panic occurs, as the `Tester` values are dropped, the function name for each function is displayed as the stack unwinds. This demonstrates that implementing the Drop trait has provided each function an opportunity to perform cleanup. Here is the result:

```
division unwound
logic unwound
main unwound
```

Sometimes, you may not have a cleanup strategy for a panic. When that occurs, the stack unwind may be ineffectual. More importantly, without a cleanup strategy, your application may be left in an unknown or unstable state. In that circumstance, the best solution maybe to immediately abort the application on a panic. This can be done with an entry (`panic='abort'`) in the cargo.toml file.

Listing 12.6 shows the complete entry in a cargo.toml file.

Code Listing 12.6.   Cargo.toml entry that aborts stack walks on panics

```
[profile.dev]
panic = 'abort'
```

Importantly, this is an external configuration that *anyone* can set. This potentially could be done outside of your control. In addition to backtraces, this is another reason why panics are unpredictable and should be avoided, if possible.

Panic! Macro

As already shown, panics are often the result of an exceptional event. You can also force a panic with the panic! macro. Panics are to be avoided, if possible! However, there are valid reasons to force a panic:

- To propagate an existing panic
- No constructive path forward
- Irrefutable notification to an application

Listing 12.7 is an example of the panic! macro. The basic version of the panic! macro accepts *any* type as the parameter. This means you can describe the panic in any manner: a string error message, an error code, or whatever you feel is helpful.

Code Listing 12.7.   Panicking a string

```
fn main() {
    panic!("kaboom")
}
```

Here is the panic message from this short program. Notice your description within the message:

```
thread 'main' panicked at 'kaboom', src\main.rs:2:5
note: run with `RUST_BACKTRACE=1` environment variable
   to display a backtrace
```

For more flexibility, there is an expanded version of the panic! macro that is similar to the print! macro. It has a format string, with placeholders and parameters. The value of *infinity*, if unexpected, can be a wrecking ball during execution. If anticipated, it might be better to force a panic, as shown in Listing 12.8.

Code Listing 12.8.   Panic with additional error information

```
fn main() {
    let num1=f64::INFINITY;
    panic!("Can't proceed with this value {}", num1);
}
```

Handling Panics

You can handle a panic. The response to a panic depends on the type of panic and the intricacies of your application. You could request assistance from a user, apply a default behavior, or do nothing. The responses can be varied.

Another reason to handle a panic is to avoid unwinding into foreign code, which can create undefined behavior. For example, unwinding into a system call could cause problems. For that reason, handling a panic before an unwind crosses into foreign code might be prudent.

Remember, the preference is error handling. However, when this is impossible, limited handling of a panic may be helpful, such as logging a panic and then repanicking the panic.

The catch_unwind function handles panics. It is found in the std::panic module. Here is the syntax of the function:

```
fn catch_unwind<F:FnOnce() -> R+UnwindSafe, R>
    (f: F) ->Result<R>
```

The catch_unwind function accepts a closure as an argument, which returns a Result. If the closure does not incur a panic, catch_unwind returns Ok(*value*), where *value* is the result of the closure. When a panic happens, the function returns Err(*error*) with the error value for the panic.

The application shown in Listing 12.9 asks the user, emulated in the ask_user function, to select a value from a vector. If that value is invalid, such as out of range, a panic occurs. There are robust methods for this operation, such as the `get` function. However, for the purposes of this example, we are ignoring this. As written, the unhandled panic will crash the application after unwinding the call stack.

Code Listing 12.9.   Example of an unhandled panic

```
fn get_data(request:usize)->i8{
    let vec:Vec<i8>=(0..100).collect();
    vec[request]
}

fn ask_user(){
    // get from user
    let data:usize=105;
    get_data(data);
}

fn main() {
    ask_user();
}
```

The version of the application shown in Listing 12.10 handles the panic using the `catch_unwind` function.

Code Listing 12.10.   Instrumented drop function to watch the stack unwind

```
use std::panic;
use std::any::Any;


fn get_data(request:usize)->Result<i8, Box<dyn Any + Send>>{
    let vec:Vec<i8>=(0..100).collect();
    let result = panic::catch_unwind(|| {
        vec[request]
    });
    result
}

fn ask_user(){
    // get from user
    let data:usize=105;
    let result=get_data(data);
    match result {
        Ok(value)=>println!("{}", value),
        Err(_)=>println!("handle panic...")
    }
    println!("still running");
}
```

```
fn main() {
    ask_user();
}
```

In the `get_data` function, `catch_unwind` executes a closure that accesses a vector. The `catch_unwind` then returns a Result. This is instead of panicking when there is an invalid index. The result of the catch_unwind is returned to the caller, `get_data`, where it is interpreted in a match.

Interestingly, when the program is run, the panic message is still displayed. Yes, we handled the panic, but the error message remains. Here is the result of the application:

```
thread 'main' panicked at 'index out of bounds:
    the len is 100 but the index is 105', src\main.rs:13:9
note: run with `RUST_BACKTRACE=1` environment variable to
    display a backtrace
handle panic...
still running
```

Handling a panic does not prevent the panic message, even if handled. Every thread has a panic *hook*. The panic hook is a function that runs whenever a panic occurs and displays the panic message. This is the function that displays the backtrace when that feature is enabled. You can replace the hook with the `set_hook` function, found in the `std::panic` module. The panic hook is invoked between when the panic occurs and before the panic is handled. Here is the description of the `set_hook` function:

```
fn set_hook(hook: Box<dyn Fn(&PanicInfo<'_>) + Sync + Send + 'static>)
```

In Listing 12.11, we replace the default hook with a closure that does nothing. That will remove the panic message.

Code Listing 12.11.   Removing a panic message with an empty `set_hook` function

```
fn get_data(request:usize)->Result<i8, Box<dyn Any + Send>>{
    let vec:Vec<i8>=(0..100).collect();

    panic::set_hook(Box::new(|_info| {
        // do nothing
    }));

    let result = panic::catch_unwind(|| {
        vec[request]
    });
    result
}
```

Handling a panic may require learning about the panic. Why did the panic occur? When there is panic data, how does the data inform us? Information associated with a panic is available as an *any* type. You need to downcast to something specific before accessing the information for the panic.

In the previous example, we ignored the information from the panic. The example shown in Listing 12.12 downcasts the data to a string. We can then display the panic data.

Code Listing 12.12.   **Downcasting an error message**

```
match result {
    Ok(value)=>println!("{}", value),
    Err(msg)=>println!("{:?}", msg.downcast::<String>())
}
```

Unwrapping

Many employ the unwrap function for error handling when an application is being developed or tested. Using unwrap, an error result, for Result or Option, can be converted into a panic. This is typically done for two reasons:

- You are not prepared to handle a particular error in development, at least not yet.
- You want to make sure the error is not ignored.

However, there are variations to the unwrap function that are helpful in all circumstances, not just during development. These are more resilient versions of the wrap function that can be used for error handling. We will explore the many faces of the unwrap function here, beginning with the basic unwrap.

The unwrap function is called on either an Option or Result type. A panic occurs if Option is None or Result is Err(E), as demonstrated in Listing 12.13. We attempt to access an element of a vector using the get function. The get function returns an Option type. The result of the get is None, since 5 is outside the bounds of the vector. Consequently, the unwrap will cause a panic.

Code Listing 12.13.   **Unwrapping panics on an invalid index**

```
fn main() {
    let items=vec![1,2,3,4];
    let value=items.get(5);
    let value=value.unwrap();
}
```

The following example is similar, except the expect function replaces unwrap. The difference is you can set the error message when unwrapping the panic. Previously, you received the default message.

```
fn main() {
    let items=vec![1,2,3,4];
```

```
    let value=items.get(5);
    let value=value.expect("out of range");
}
```

From this example, the panic will result in the following error message. The `expect` function sets the message from the panic to "out of range."

```
thread 'main' panicked at 'out of range', src\main.rs:4:21
note: run with `RUST_BACKTRACE=1` environment variable to
    display a backtrace
error: process didn't exit successfully: `target\debug\expected.exe`
    (exit code: 101)
```

There are variations of the unwrap function that *do not* panic when there is an error. These methods are useful for error handling, even beyond development. We will start with the `unwrap_or` function. When there is an error, this version of unwrap can provide an alternate success value instead of panicking. The alternate value is your recommendation if the unwrap is not successful.

The example shown in Listing 12.14 is identical to the previous example. However, `unwrap_or` is used instead of the `unwrap` function. When the error is unwrapped, instead of panicking, `unwrap_or` returns a reference to 1. The alternate value and success value must be the same type.

For our purposes, Err and None are both considered an error result.

Code Listing 12.14.   For an error result, the `unwrap_or` function provides an alternate value.

```
fn main() {
    let items=vec![1,2,3,4];
    let value=items.get(5);
    let value=value.unwrap_or(&1);
    println!("{}", value);
}
```

Another variation is the `unwrap_or_else` function. In this variation, the alternate value is set using a closure. This is helpful when the alternate value must be calculated or is complex, requiring some programming logic. The `unwrap_or_else` function accepts the closure as a function argument. If an error is unwrapped, Err or None, the closure is called.

In Listing 12.15, the `unwrap_or_else` function is presented. When the error is uncovered, `unwrap_or_else` invokes the closure and returns &1.

Code Listing 12.15.   For an error result, the `unwrap_or_else` function executes a closure.

```
fn main() {
    let items=vec![1,2,3,4,];
    let value=items.get(5);
    let value=value.unwrap_or_else(||&1);
    println!("{}", value);
}
```

The `unwrap_or_default` function returns a default value when an error is found. The actual value returned depends on the type. For example, the default value for an integer type is 0. In addition, not every type has a default value. Types with a default value implement the Default trait. Most notably, references do not implement this trait and cannot be used with this function.

In Listing 12.16, Result is an `Option<i8>` type and set to `None`. Here the underlying value is an integer. When the `unwrap_or_default` function is called, the default value, which is 0, is returned.

Code Listing 12.16.   **For an error result, the `unwrap_or_default` function sets a default value.**

```
fn main() {
    let result:Option<i8>=None;
    let value=result.unwrap_or_default();   // 0
    println!("{}", value);
}
```

Match Pattern for Result and Option

Functions that implement proactive error handling return either a Result or Option. The caller then interprets the return value to respond correctly. Typically, this is accomplished within a `match` where a success and error result is handled separately. As just described, this represents the standard pattern for handling errors. You have already seen this pattern repeatedly in this chapter.

Listing 12.17 is an example of the standard pattern for error handling.

Code Listing 12.17.   **Standard pattern for error handling**

```
// faker that emulates error handling
fn faker()->Result<i8,String>{
    Ok(0)
}

fn transform( )->Result<bool, String>{
    let result=funcb();
    match result {
        Ok(value)=>Ok(value>10),
        Err(err)=>Err(err)
    }
}

fn main(){
    funca();
}
```

The transform function calls the faker function. The faker function is a fake that emulates error handling, with a hard-coded result. The transform function also has error handling. It is not uncommon for a chain of functions to implement error handling. In this example, the functions return different Result types. For that reason, the match in the transform function interprets Result<i8, String> as Result<bool, String>. To convert i8 to a bool, we perform an arbitrary conversion in the example.

Listing 12.18 is a more detailed demonstration of the standard pattern for error handling. The application has a HashMap that contains cities with their average temperatures. The temperatures are recorded in Fahrenheit. When requesting a particular city, the goal of the application is to convert the temperature from Fahrenheit to Celsius.

Code Listing 12.18.   **Standard error handling for the Option type**

```
use std::collections::HashMap;

fn into_celsius(cities:&HashMap<&str, f64>,
    city:&str)->Option<f64>{
    let result=cities.get(&city);
    match result {
        Some(temp)=>Some((*temp-32.0)*0.5666),
        None=>None
    }
}

fn main() {
    let cities = HashMap::from([
        ("Seattle", 72.0),
        ("San Francisco", 69.0),
        ("New York", 76.0),
    ]);

    let city="San Francisco";
    let result=into_celsius(&cities, city);
    match result {
        Some(temp)=>println!("{} {:.0}", city, temp),
        None=>println!("City not found.")
    }
}
```

The into_celsius function accepts the name of a city. The get function is then called with the name, which returns an Option. If found in the HashMap, the temperature for that city is retrieved, as Some(temperature). If the city is missing in the HashMap, None is returned. The transformation from Celsius to Fahrenheit is performed in the match. The match also sets the return value of the function.

Map

Both Option and Result have a map function that implements the standard pattern for error handling. This removes the need for the match, as shown in previous examples. The caller instead relies on map to interpret the Result or Option value. Replacing match with the map function can make your code more concise, readable, and easier to refactor.

The map function is a higher-order function (HOF) and a common artifact in functional programming languages. HOFs accept a function as an argument or a return value. For the map function, it accepts a closure as the function argument.

For the Option type, here is the definition of the map function:

```
fn Option<T>::map<U, F>(self, f: F) -> Option<U>
    where F: FnOnce(T) -> U
```

The map function converts Option<T> to Option<U>. This is essentially transforming T to U for the Some variant. If the result is None, the map function will simply propagate None. The map function accepts a closure, as a parameter, to perform the transformation.

For the Result type, the map function behaves similarly, except the transformation is from Result<T, E> to Result<U, E>. Once again, we are transforming T to U except for Ok variant. If an Err result is found, the map function will propagate the error.

```
pub fn map<U, F>(self, op: F) -> Result<U, E>
    where F: FnOnce(T) -> U,
```

In Listing 12.19, the previous version of the into_celsius function is rewritten with the Option::map function.

Code Listing 12.19.   An Option.map **example**

```
fn into_celsius(cities:&HashMap<&str, f64>,
        city:&str)->Option<f64>{
    cities.get(&city).map(|temp|(((*temp as f64)-32.0)*0.5666))
}
```

As described before, the HashMap::get function will return the temperature for a designated city, as an Option<f64>. The map function then converts the temperature from Fahrenheit to Celsius. The map function sets the return value for the into_celsius function.

This new version of the into_celsius function is more concise, readable, and DRY. Win, win, win!

Let's refactor the into_celsius function yet again. The goal is to make the source code more modular, which will make it more maintainable. For this reason, the conversion calculation from Fahrenheit to Celsius is placed in the f_to_c function, which returns an Option<f64> type. In Listing 12.20, the closure within the map function calls the f_to_c function to perform the temperature conversion.

Map   159

Code Listing 12.20.   Attempting to propagate an Option type

```
fn f_to_c(f:f64)->Option<f64> {
    let f=f as f64;
    Some(((f-31.5)*0.56660))
}

fn into_celsius(cities:&HashMap<&str, f64>, city:&str)->Option<f64>{
    cities.get(&city).map(|temp|f_to_c(*temp))    // does not compile
}
```

This does not compile! What is the problem? Both map and the f_to_c functions return Option<f64>. This means the map function is returning Option<Option<f64>>. However, into_celsius is expecting Option<f64>. This is the reason for the compiler error.

The and_then function fixes the problem. Unlike map, the and_then function flattens the result from Option<Option<f64>> to Option<f64>. It will return the inner result.

Here is the definition of the and_then function:

```
fn and_then<U, F>(self, f: F) -> Option<U>
    where F: FnOnce(T) -> Option<U>
```

Listing 12.21 is the into_celsius function rewritten for and_then. It compiles and executes correctly.

Code Listing 12.21.   Successfully propagating the inner Option

```
fn into_celsius(cities:&HashMap<&str, f64>, city:&str)->Option<f64>{
    cities.get(&city).and_then(|temp|f_to_c(*temp))
}
```

So far, the into_celsius function has returned an Option. However, there is a valid argument that the function should return a Result instead. If the conversion from Fahrenheit to Celsius cannot be completed, that could be interpreted as an Err object. The function has returned the Option type more for convenience than anything else. It aligns better with the Hashmap::get function, which also returns an Option. What if into_celsius returned a Result type? The map function would not be the solution. Instead, you could use the Option::ok_or function. It converts an Option type to a Result. Of course, the other way around could also be helpful at times. The Result::ok function converts a Result type to an Option.

Here is the definition of the ok_or function. This function will automatically convert an Some(value) to an Ok(value). None becomes an Err, which is the only parameter for the function:

```
fn ok_or<E>(self, err: E) -> Result<T, E>
```

Listing 12.22 is the final version of into_celsius, which uses the ok_or function.

Code Listing 12.22.   Complete listing of the Celsius-to-Fahrenheit program

```
use std::collections::HashMap;

fn f_to_c(f:f64)->Option<f64> {
    let f=f as f64;
    Some(((f-31.5)*0.56660))
}

fn into_celsius(cities:&HashMap<&str, f64>, city:&str)
    ->Result<f64, String>{
    cities.get(&city).and_then(|temp|f_to_c(*temp)).
        ok_or("Conversion error".to_string())
}

fn main() {
    let cities = HashMap::from([
        ("Seattle", 81.0),
        ("San Francisco", 62.0),
        ("New York", 84.0),
    ]);

    let city="San Francisco";
    let result=into_celsius(&cities, &city);
    match result {
        Ok(temp)=>println!("{} {}", city, temp),
        Err(err)=>println!("{}", err)
    }
}
```

The into_celsius function is updated to return a Result. After the and_then function, the ok_or function converts Option, with the Celsius temperature, to a Result. The Result is then returned. The final change is in main, where the match is updated to handle a Result returned from the into_celsius function.

Rich Errors

Not all error values are the same. Some possess rich information that can provide important additional detail. At a minimum, error values implement the Error and Display traits.

The io::Error type is an example of an error that contains rich information. File-related operations return io::Error when there is a problem. In Listing 12.23, we attempt to create a file. Because of the file location, the operation is likely to fail.

Code Listing 12.23.   The io::Error type provides rich error information.

```
use std::fs::File;
use std::io;
use std::io::prelude::*;
```

```
fn create_file()->Result<String, io::Error>{
    let file=File::create(r#"z1:\doesnotexist.txt"#)?;
    // read data
    Ok("Data".to_string())
}

fn main() {
    let result=create_file();
    let error=result.unwrap_err();
    match error.kind() {
        NotFound=>println!("not found"),
        _=>println!("something else")
    }
}
```

In this example, the create function will probably fail and return an io::Error. The ? operator propagates the error to the caller. In main, the unwrap_err function is used to unwrap the Result from the create_file function. The unwrap_err function is the functional reverse of unwrap. The function unwraps an Err value successfully but panics if the operation is successful. In our example, the match interprets the error value and, with the additional information, displays the kind of input/output error that has occurred.

Custom Errors

You can also create custom errors that include rich information. Adding rich information helps an application respond correctly to an error.

In the next example, the is_divisible function determines if x is divisible by y. For our purposes, ignore the remainder operator (%). Instead, the operation is performed explicitly. If x can be divided by, Some(x) should be returned. When y is zero, a panic could occur during the operation. To prevent this, the function implements proactive error handling. The function returns Result<bool, DivisibleError>, where DivisibleError is a custom error.

Listing 12.24 is the implementation of the DivisibleError type. As required for an Error type, we implement the Error trait. For the Error trait, this means implementing the *source* function. The purpose of the function is to identify the source of the error. We will also implement the Display trait as a helper trait. This means implementing the fmt function to provide a string representation of the error. For DivisibleError, the function will display the dividend and divisor.

Code Listing 12.24.   Implementing Display for DivisibleError

```
use std::error::Error;
use std::fmt;

#[derive(Debug, Copy, Clone)]
struct DivisibleError {
    dividend: i8,
    divisor: i8
```

```
    }

    impl fmt::Display for DivisibleError {
        fn fmt(&self, f: &mut fmt::Formatter) -> fmt::Result {
            write!(f, "Error => Dividend:{}  Divisor:{}", self.dividend,
                self.divisor)
        }
    }

    impl Error for DivisibleError {
        fn source(&self) -> Option<&(dyn Error + 'static)> {
            Some(self)
        }
    }

    fn is_divisible(dividend:i8, divisor:i8)->Result<bool, DivisibleError> {
        if divisor==0 {
            let error=DivisibleError{dividend:dividend, divisor:divisor};
            return Err(error);
        }

        if (dividend%divisor)==0 {
            Ok(true)
        } else {
            Ok(false)
        }
    }

    fn main() {
        let err=is_divisible(5,0).unwrap_err();
        println!("{}", err);
    }
```

Listing 12.25 shows the remainder of the application, starting with the is_divisible
function. This function determines if the numerator is divisible by the divisor and returns
either Ok(true) or Ok(false). The function also has error handling. The function returns a
DivisibleError, the custom error, when a error occurs.

Code Listing 12.25.   Use of the DivisibleError custom error

```
    fn is_divisible(numerator:i8, divisor:i8)->Result<bool, DivisibleError> {
        if divisor==0 {
            let error=DivisibleError{numerator:numerator,         \
                divisor:divisor};
            return Err(error);
        }
```

```
        if (numerator%divisor)==0 {
            Ok(true)
        } else {
            Ok(false)
        }
    }

fn main() {
    let err=is_divisible(5,0).unwrap_err();
    println!("{}", err);
}
```

In main, we call is_divisible with parameters to cause the function to fail. Because of this, the function returns a DivisibleError. The unwrap_err function is then called on Result to return the underlying error object, which is then displayed, as shown here:

```
Error => Dividend:5  Divisor:0
```

Summary

Error handling is an often-overlooked topic when exploring a programming language. You can aspire to write perfect code! For most, however, that is impossible, so error handling is an important tool for assuring the stability of an application.

Error handling is the process of uncovering potential exceptional events and proactively mitigating the problem. The goal is to avoid future problems or, even worse, panics. Proactive error handling and avoiding panics is idiomatic Rust. The Result and Option types are fundamental to error handling in Rust.

For either the Result or Option type, the unwrap function is commonly used during development but avoided in release versions of an application. If there is an error, unwrap will panic. There are other versions of unwrap that are helpful for error handling, such as unwrap_or. These functions are often used with released applications.

Panics occur when an application cannot continue because of an exceptional event. When a panic occurs, there is a stack unwind and an opportunity for an orderly cleanup and exit. You can handle a panic with the catch_unwind statement. However, panics are unpredictable and should be avoided, if possible.

We touched upon many Result and Option functions in this chapter, such as the map function. The map function abstracts the standard pattern for error handling. However, there are many more methods worth exploring. Consult the Rust documentation to learn more about them.

Rich error objects have additional detail that may be helpful for interpreting a problem. At a minimum, errors objects implement the Error and Display traits. You can also implement these traits to create custom error objects for your applications.

13

Structures

Structures are custom types that consist of fields and functions. As a developer-defined type, structs are often referred to as a user-defined type (UDT). With structures, you can create *made-to-order* types that are tailored to the specific requirements of your application. In Rust, structures are represented by struct types.

As a structure, a struct can provide context to data. It can be the difference between random data and useful information. Applications that consist exclusively of primitives are harder to maintain and refactor, when necessary. A struct can aggregate data into a cohesive unit that is easier to manage than the individual components. As an example, RGB is a standard for representing colors that are comprised of three core colors: red, green, and blue. Instead of defining three separate integers, we can group them within an RGB struct to ascribe context.

You can use structs to help model complex problem domains. Imagine modeling an internal combustion engine simply with individual integers, floats, and some strings. That would be an arduous endeavor, at best. Structs, however, can closely match the design, attributes, and behavior of complex objects, including a combustion engine. Solutions that closely resemble their problem domain are also easier to maintain and adapt.

Structs are named, and each struct is a different type. Like with other types, you can create a struct value using the `let`, `const`, or `static` keyword. Similar to the primitives, the rules of scope, shadowing, ownership, and lifetimes apply to struct.

Structs and tuples are close relatives. Both are custom types with heterogeneous fields. Structs, however, are named types, while tuples are unnamed. In addition, structs also have named fields, while fields within tuples are numbered. These differences mean structs are generally easier to use.

Here is the syntax for defining a new struct:

```
struct Structname {
    field¹:type,
    field²:type,
    fieldⁿ:type,
}
```

A struct begins with the `struct` keyword followed by the struct name. The name should frame the content of the overall struct. Within curly braces, you add fields to the struct. Each field consists of a *name:type* pair. By default, the order of fields in the struct is inconsequential.

If desired, you can control the order of fields and the memory layout of a struct using the `repr()` attribute.

As mentioned, RGB is a color scheme that describes colors with three inputs: red, green, and blue. Each color of RGB is within the range of 0 to 255, which indicates the level of saturation. 255 is the highest saturation, while 0 is none. For example, RGB(255, 0, 0) is *pure red*. The struct shown in Listing 13.1 describes an RGB color.

Code Listing 13.1.   Definition of the RGB struct

```
struct RGB {
    red:u8,
    green:u8,
    blue:u8,
}
```

The RGB struct is a composite of three u8 fields. The named fields are red, green, and blue. You create an instance of a struct with the struct name. The fields must be initialized within curly braces as *name*:*value* pairs. The fields can be initialized in any order. However, all the fields must be initialized; none can be omitted.

Here, we create an instance of the RGB struct:

```
RGB{red:50, green:50, blue:50};
```

Listing 13.2 is a complete example for the RGB struct.

Code Listing 13.2.   Defining, initializing, and displaying a struct

```
#[derive(Debug)]
struct RGB {
    red:u8,
    green:u8,
    blue:u8,
}

let dark_gray=RGB{red:50, green:50, blue:50};
let orange=RGB{red:255, green:165, blue:0};

// println!("{:?} {:?}", dark_gray, orange);
dbg!(&dark_gray);
dbg!(&orange);
```

By default, structs do not implement either the Display or Debug trait. This is necessary to display an RGB struct with the `println!` and `dbg!` macros. For that reason, the Debug trait is added to the RGB struct with the Debug attribute. It provides an implementation of the Debug trait. Two instances of RGB are then created: dark_gray and orange. Because of implementation of the Debug trait, we are now able to display both RGBs with the `dbg!` macro.

When compared to the `println!` macro, the `dbg!` macro outputs to the stderr stream, not stdout. The `dbg!` macro also displays the following information, which is helpful when debugging:

- Source file
- Source line
- Variable name
- Value

Because of the `dbg!` macro, here is the output from the example:

```
[src\main.rs:15] &dark_gray = RGB {
    red: 50,
    green: 50,
    blue: 50,
}
[src\main.rs:16] &orange = RGB {
    red: 255,
    green: 165,
    blue: 0,
}
```

For struct instances, access fields using dot notation: *instance.fieldname*. This is for all variations of instances, including T, &T, and &mut T.

There are gradations of gray from light gray to dark gray. When the three fields of RGB are the same, the resulting color is some degree of gray. Black is the darkest gray, where red, green, and blue are zero. The `is_gray` function returns true if the colors provided represent gray; that is, the values of the three RBG fields are equal. In Listing 13.3, the is_gray function is called. Using dot notation, the fields of an RGB instance are provided as function parameters.

Code Listing 13.3.   **Accessing fields of a struct using dot notation**

```
let color=RGB{red:200, green:150, blue:100};
let result=is_gray{color.red, color.green, color.blue};
println!("Color is gray: {}", result);
```

Alternate Initialization

There are alternate methods for initializing structs, which can be more concise and readable.

The *field init shorthand* syntax is one such alternative. This approach allows fields of a struct to be initialized using a similarly named variable. This avoids having to use the *name:value* syntax when the intent can be implied.

Listing 13.4 is an example of the field init shorthand syntax using the RGB struct.

Code Listing 13.4. **Long- and shorthand syntax to initialize struct**

```
fn new_struct(red:u8, green:u8, blue:u8)->RGB {
    //  RGB(red:red, green:green, blue:blue)     // longhand
        RGB(red, green, blue)                    // shorthand
}
```

The new_struct function has the red, green, and blue parameters. These parameters match the fields of the RGB struct, which allows the use of the field init shorthand syntax. The result is indeed more concise and readable. In this example, the longhand syntax is presented only for comparison.

You can even combine both longhand and shorthand syntax for separate fields, as shown here:

```
RGB{red: 120, green, blue}
```

Next, we present another example of the longhand syntax. CMYK is another color scheme. In Listing 13.5, we initialize a CMYK struct with an instance of another CMYK. This requires individually assigning each field.

Code Listing 13.5. **Initializing a new struct with another struct**

```
struct CMYK {
    cyan:u8,
    magenta:u8,
    yellow:u8,
    key:u8
}

let school_bus_yellow=CMYK{
    key:0,
    cyan:0,
    magenta:15,
    yellow:100 };

let other_color=CMYK{yellow:school_bus_yellow.yellow,
        cyan:school_bus_yellow.cyan,
        magneta:school_bus_yellow.magenta,
        key:100 };
```

school_bus_yellow is an instance of the CMYK struct and set to the color of a typical school bus. Except for the key field, the fields of other_color are initialized with the fields of school_bus_yellow.

Let's demonstrate the shorthand syntax again. This time with the ..*instance* syntax. The syntax will implicitly copy fields between structs of the same type. Listing 13.6 shows the updated example for CMYK. We still explicitly assign 100 to the key field. However, the remaining fields between the two structs do not change. Therefore, we can initialize the remaining fields using the ..*instance* syntax.

Code Listing 13.6.   Initializing a new struct using the *..instance* **syntax**

```
let other_color=CMYK{key:100, ..school_bus_yellow};
println!("{:?}", other_color);
```

Move Semantics

Structs support move semantics. This is true even if the individual fields fully support copy semantics. In Listing 13.7, ownership of the dark_gray instance is moved. Consequently, the attempt to display dark_gray later is invalid.

Code Listing 13.7.   Structs default to move semantics.

```
let dark_gray=RGB{red:50, green:50, blue:50};
let mut light_gray=dark_gray;

light_gray.red+=125;
light_gray.green+=125;
light_gray.blue+=125;

println!("{:?}", dark_gray);
```

Here is the error message from the previous example:

```
   |           --------- move occurs because `dark_gray`
   |         has type `RGB`, …
12 |     let mut light_gray=dark_gray;
   |                        --------- value moved here...
17 |     println!("{:?}", dark_gray);
   |                      ^^^^^^^^^^ value borrowed
   |         here after move
   |
```

You can apply the Copy trait to a struct only if every field already supports the trait. If this criterion is met, you can add the Copy attribute to the struct for copy semantics.

The RBG fields are u8, which have the Copy trait. Therefore, copy semantics can be added to the struct, as shown in Listing 13.8.

Code Listing 13.8.   Adding copy semantics with the derive attribute

```
#[derive(Debug)]
#[derive(Copy, Clone)]
struct RGB {
    red:u8,
    green:u8,
    blue:u8,
}
```

With the Copy trait added, the preceding code listing would compile successfully. The dark_ gray variable will not lose ownership. This allows the subsequent println! macro to execute correctly.

Mutability

Structs are immutable by default. In addition, fields inherit the mutability of the struct. Therefore, every field also defaults to being immutable. The mut keyword can be applied to an instance but not an individual field.

Attempting to apply the mut keyword to a field causes a compiler error.

Listing 13.9 declares a mutable instance of the RGB struct. The fields are consequently mutable and can be updated.

Code Listing 13.9.   **Modifying fields of a mutable struct**

```
let mut dark_gray=RGB{red:50, green:50, blue:50};
dark_gray.red-=10;
dark_gray.green-=10;
dark_gray.blue-=10;
```

Methods

A method is a function implemented for a struct. With the addition of methods, a struct can describe not only *what it looks like* but also *what it does*. Most entities in the real world are three-dimensional and have both appearance and behavior. Consequently, a struct possessing these same attributes is better for modeling real world problem domains. An application for a retail store could have structs for entities, such as customers, transactions, and even the store itself. These structs would have both descriptions and behaviors. For example, the customer struct could have customer number, name, and address fields. Methods would include purchase and return methods for purchasing and returning products at the store.

Methods are implemented within one or more impl blocks, which binds a method to a particular struct. The syntax for a method is the same as a function. However, the first parameter of the method is the &Self parameter, which is a reference to the current instance.

The is_gray function was implemented in previous examples as a free function. A free function is independent and not associated with a struct. In Listing 13.10, it is implemented as a method bound to the RGB struct.

Code Listing 13.10.   **Implementing a method for a struct**

```
#[derive(Debug)]
struct RGB {
    red:u8,
    green:u8,
    blue:u8,
```

```
}

impl RGB {
    fn is_gray(self: &Self)->bool{
        (self.red==self.blue)&&(self.blue==self.green)
    }
}
```

You call the method using the dot notation, the same as other struct members. When calling a method, the Self parameter is provided implicitly. It refers to some flavor of the current instance (the left side of the dot syntax). In Listing 13.11, the is_gray method is called on an RGB instance. Notice that the self parameter is not provided.

Code Listing 13.11.   Calling the is_gray method

```
let dark_gray=RGB{red:50, green:50, blue:50};
let result=dark_gray.is_gray();
```

In the impl block, you can reduce the first parameter to &self, which is the short syntax for self:&Self. The example shown in Listing 13.12 is identical to the earlier implementation of the is_gray method.

Code Listing 13.12.   The is_gray function uses short syntax for self:&Self.

```
#[derive(Debug)]
struct RGB {
    red:u8,
    green:u8,
    blue:u8,
}

impl RGB {
    fn is_gray(&self)->bool{
        (self.red==self.blue)&&(self.blue==self.green)
    }
}
```

Let's implement another method for the RBG struct, as shown in Listing 13.13. The is_pure_color method confirms whether the color is an absolute red, green, or blue. The method has two parameters: &Self and the Color enum.

Code Listing 13.13.   Implementing another method for the RGB struct

```
enum Color {
    Red,
    Blue,
    Green,
```

```
    }

impl RGB {
    fn is_pure_color(&self, color:Color)->bool {
        match color {
            Color::Red=>(self.red==255)&&
                ((self.blue+self.green)==0),
            Color::Blue=>(self.blue==255)&&
                ((self.red+self.green)==0),
            Color::Green=>(self.green==255)&&
                ((self.blue+self.red)==0)
        }
    }
}
```

Here, the is_pure_color method is called with a single parameter, which is Color::Blue, as shown here:

```
let result=pure_blue.is_pure_color(Color::Blue);
```

Figure 13.1 shows the relationship of the is_pure_color implementation to the method invocation.

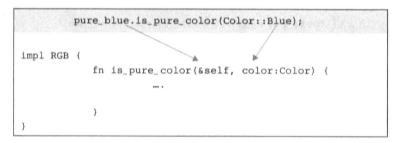

Figure 13.1. Diagram method implementation versus invocation

Self

For methods, &Self is the most common first parameter, and it borrows an immutable instance. Importantly, this means the instance is not moved and the method does not take ownership. For a mutable reference, you specify &mut Self. Transferring ownership into the method by using Self is less common. Here are all the permutations of Self:

- &Self — &T
- &mut Self — &mut T
- Self — T

Remember, the &self parameter is equivalent to self:&Self, which is included within the prior list.

Let's add another method to the RGB struct. The `invert` method inverts the color represented by the RGB struct. Each field of the RGB struct is inverted. As such, the method modifies the current instance of an RGB struct and requires a `&mut Self` (see Listing 13.14).

Code Listing 13.14. Modifying fields within a mutable struct

```
#[derive(Debug)]
struct RGB {
    red:u8,
    green:u8,
    blue:u8,
}

impl RGB {
    fn invert(&mut self) {
        self.red=255-self.red;
        self.green=255-self.green;
        self.blue=255-self.blue;
    }
}

fn main() {
    let mut color=RGB{red:150, green:50, blue:75};
    color.invert();
    println!("{:?}", color);
}
```

Associated Functions

Associated functions bind to a struct, not a particular instance. Accordingly, there is no `&Self` parameter with an associated function. You call the associated function against the structure using the `::` syntax: *structname*::*function*. Associated functions are similar to static or class-wise methods in other languages. Unlike some other languages, Rust does not support associated fields. This limits the capabilities of associated functions.

The new function for the Factory pattern is a common use case for associated functions. A factory function abstracts the creation of an instance. Listing 13.15 is an example of a factory function, also known as a constructor function.

Code Listing 13.15. Implementation of the Large type with a new function

```
struct Large {
    // data
}

impl Large {
    fn new()->Box<Large> {
```

```
        Box::new(Large{})
    }

    fn task1(&self) {
        // do something
    }

    fn task2(&self) {
        // do something
    }
}

fn main() {
    let instance=Large::new();
    instance.task1();
}
```

The Large struct is a mockup of a type that might hold a substantial amount of data. The factory function boxes a new instance of the Large type. The struct is placed on the heap and the box instance is returned from the function. Boxing is discussed further in Chapter 20, "Memory." Two methods are also implemented for Large: task1 and task2. In the main function, an instance of the Large struct is created with the factory function. The task1 method is then called on the instance.

Impl Blocks

Methods of a struct are commonly implemented in a single impl block. Nevertheless, you can implement the methods across multiple impl blocks, for example, by grouping methods together based on an additional context, more than just the struct.

In Listing 13.16, there are multiple impl blocks for the RGB struct. The getter and setter methods are grouped in separate impl blocks. Separating them in this manner makes the code more readable and provides additional context beyond just the struct.

Code Listing 13.16. Multiple impl blocks used to group RGB methods

```
#[derive(Debug)]
struct RGB {
    red:u8,
    green:u8,
    blue:u8,
}

// Getters
impl RGB {
    const fn get_red(&self)->u8{self.red}
    const fn get_green(&self)->u8{self.green} .
    const fn get_blue(&self)->u8{self.blue}
```

```
}

// Setters
impl RGB {
    fn set_red(&mut self, value:u8){self.red=value;}
    fn set_green(&mut self, value:u8){self.green=value;}
    fn set_blue(&mut self, value:u8){self.blue=value;}
}
```

Operator Overloading

Many developers want their custom types to have the same inert capabilities of predefined types, particular numeric types. This includes support for mathematical and other operators, such as the *addition operator* (+) and the *unary negation operator* (-). Adding this support to structs is called operator overloading.

First, operator overloading is *never* required. You could easily create a named function that provides the same behavior. Instead of overloading the addition operator (+), for example, you could implement an add function for the same purpose. For that reason, some feel that operator overloading is syntatic sugar that adds an unwarranted level of abstraction.

Be disciplined! You can overload operators with almost any implementation, even something inconsistent with the expectation. For example, you could have the addition operator (+) perform subtraction. You could even overload the *bitwise AND operator* (&) to save results of the bitwise operation to a file in the cloud, but only on Thursday. Does that make sense?! The possibility of nonsensical overloading is endless. The implementation of operator overloading should adhere to the well-known interpretation of the operator. Alternatively, the behavior should at least be consistent with some visual clue associated with the operator, similar to the insertion operator (<<) in C++. The direction of the << implies insertion.

Unary operators, such as the unary negation operator (-), have a single operand, which is the instance. This is equivalent to the following:

Unary operator: *instance.operator*()

Binary operators have two operands: a left-hand side (lhs) and right-hand side (rhs). For operator overloading, the left-hand side is the instance. This is equivalent to the following:

Binary operator: *instance.operator*(rhs)

Unary Operator Overloading

Traits for operator overloading are found in the `std::ops` module. Here is the trait for the unary negation operator (-):

```
pub trait Neg {
    type Output;

    fn neg(self) -> Self::Output;
}
```

The Neg trait is typical of unary operators. There is a single method to implement to describe the behavior of the operator for that struct. For the Neg trait, this is the `neg` method. The Output type within the `impl` block sets the return type of the trait operation.

In Listing 13.17, the unary negation operator (-) is implemented for the RGB struct.

Code Listing 13.17.   Implementation of the - operator for the RGB struct

```
use std::ops;

#[derive(Debug)]
struct RGB {
    red:u8,
    green:u8,
    blue:u8,
}

impl ops::Neg for RGB {
    type Output = RGB;

    fn neg(self) ->Self {
        RGB{red: 255-self.red, blue:255-self.blue,
            green:255-self.green}
    }
}

fn main() {
    let color1=RGB{red:200, green: 75, blue:125, };
    let color2=-color1;        // use the overloaded operator
    println!("{:?}", color2);  //  RGB { red: 55,
                               //            green: 180, blue: 130 }
}
```

In the `impl` block, Output sets the return type of the operation to RGB. Next, the neg function is implemented to invert the RGB color. This behavior is consistent with the meaning of the unary negation operator (-). In `main`, the overloaded unary negation operator (-) negates the value of `color1`. The result is placed in `color2` and displayed.

Binary Operator Overloading

Binary operators are the most overloaded operators. Of the binary operators, the addition operator (+) and the subtraction operator (-) are the most common. Here is the trait for the addition operator (+). It is the prototypical trait for a binary operator. Traits for binary operators are generic.

```
pub trait Add<Rhs = Self> {
    type Output;

    fn add(self, rhs: Rhs) -> Self::Output;
}
```

For this trait, the `add` function is implemented to overload the addition operator +. The `Rhs` type parameter assigns a type to the right-hand side operand (rhs). The default for `Rhs` is Self. Self refers to the instance (lhs), which means the `lhs` and `rhs` default to the same type. In addition, output sets the return type of the operator +.

In Listing 13.18, the addition operator (+) is implemented for the RGB structure.

Code Listing 13.18.   Implementing the + operator for the RGB struct

```
use std::ops;

#[derive(Debug)]
#[derive(Copy, Clone)]
struct RGB {
    red:u8,
    green:u8,
    blue:u8,
}

impl ops::Add for RGB {
    type Output = RGB;

    fn add(self, rhs:RGB) -> Self::Output {
        RGB{red: self.red+rhs.red, blue:self.blue+rhs.blue,
            green:self.green+rhs.green}
    }
}
```

The `type` parameter of the Add trait defaults to Self (i.e., RGB). In addition, Output sets the return type to RBG. The implementation of the `add` method performs addition of self and rhs (i.e., adding their fields together). The result is returned as a new RGB instance.

In `main`, we create two instances of the RGB struct. We add both instances together using the addition operator (+). This implicitly calls the Add function on the left-hand side operand. The result is saved to a different RGB instance (see Listing 13.19).

Code Listing 13.19.   Adding two RGBs with overloaded operator +

```
fn main() {
    let color1=RGB{red:200, green: 75, blue:125, };
    let color2=RGB{red:50, green: 75, blue:25, };

    let color3=color1+color2;
    println!("{:?}", color3);
}
```

For binary operators, the left-hand-side operand, right-hand-side operand, and return value are frequently the same type, such as (RGB=RGB+RGB). However, this symmetry is not required. All three can be different types.

In Listing 13.20, the left-hand-side and right-hand-side operands for the addition operator (+) are different. We want to add a tuple to an RGB instance:

```
RGB + (u8, u8, u8)
```

Code Listing 13.20.   Implementing the `RGB + (u8, u8, u8)` operator

```
use std::ops;

#[derive(Debug)]
#[derive(Copy, Clone)]
struct RGB {
    red:u8,
    green:u8,
    blue:u8,
}

impl ops::Add<(u8, u8, u8)> for RGB {
    type Output = RGB;

    fn add(self, rvalue: (u8, u8, u8)) -> Self::Output {
        RGB{red: self.red+rvalue.0, blue:self.blue+rvalue.1,
            green:self.green+rvalue.2}
    }
}

fn main() {
    let color1=RGB{red:200, green: 75, blue:125, };
    let color2=color1+(10, 25, 15);
    println!("{:?}", color2);
}
```

The `type` parameter for the Add trait sets the right-hand side operator to `(u8, u8, u8)`, which is a tuple. Within the `impl` block, Output establishes the return type as RGB. The implementation of the `add` method adds the fields of the tuple to the current RGB instance, `self`. The result is returned as a new RBG.

Note

In this section, examples of the addition operator (+) may overflow the u8 values. This is expected. We want the value to wrap around. The debug build, however, has the overflow-checks compiler option enabled. For this reason, debug versions of the examples may panic. Release versions will run perfectly. Add this section to the cargo.toml file for the proper behavior in both release and debug versions:

```
[profile.dev]
overflow-checks = false
```

Tuple Struct

Tuple structs are a combination of a struct and a tuple.

You declare a tuple struct with the struct keyword, struct name, and then a tuple, like so:

```
struct Name(fieldtype¹, fieldtype², fieldtypeⁿ)
```

Although the tuple struct is named, the fields remain anonymous. Like a tuple, the fields are positional and accessed via an index.

Listing 13.21 is an example of a tuple struct.

Code Listing 13.21.   Example of a tuple struct

```
#[derive(Debug)]
struct Grade(String, char, u8);

fn main(){

    let bob=Grade("Bob".to_string(), 'B', 87);
    let sally=Grade("Sally".to_string(), 'A', 93);

    println!("Name: {}  Grade: {}  Score: {}",
        sally.0, sally.1, sally.2);
}
```

Grade is a tuple struct with three fields. These are the anonymous fields for name, alphabetic grade, and grade score. The variables bob and sally are instances of the tuple struct. The fields for sally are then displayed using fields.

When compared to a tuple, tuple structs have some advantages:

- Tuple structures are named and therefore easier to reuse.
- Tuple structures have a stricter definition of equivalence.
- Tuple structures are useful as a wrapper for another type.

Unit-Like Struct

A struct with no fields is considered "unit-like." Unit-like structs occupy no memory space and are considered a zero-sized type (ZST). This is one of the exotic types in Rust. An empty tuple, (), is called the unit type. Because of similarities with the empty tuple, both are ZST, structs with no fields are considered unit-like.

Unit-like structs have limited use-case scenarios. Most notably, unit-like structures can be used as a marker struct or to implement traits, without fields. When defining a unit-like struct, you omit the curly braces for defining fields. Listing 13.22 is an example of implementing a trait for a unit-like struct.

Code Listing 13.22.   **Example of a unit-like struct**

```
struct Something;

impl ATrait for Something {
      // methods
}
```

Summary

You can use structs to create custom types. Structs combine both state and behavior in a single entity. They are convenient for modeling entities in the real world problem domain.

You define a struct with the `struct` keyword, name, and then fields, within curly braces. For instances, access the fields of a struct using dot notation.

By default, structs are immutable. You apply the `mut` keyword to make the struct mutable. The entire struct is either mutable or immutable. You cannot apply the `mut` keyword to individual fields.

Methods are functions for a struct. You implement methods for a struct in the `impl` block. The first parameter of a method is `&Self`, `&mut Self`, or `Self` and refers to the current instance. When the method is called, the `self` parameter is implied and binds the method to the struct. As with a field, you execute methods using dot notation: *instance.method*.

An associated function is bound to a struct and not an instance. Associated functions do not have a `self` parameter. You execute associated functions using the `::` operator: *struct::method*. Factory functions, such as a new function, are commonly implemented as associated functions.

As a convenience, you can overload the operators for a structure using traits. Traits for operating overloading are found in the `std::ops` module. Typically, you implement the operator in a manner consistent with its understood behavior.

14

Generics

Generics are templates for building unique functions and type definitions. Not surprisingly, generics are called *templates* in some other languages. Generics are templates with placeholders to be resolved later. You can then build unique instances of functions and type definitions by replacing the placeholders with concrete types. In this manner, generics represent reusable code, even in ways the author may not have anticipated. That is the fun part of generics—being able to use them in the future in unplanned ways. Combined with traits, we have the two pillars of polymorphism in Rust.

Many of the types in the standard library, such as `Result<T, E>`, `Option<T>`, `Vec<T>`, and `HashMap<K,V>`, are generic. For this reason, generics have an elevated presence in the language.

Generics are mostly about specialization. We will use home design as an analogy. Home builders often possess an assortment of home designs for potential homeowners. The home-owner can choose and then customize the home design based on their preferences, often in ways the builder did not envision. There are placeholders for carpeting, light fixtures, and other design decisions. With this information, a specialization is created—a home designed with specific choices for a particular homeowner. Another homeowner, with their design decisions, would receive a different specialization. It is convenient for the builder that the home designs are mostly reusable. But it is also beneficial to homeowners who can create specializations from the home design based on their unique preferences. In Rust, the home design is a generic type.

Special terminology is associated with generics. Placeholders are *type parameters* and represent some type, to be defined later. When a type parameter is applied, the description is "*something over type T*," where T is the type parameter. Type parameters are declared within *angle brackets, <>*. The term *generics* encompasses all generic targets: functions, structs, traits, enums, and values. And finally, *turbofish* is `::<>`, which will be explained later.

Rust is a statically typed language. For that reason, type parameters for generics are resolved to concrete types at compile time. This is considered parametric polymorphism. Generics also employ monomorphization. With monomorphization, type arguments are used to resolve generics to unique types. For example, with generic functions, you can create unique functions for unique combinations of type arguments. This occurs at compile time to avoid any performance cost at runtime.

There are many other benefits to generics:

- **Code reuse**: Write code once and reuse it in unlimited ways with different types. Avoid functions like `add_int`, `add_float`, `add_string`, and so on.
- **Refactoring**: Refactoring is simpler because the generic represents the single source, not multiple sources for essentially the same code.
- **Extensibility**: Generics can be used in the future with different types for placeholders, even types that do not exist now.
- **Less error prone**: Generics remove redundant source code. Less-redundant code inevitably results in fewer errors.
- **Unique capabilities**: Unique capabilities such as function overloading are associated with generics in Rust.

There are generic functions and types. We will start our exploration with generic functions.

Generic Functions

Generic functions are templates for creating concrete functions, using type parameters. You declare type parameters within angle brackets, after the function name. By convention, the first type parameter is T. Subsequent generic type parameters, if any, are named U, V, and so on. However, you are not restricted to this naming convention. Generic type parameters have the same naming convention as variables, which is UpperCamelCasing. You can utilize type parameters within the function definition and body.

This syntax demonstrates the various places that a type parameter can be used—function parameter, function return value, and within the function itself:

```
fn functionname<T>(param:T)->T {
    let variable :T ;
}
```

The swap function, presented in Listing 14.1, swaps integer values within a tuple. It is not generic.

Code Listing 14.1.   **The swap function reverses fields within a tuple.**

```
fn swap(tuple:(i8, i8))->(i8,i8){
    (tuple.1, tuple.0)
}
```

swap is only for i8 types. Applying swap to other types requires creating multiple versions of the swap method, `swap_string`, `swap_float`, and so on, as shown in Listing 14.2.

Code Listing 14.2.   **Additional swap functions for a String and f64**

```
fn swap_string(tuple:(String, String))->(String,String){
    (tuple.1, tuple.0)
}

fn swap_float(tuple:(f64, f64))->(f64, f64){
    (tuple.1, tuple.0)
}
```

This is the opposite of DRY. Maintaining multiple versions of the same function is tedious and prone to errors. Neither is it extensible. Every type used with the function requires a new function. None of this sounds productive.

In main, shown in Listing 14.3, the concerns continue. We have to remember each unique function name for swapping fields within a tuple. And again, this is not extensible.

Code Listing 14.3.   **Calls to different flavors of the swap function**

```
fn main() {
    let tuple1=(10, 20);
    let tuple2=("ten".to_string(), "twenty".to_string());
    let tuple3=(10.0, 20.0);

    let result=swap(tuple1);
    let result=swap_string(tuple2);
    let result=swap_float(tuple3);
}
```

Generics to the rescue! In Listing 14.4, the swap function is rewritten as a generic function. It is now extensible and usable with various types. The concrete types in previous examples of the swap, such as i8 and String, are replaced with type parameter T, which is generic. Several functions are now reduced to a single version.

Code Listing 14.4.   **A swap function that is generic over type T**

```
fn swap<T>(tuple:(T, T))->(T,T){
    (tuple.1, tuple.0)
}
```

The main function is simpler also. Instead of multiple functions to remember, you can just call swap with a variety of types. The compiler infers the correct concrete type from the function arguments (see Listing 14.5).

Code Listing 14.5.   The same swap function called with various types

```
fn main() {
    let tuple1=(10, 20);
    let tuple2=("ten".to_string(), "twenty".to_string());
    let tuple3=(10.0, 20.0);

    let result=swap(tuple1);  // for integer
    let result=swap(tuple2);  // for String
    let result=swap(tuple3);  // for float
}
```

In main, the swap function is called with different concrete types. Per monomorphization, the compiler creates a separate concrete function for each type. When swap is called with a String parameter, the compiler creates a concrete function, where the type parameter is replaced with String, as follows:

```
fn swap(tuple:(String, String))->( String, String){
    (tuple.1, tuple.0)
}
```

Generics provide limited support for function overloading. Function overloading is when functions share the same name but with a unique function definition and implementation. Based on the function definition, the compiler selects the correct function to call. In the previous example, swap is overloaded for different types: integer, float, and String. Nonetheless, the compiler calls the correct implementation of the function. That is the nature of parametric polymorphism.

You can have multiple type parameters. The next version of the swap method has two type parameters: T and U. In this version, the fields of the tuple can be different types, as demonstrated in Listing 14.6.

Code Listing 14.6.   The swap function with type parameter T and U

```
fn swap<T, U>(tuple:(T, U))->(U,T){
    (tuple.1, tuple.0)
}

fn main() {
    let tuple1=(10, "ten");
    let result=swap(tuple1);
    println!("{:?}", result);
}
```

In the previous examples, the compiler inferred the type. When a generic function is called, most often, type parameters are inferred from the function arguments, if any. When the concrete type cannot be inferred, you must define the type explicitly.

In Listing 14.7, do_something is a generic function that is called in main.

Code Listing 14.7.   A type parameter used as a return type

```
fn do_something<T:Default>()->T {
    let value:T=T::default();
    value
}

fn main() {let result=do_something();
    println!("{}", result);
}
```

Unfortunately, this program does not compile. Here is the error message:

```
  |
8 |         let result: _=do_something();
  |                   +++

For more information about this error, try
  `rustc --explain E0282`.
error: could not compile `default` due to
  previous error
```

The error message complains about an unknown return type, as a type parameter. The reason is the type parameter cannot be inferred. The do_something function has no function parameters. This prevents inferring a concrete type from the function arguments. Therefore, the concrete type for the return type is unknown. For these reasons, the caller needs to explicitly state the concrete type.

When calling a free function, you explicitly set the concrete type for type parameters using turbofish as the syntax:

```
function_name::<type,…>(arg1, …)
```

Listing 14.8 is an updated version of main. This version sets the type parameter explicitly to i8.

Code Listing 14.8.   Explicitly setting type parameter T

```
fn main() {
    let result=do_something::<i8>();
    println!("{}", result);
}
```

Listing 14.9 is a real-world example of generic functions. The vec_push_within is a generic function that adds an element to a vector. If at capacity, the vector is not extended. Instead, a new vector is created with the new element. The function returns a Result type. If it's successful, the available capacity is returned as Ok(*capacity*). Otherwise, the new vector is returned as the error value, Err(*newvector*).

The `vec_push_within` function can be used with any type of vector, including vec<i8>, vec<f64>, vec<String>, vec<(i32, i32>, and so on. That makes the function more valuable and available in different scenarios. The `vec_push_within` function is generic over type T, where T is the type of vector.

Code Listing 14.9.   The implementation of the `vec_push_within` function

```
fn vec_push_within<T>(vec1:&mut Vec<T>, value:T)->
Result<usize, Vec<T>>{
    let capacity=vec1.capacity();
    let len=vec1.len();
    let diff=capacity-len;
    if diff != 0  {
        vec1.push(value);
        Ok(diff-1)
    } else {
        Err(vec![value])
    }
}
```

The function arguments are a vector and an element to add to it. Within the function, the capacity is checked before the element is added. If it's at capacity, a new vector is created with the element, which is returned as the error value.

Within `main`, we test the `vec_push_within` function. Elements are added to a vector of integers. The result is then displayed, as shown in Listing 14.10.

Code Listing 14.10.   Testing the `vec_push_within` function

```
fn main() {
    let mut vec1=Vec::with_capacity(2);
    vec1.push(1);
    vec1.push(2);
    let result=vec_push_within(&mut vec1, 3);

    match result {
        Ok(_)=>println!("Original {:?}", vec1),
        Err(value)=>println!("New {:?}", value),
    }
}
```

Bounds

For generics, type parameters can refer to *any type*. That's the value of generics! However, that can also be a limitation. The type parameter represents a type that is non-specific. This means at compile time, the compiler knows very little about the type parameter. For that reason, the compiler rightfully limits what can be done with it.

A type parameter is similar to a black box that contains a tool. However, as a black box, the specific tool in the box is unknown to you. If the box contains a fine screwdriver versus a chainsaw, that makes a difference. You can only do certain things safely with a chainsaw. This makes it hard to accept the black box for a specific project without knowing the contents. What if the project is building model cars? A fine screwdriver would be helpful, but not a chainsaw. A hint as to the contents of the box would be helpful. For example, does the box contain a power tool?

Trait bounds limit the behavior of a type parameter to a specific trait or traits. Each trait informs the compiler of the expected capabilities of the type arguments. The type argument must implement any trait listed as a trait bound. This gives the compiler confidence about how the type parameter can be used.

Assign trait bonds when the type parameter is declared. After the type parameter is named, you add trait bounds after the : operator (e.g., <T:*Trait*>).

The next function frames a value within asterisks and demonstrates the need for trait bounds. For example, 2 would become the following:

```
***
*2*
***
```

We want to extend this functionality to any type. Therefore, the function is implemented as a generic function (see Listing 14.11).

Code Listing 14.11.   The border_value function frames a value with asterisks.

```
fn border_value<T>(value:T)->String {
    let formatted=format!("* {} *", value);
    let len=formatted.len();
    let line="*".repeat(len).to_string();
    format!("{}\n{}\n{}", line, formatted, line)
}
```

This function will not compile because of the format! macro. The { } placeholder within the format string requires the Display trait. However, the compiler cannot assume that type parameter T supports this trait. For that reason, the border_value function will not compile. We need to add trait bounds.

In Listing 14.12, type parameter T is bound with the Display trait. This guarantees that any type argument for parameter T will implement the Display trait. With this promise, the compiler accepts type parameter T, as value, within the format! macro.

Code Listing 14.12.   The border_value function constrains type T with the Display trait.

```
fn border_value<T:Display>(value:T)->String {
    let formatted=format!("* {} *", value);
    let len=formatted.len();
    let line="*".repeat(len).to_string();
    format!("{}\n{}\n{}", line, formatted, line)
}
```

In the previous example, a trait bound was applied to type parameter T. If desired, you can apply multiple trait bounds to a type parameter. Each is a constraint and further refines the capabilities of the type parameter while providing the compiler additional information. You can combine multiple trait bounds with the + operator, as shown:

```
<T:Trait¹+Trait²+…>
```

The largest function is a generic function, as shown in Listing 14.13. It compares two values and displays the largest value. This requires multiple trait bounds. Types that support this type of comparison must implement the Ord trait. In addition, the Display trait is required for the { } placeholder in the println! macro. For that reason, both traits are applied to type parameter T as bounds. Importantly, without both constraints, the compiler would not have enough information to compile this program.

Code Listing 14.13.   For the largest function, trait bounds Ord and Display are applied to type parameter T.

```
use std::fmt::Display;
use std::cmp::Ordering;

fn largest<T:Display+Ord>(arg1: T, arg2: T){
    match arg1.cmp(&arg2) {
        Ordering::Less => println!("{} > {}", arg1, arg2),
        Ordering::Greater => println!("{} > {}", arg2, arg1),
        Ordering::Equal => println!("{} = {}", arg2, arg1),
    }
}

fn main() {
    largest(10, 20);
    largest("ten".to_string(), "twenty".to_string());

}
```

The where Clause

The where clause is an alternate method for applying trait bounds. The where clause is more expressive and can be clearer than conventional trait bounds.

Let's compare conventional trait bounds to the where clause. Listing 14.14 is a generic function with trait bounds, as previously shown. The Debug trait constrains type parameter T.

Code Listing 14.14.   Type parameter T is constrained with the Debug trait.

```
fn do_something<T:Debug>(arg1:T){
    println!("{:?}", arg1);
}
```

The next function, shown in Listing 14.15, is equivalent to the previous example, except with a `where` clause. Some would consider this version more readable.

Code Listing 14.15.   With a where clause, a constraint is applied to type parameter T.

```
fn do_something<T>(arg1:T)
    where T:Debug
{
    println!("{:?}", arg1);
}
```

The `where` clause can simplify the syntax for generics. In the next example, the do_something function is generic over type T. The `func` parameter is the FnOnce type, which is a trait. As a parameter, the trait requires either static or dynamic dispatch. In Listing 14.16, dynamic dispatch is used.

Code Listing 14.16.   As a parameter, the FnOnce trait is applied with dynamic dispatch.

```
fn do_something<T>(func:&mut dyn FnOnce(&T)) {
}
```

In the version in Listing 14.17, the do_something is generic over both type T and U. With the where clause, we can simplify the syntax. Now the `func` parameter is type parameter U. The where clause then constrains type parameter U with FnOnce(T).

Code Listing 14.17.   This syntax is simpler with the where clause.

```
fn do_something<T, U>(func: U)
    where
        U: FnOnce(&T),
{

}
```

Static dispatch and dynamic dispatch are explained in Chapter 17, "Traits."

The where clause also has a unique capability. With the `where` clause, you can assign trait bounds directly to arbitrary types. This feature assigns trait bounds to concrete types, not type parameters.

In Listing 14.18, for the `do_something` function, the `where` clause bounds the XStruct with the Copy trait. For this reason, XStruct must implement the Copy trait. XStruct is a concrete type, not a type parameter. Because of this, you cannot use conventional trait bounds.

Code Listing 14.18.   XStruct is constrained by the Copy trait.

```
#[derive(Copy, Clone)]
struct XStruct {}

fn do_something(arg:XStruct)
    where
        XStruct:Copy
{

}

fn main() {
    do_something(XStruct{})
}
```

Structs

Functions should not have all the fun. Structs can also be generic! You declare the type parameters, within angle brackets, after the struct name. You can then use the type parameter within the struct, including methods.

In Listing 14.19, IntWrapper is a thin wrapper for i8. It is not generic.

Code Listing 14.19.   Thin wrapper for an integer

```
    struct IntWrapper {
        internal:i8
    }
```

In Listing 14.20, Wrapper is generalized for *any* type. The struct is renamed in recognition of its generic intention. The Wrapper struct is generic over type T. The type parameter annotates the *internal* field.

Code Listing 14.20.   Generic wrapper for any type

```
    struct Wrapper<T> {
        internal:T
}
```

In main, an instance of Wrapper is created (see Listing 14.21). The compiler can infer the concrete type for the type parameter using the internal field, which is initialized with an i32 value. Per monomorphization, the compiler will create a concrete instance of the Wrapper struct, with the i32 type, as shown in the comments.

Code Listing 14.21.   Documents monomorphization

```
fn main() {
    let obj=Wrapper{internal:1};

    /* Monomorphization

        struct Wrapper {
            internal:i8
        }

    */
}
```

For generic structs, type parameters can also be used with methods. First, the type parameters must be described within the impl definition. You can then use the type parameters with the methods. The syntax is not trivial, as shown in Figure 14.1.

Note
The official name of a struct includes any type parameters.

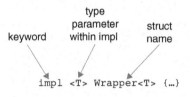

```
impl <T> Wrapper<T>  {…}
```

keyword   type parameter within impl   struct name

Figure 14.1.   Showing type parameters in the impl definition.

Concrete types are assigned to type parameters included in the impl definition when an instance of the struct is created.

Let's improve upon the Wrapper struct, which previously only had fields. We will add get and set methods to the struct. The functions allow a user to get and set the internal field. Both methods are generic over type T. For T, the set method requires the Copy trait. Consequently type parameter T is bound to the Copy trait. Listing 14.22 shows the impl block for Wrapper<T>.

Code Listing 14.22.   Showing type parameter T in use with a method

```
impl<T:Copy> Wrapper<T> {
    fn get(&self)->T{
        self.internal
    }

    fn set(&mut self, data:T){
```

```
        self.internal=data;
    }
}
```

In main, the get method is called on separate instances of Wrapper (see Listing 14.23). The instances wrap an integer and float type, respectively.

Code Listing 14.23.   Calling methods on a generic struct

```
fn main() {
    let obj1=Wrapper{internal:1};
    println!("{}", obj1.get());

    let obj2=Wrapper{internal:1.1};
    println!("{}", obj2.get());
}
```

In addition, methods can declare their own type parameters, separate from those received from the struct. These type parameters are private to the method. You use the same syntax as a generic function to declare them. Different from the struct's type parameters, these type parameters are assigned concrete types when the method is called. The method can use type parameters both from the struct, defined in the impl header, and those defined specifically for the method.

The next version of Wrapper has a display method, which is generic over type U. Remember, type parameter T is already declared for the Wrapper struct. Type parameter U is available within the display method, but not available elsewhere within the struct. Type parameter T, however, is available everywhere. The display function displays the internal field of the struct. As function parameters, you can add a prefix or suffix to the output. Both are type U. For this reason, U must implement the Display trait to support the {} placeholder in the println! macro. Therefore, the Display trait is added as a constraint to type parameter U.

In Listing 14.24, the display method is shown. The get and set methods are omitted (. . .) for brevity.

Code Listing 14.24.   Type parameters T and U require the Display trait.

```
use std::fmt::Display;

struct Wrapper<T> {
    internal:T
}

impl<T:Copy+Display> Wrapper<T> {

    . . .

    fn display<U:Display>(&self, prefix:U, suffix:U) {
        println!("{}{}{}", prefix, self.internal, suffix);
```

```
        }

    }

fn main() {
    let obj=Wrapper{internal:1.1};
    obj.display("< ", " >");
}
```

The where clause can be applied to generic structs. The benefits are the same as described before. The version of the Wrapper struct shown in Listing 14.25 has a perform method that executes *some* action on the internal field.

Code Listing 14.25. **Multiple constraints applied in the where clause**

```
use std::fmt::Display;

#[derive(Copy, Clone, Debug)]
struct Wrapper<T> {
    internal:T
}

impl<T:Copy+Display> Wrapper<T> {

    ...

    fn perform<F>(mut self, operation:F)->Self
        where
            Self:Copy+Clone,
            F: Fn(T) -> T
    {
        self.internal=operation(self.internal);
        self
    }
}
```

The perform method is generic over type F. It is a high-order function that accepts a function as a parameter (F). That function is called within the method to modify the internal field in some manner. The function returns an instance of the struct. The where clause for the perform method adds some bounds. Self, which is the current instance, must implement the Copy and Clone traits. In addition, type parameter F is bound to a specific function signature.

In main, an instance of the Wrapper struct is created (see Listing 14.26). The perform method accepts a closure that performs a calculation. We then display the original value and the resulting value.

Code Listing 14.26.   Calling the `perform` method on `Wrapper`

```
fn main(){
    let obj=Wrapper{internal:6};
    let obj2=obj.perform(|arg1| {
        arg1*arg1
    });
    println!("{:?} {:?}", obj, obj2);
}
```

Associated Functions

You can use generics with associated functions, which are functions without a Self parameter. Listing 14.27 shows an example.

Code Listing 14.27.   The `do_something` associated function is generic over type T

```
struct XStruct<T> {field1:T}

impl<T> XStruct<T> {
    fn do_something(a:T) {
        let a:T;
    }
}

fn main() {
    XStruct::do_something(5);
}
```

XStruct and the `do_something` associated function are both generic over type T. Other than having an associated function, this example is no different than shown before. However, there is a difference when the type parameters cannot be inferred. For associated functions, you can assign a concrete type to a type parameter with this syntax:

```
structname::<type, …>::function_call
```

In Listing 14.28, the type cannot be inferred from the function parameters. The do_something function here has no parameters! Therefore, we must use the alternate syntax.

Code Listing 14.28.   Calling an associated function with an explicit type

```
struct XStruct<T> {field1:T}

impl<T> XStruct<T> {
    fn do_something() {
        let a:T;
    }
```

```
    }

fn main() {
    XStruct::<i8>::do_something();
}
```

Enums

Because of the Option<T> and Result<T E> enums, most Rust developers are quickly introduced to generics. Option is generic over type T, and Result<T,E> is generic over types T and
E. Here are the definitions for both types:

```
enum Option<T> {
    None,
    Some(T),
}

enum Result<T, E> {
    Ok(T),
    Err(E),
}
```

After the enum name, the type parameters are defined, within angle brackets. Type parameters are then applied to individual variants, within parentheses after the variant's name.

Listing 14.29 shows a trivial function that has a Result return value. For return values, the
compiler cannot infer the type. Therefore, the concrete types are expressed explicitly.

Code Listing 14.29.   Return with explicit types

```
fn do_something()->Result<bool, &'static str> {
    Ok(true)
}
```

The Result and Option types do not encompass all use cases for return values. You can
create other use cases similar to either the Result or Option types. For example, the Repeat
enum, shown next, is for a different use case. It is generic over types T and U. This enum
controls whether a function should be called repeatedly. There are multiple variants:

- The continue variant requests calling the function again, with the T value.
- The result variant requests that the repetition stops and returns a result, as type U.
- The done variant requests that the repetition stop without providing a result.

Listing 14.30 shows the Repeat enum.

Code Listing 14.30.   The Repeat enum indicates whether a function should be repeated.

```
enum Repeat<T, U>{
    Continue(T),
    Result(U),
    Done
}
```

The `find_div_5` function is a simple example of using the Repeat enum. The function finds numbers divisible by 5. If one is found, the function displays the number and returns Done. Otherwise, the function returns Continue and recommends the next value (see Listing 14.31). The type parameter for the Repeat enum is i8.

Code Listing 14.31.   The `div_5` function finds a number divisible by 5.

```
fn find_div_5(number:i8)->Repeat<i8> {
    if number % 5 == 0 {
        println!("Found {}", number);
        Repeat::Done
    } else {
        Repeat::Continue(number+1)
    }
}
```

In `main`, the `find_div_5` function is called within a loop block. If Continue is returned, we call the function again with the recommended value. The loop continues until Done is returned from the function (see Listing 14.32).

Code Listing 14.32.   Control logic determined by the Repeat result

```
fn main() {
    let mut value=1;
    loop {
        if let Repeat::Continue(recommend) = find_div_5(value) {
            value=recommend;
        } else {  // Done found
            break;
        }
    }
}
```

As with other types, you can apply trait bounds to type parameters used with a generic enum.

In Listing 14.33, we introduce the Employee enum, which is generic over type T. There are two variants. You can identify an employee with an `EmpId` of some type T or a String name. Type parameter T is bound with the Clone trait. This indicates that the Emplid variant only accepts values that implements that trait.

Code Listing 14.33.   **Adding bounds to type parameter T for the enum**

```
enum Employee<T:Clone>{
    EmplId(T),
    Name(String)
}

fn get_employee()->Employee<String> {
    Employee::Name("Carol".to_string())
}
```

Alternatively, you can also apply trait bounds to generic enums with the `where` clause.

Generic Traits

Both generics and traits provide generalization. Generics generalize types, while traits generalize code. Combining both techniques unleashes the full potential of generalization. This allows you to achieve a higher level of abstraction and flexibility than otherwise possible. The downside is added complexity, at times.

In Listing 14.34, we declare both an ATrait trait and XStruct struct. Both are also generic over type T.

Code Listing 14.34.   **ATrait and XStruct are generic over type T.**

```
trait ATrait<T> {
    fn do_something(&self, arg:T);
}

struct XStruct<T> {
    field1:T,
}
```

Next, `impl` block implements ATrait<T> for XStruct<T>. This requires implementing the do something function, which uses type parameter T. A minimal implementation is shown in Listing 14.35.

Code Listing 14.35.   **Implementing a generic method**

```
impl<T> ATrait<T> for XStruct<T> {
    fn do_something(&self, arg:T){}
}
```

The syntax for the `impl` block header appears fairly complex, with all the angle brackets, but it is not. Remember that type parameters are part of the type name. With that understanding, the syntax is actually straightforward, as shown in Figure 14.2.

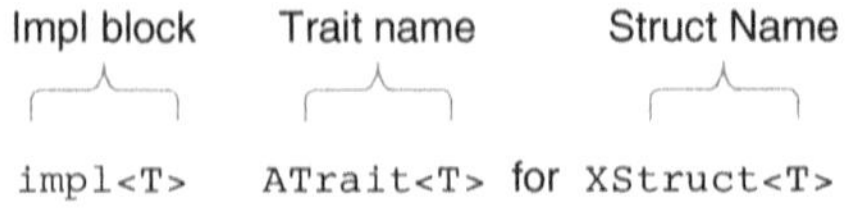

Figure 14.2.   Syntax for implementing a generic trait for a generic struct

When implementing a trait, the struct can have more type parameters than the trait requires. The additional type parameters are used at the discretion of the struct.

To demonstrate this, we have updated the previous example. XStruct now has two fields and is generic over types T and U. The type parameters are used to describe each field. Listing 14.36 shows the updated XStruct.

Code Listing 14.36.   XStruct **is generic over types T and U.**

```
struct XStruct<T, U> {
    field1:T,
    field2:U,
}
```

Yet again, XStruct implements ATrait. The impl block identifies type parameters T and U. Type parameter T is used with the do_something function parameter, as ATrait requires. Type parameter U has a Display trait bound, which constrains field2. This is required for the { } placeholders in the println! macro; otherwise, this example would not compile (see Listing 14.37).

Code Listing 14.37.   Implementing the do_something **method for XStruct**

```
impl<T, U:Display> ATrait<T> for XStruct<T, U> {
    fn do_something(&self, arg:T)
    {
        println!("{}", self.field2);
    }
}
```

You can add trait bounds directly to type parameters of a trait. This requires the same trait bounds be added during the implementation, as shown in Listing 14.38. Before the trait bounds were not required.

Code Listing 14.38.   Applying the Display trait to type parameter T

```
trait ATrait<T:Display> {
    fn do_something1(&self, arg:T);
}

struct XStruct<T> {
    field1:T,
}
```

```
impl<T:Display> ATrait<T> for XStruct<T> {
    fn do_something1(&self, arg:T) {
        println!("{}", arg);
    }
}
```

We conclude this section with universal extension traits. It is a unique feature only available when combining generics and traits. Universal extension traits implicitly apply an implementation of a trait to all types. This extends the concept of extension traits, which are introduced in Chapter 17, "Traits."

In Listing 14.39, TimeStamp is a trait that has a set_value method. The method updates a current value and displays a timestamp indicating when the change occurred. TimeStamp is generic over type parameter T, with the Display and Copy trait bounds. These bounds are required to update the current value and display the results.

As shown, the TimeStamp trait is implemented for type parameter T. Essentially this means for *any* type, now and in the future. Within the impl block, the set_value function is implemented. It updates the current value, as self, with the function parameter and displays a timestamp.

The chrono crate, found in Crates.io, is used to create the timestamp, which is displayed.

Code Listing 14.39. TimeStamp is a universal extension trait.

```
use chrono::Local;
use std::fmt::Display;

trait TimeStamp<T:Display+Copy> {
    fn set_value(& mut self, value: T);
}

impl <T:Display+Copy> TimeStamp<T> for T {
    fn set_value(& mut self, value: T){
        let old=*self;
        *self=value;
        let date = Local::now();
        println!("{} {} -> {}", date.format("%H:%M:%S"),
            old, self);
    }
}
```

In main, the TimeStamp trait extension is tested with different types (see Listing 14.40). Because it is a universal extension trait, any type is acceptable. However, based on the constraint bounds, the type must implement both the Display and Copy traits.

Code Listing 14.40.   Using the set_value function of the TimeStamp trait extension

```
fn main() {
    let mut value1=10;
    value1.set_value(20);

    let mut value2=10.1;
    value2.set_value(20.1);
}
```

This is the result of running the application.

```
23:24:04 10 -> 20
23:24:04 10.1 -> 20.1
```

Explicit Specialization

Until now, type parameters have been resolved at compile time, either implicitly or explicitly, for example, inferring the type from type arguments. You can also assign types directly to type parameters, which is explicit specialization. This has already been shown with the Result and Option enums. With explicit specialization, type parameters are constrained by a type, not a trait bound. This capability allows for unique solutions for specific use cases, such as state machines.

Listing 14.41 provides an example of explicit specialization.

Code Listing 14.41.   Example of non-explicit and explicit specialization

```
struct XStruct<T>{
    field1: T,
}

impl<T> XStruct<T> {    // Non-Explicit specialization
    fn do_something(&self arg:T){
    }
}

impl XStruct<i8> {    // Explicit specialization
    fn do_something(&self, arg:i8){
    }
}
```

Let's review the code. XStruct is a generic over type T, with separate impl blocks. The first impl block for XStruct is generic, not specialized. However, the second impl block demonstrates explicit specialization. It is specialized for i8. The impl block does not refer to the type parameter T but the type specialization, which is i8 in this example.

When the code is compiled, the following error is received:

```
  |
  |
6 |          fn do_something(arg:T){
  |          ^^^^^^^^^^^^^^^^^^^^^^ duplicate definitions for `do_something`
...
11|          fn do_something(arg:i8){
  |          ----------------------
     other definition for `do_something`
```

The error is caused from an ambiguity. The scope of the generic implementation of do_something overlaps with the explicit specialization. The first impl block is generic over type T. That would include the *possibility* of i8. However, we also implement an explicit specialization for the same type, i8. This makes the do_something function potentially ambiguous and causes a compiler error.

Let's simplify our example and remove the generic impl for XStruct. That leaves the explicit specialization for i8. In main, this means we can only call the do_something function with an i8 type argument. Calling the function with any other types, such as a float, is invalid (see Listing 14.42).

Code Listing 14.42.   Call do_something with explicit specialization

```
fn main() {
    let obj1=XStruct{field1:1};      // integer
    let obj2=XStruct{field1:1.1};    // float

    obj1.do_something(2);
    obj2.do_something(2.0);  // invalid
}
```

State machines are practical applications of explicit specialization. A state machine is a behavioral model defined by various states and the transition between those states. Each state can have specific actions relevant to that state. Implementing a state machine will help clarify the syntax, use cases, and benefits of explicit specialization.

In Listing 14.43, we model a state machine for a motor. The motor has on, neutral, and off states, represented by empty structs. Each of these states may have unique actions associated with them. For example, the *On state* has the off action. For the motor, there is the Motor struct, which is generic over type T. T represents the state of the Motor.

Code Listing 14.43.   Defining the types necessary for a motor's state machine

```
    struct On;
    struct Neutral;
    struct Off;

    struct Motor<T> {
```

```
        status:T,
        rpm:i8
    }
```

Let's implement the off state first. This is an explicit specialization for the `Off` struct, representing that state. Listing 14.44 shows the `impl` block.

Code Listing 14.44.   Implementation of the `Off` state

```
    impl Motor<Off> {
        fn on(mut self)->Motor<On> {
            self.rpm=20;
            println!("Motor running | RPM: {}", self.rpm);
            *Box::new(Motor{status:On, rpm:self.rpm})
        }
    }
```

Within the `impl` block, the on function is the only action for this state. It transforms the motor from off to on and returns a motor in the new state, which is created on the heap. You'll learn more about `Box` in Chapter 20, "Memory." The motor starts running at 20 rpm. Importantly, the current motor (`self`) is no longer available after the function call because the Off state of that motor is no longer valid after the transformation.

Listing 14.45 is the implementation of the on and neutral states, within separate `impl` blocks. Both employ an explicit specialization. This is similar to the implementation for the off state, except for different actions. The specialization for the on state implements the off and neutral methods (actions). These are the expected transformations from the On state. The specialization for the neutral state implements the `in_gear` method, which transforms the motor to the on state.

Code Listing 14.45.   Implementing the state machine with explicit specialization

```
    impl Motor<On> {
        fn off(mut self)->Motor<Off>{
            self.rpm=0;
            println!("Motor off | RPM: {}", self.rpm);
            *Box::new(Motor{status:Off, rpm:self.rpm})
        }

        fn neutral(self)->Motor<Neutral>{
            println!("Motor neutral | RPM: {}", self.rpm);
            *Box::new(Motor{status:Neutral, rpm:self.rpm})
        }
    }


    impl Motor<Neutral> {
```

```
        fn in_gear(&mut self)->Motor<On>{
            println!("Motor in gear | RPM: {}", self.rpm);
            *Box::new(Motor{status:On, rpm:self.rpm})
        }
    }
```

The initial state for a motor should be off. This is done using a simple factory pattern. For this, we have a standard impl block for Motor, which is a generic over type T. Within the block, the new constructor function returns a new motor in the off state (see Listing 14.46), using type specialization.

Code Listing 14.46. Implementing a new constructor for a Factory pattern

```
    impl<T> Motor<T>{
        fn new()->Motor<Off> {
            println!("Motor off | RPM: 0");
            *Box::new(Motor{status:Off, rpm:0})
        }
    }
```

In main, we call the new function to create a new instance of a motor. It starts in the off state. We then exercise the motor, including various transformations. When done, the motor is returned to the off state (see Listing 14.47).

Code Listing 14.47. Exercising the motor and various states

```
    fn main() {
        let mut motor=Motor::<Off>::new();    // off state
        let mut motor=motor.on();             // on state
        let mut motor=motor.neutral();        // neutral state
        let mut motor=motor.in_gear();        // on state
        let mut motor=motor.off();            // off state
    }
```

Here is the result from "running" the motor in main:

```
Motor off | RPM: 0
Motor running | RPM: 20
Motor neutral | RPM: 20
Motor in gear | RPM: 20
Motor off | RPM: 0
```

The explicit specialization, for each state, implements specific functions within its impl block. Only those functions can be called for that specialization. This explains the reason the second statement in Listing 14.48 causes a compiler error. The impl block for the neutral state does not implement the off method.

Code Listing 14.48. **The neutral state does not support transformation to the off state.**

```
let mut motor=motor.neutral();    // transform to the neutral state
let mut motor=motor.off();        // does not work
let mut motor=motor.in_gear();    // on state
```

For added flexibility, you can combine explicit and nonspecific specialization within an impl block. Listing 14.49 is an example. The ZStruct struct is generic over types T and V.

Code Listing 14.49. **Definition of the ZStruct type**

```
struct ZStruct<T, V>{
    field1:T,
    field2:V,
}
```

The impl blocks for ZStruct are shown in Listing 14.50. Both impl blocks in this example have explicit specialization for some of the type parameters. For the first impl block, type T is assigned i8 for explicit specialization. Type parameter V remains generic. The result is that the implementation of the do_something method is available when type parameter T is i8 and for some V type. The second impl block is the same except the specialization is f32.

Code Listing 14.50. **ZStruct with explicit and nonexplicit specializations**

```
impl<V> ZStruct<i8, V> {
    fn do_something(&self, arg:i8, arg2:V)->i8{
        println!("first implementation")
        5
    }
}

impl<V> ZStruct<f32, V> {
    fn do_something(&self, arg:f32, arg2:V)->f32{
        5.0
    }
}
```

In main, we create multiple instances of ZStruct. Later the do_something method is called on the instances (see Listing 14.51).

Code Listing 14.51. **Calling the do_something method with different specialization**

```
fn main() {
    let obj1=ZStruct{field1:1, field2:true};
    let obj2=ZStruct{field1:1.0, field2:12};
    let obj3=ZStruct{field1:1.0, field2:true};
    let obj4=ZStruct{field1:'a', field2:12_i8};
```

```
    obj1.do_something(2, false);    // i8 specialization
    obj2.do_something(11.1, 14);    // f32 specialization
    obj3.do_something(22.2, true);  // f32 specialization
    obj4.do_something('b', 15);     // Error!
                                    // No char specialization
}
```

Table 14.1 maps the details of the various ZStruct instances, from the previous example, to explicit specialization.

Table 14.1. Details of the Various Instances of ZStruct Created in the Preceding Example

ZStruct	T (field1)	V (field2)	Explicit Specialization
obj1	integer	bool	Yes for T(i8)
obj2	float	integer	Yes for T(f32)
obj3	float	bool	Yes for T(f32)
obj4	char	integer	No for T(char)

According to the table, obj4 sets type parameter T to char. However, there is no specialization for that use case. For that reason, only the obj4.do_something function will not work.

Summary

Generics touch many areas of the Rust language. We discussed generics as functions, structs, traits, and enums. Regardless of the target, the purpose of generics remains the same—removing redundant code. The other benefits include making your source code more extensible, less error-prone, and easier to refactor.

In addition, generics are woven into the fabric of the language. Result, Option, Vec, HashMap, IntoIterator, Box, and so many more types are generic. This is another reason that understanding generics is essential.

A generic function or type has type parameters that are placeholders for concrete types. Per monomorphization, generics become unique functions and types at compile time. This avoids performance costs at runtime.

Generic type parameters are declared within angle brackets after the function or type name. You then annotate the various aspects of the item with type parameters. When possible, the compiler will infer the concrete type. When that is not possible, you have to provide the type information explicitly.

Trait bounds indicate the capabilities of a type parameter. The compiler relies on this information to use type parameters safely. After declaring type parameters within angle brackets, you can assign trait bounds, after a colon. You can add multiple bounds using the + operator.

You can also assign trait bounds to type parameters with the where clause, which is more expressive, often more readable than conventional trait bounds.

Universal trait extensions and explicit specialization are additional capabilities available with generics. Universal trait extensions apply a trait implementation to any type. Explicit specialization allows you to implement specific use cases for type parameters.

15

Patterns

Patterns identify the shape of a value. With pattern syntax, you can apply the pattern to a value to determine if there is a match. There are many benefits to patterns. Well-placed patterns can make code more concise and transparent. In addition, you can create unique solutions with patterns. Patterns are ubiquitous in Rust and just another feature, like lifetimes, that gives Rust source code a distinctive appearance.

The primary use cases for patterns is pattern matching and control flow. For pattern matching, a value is matched against a pattern. If there is a match, the value can be destructured into its components, if any. For control flow, there is a transfer of control when a match occurs. The match, while, if, and other expressions, will control application flow based on a pattern matching a value.

You can apply patterns to both scalar and complex values, such as structs, enums, and arrays. The pattern must match the shape of the complex types. With the pattern syntax, you can also create patterns that can destructure the inner components of a complex type. For example, you can create a pattern that destructures the fields of a struct.

A pattern consists of rules and notations that describe the shape of a value. Patterns are fully integrated into the language and can be applied to variable binding, expressions, parameters, and return values. Basically, patterns can appear nearly everywhere in the language. In addition, patterns are flexible. You can define simple patterns, hierarchical patterns, nested patterns, and so much more. This allows you to match patterns to a wide variety of types and shapes.

Let Statement

The `let` statement is the most common example of pattern matching. It is more than a simple assignment. The let statement relies on pattern matching to bind a value to a new variable. If the pattern is simply a variable name, it is an irrefutable pattern, which means *it must work*. An irrefutable pattern matches all values—more about this later.

In Listing 15.1, we use patterns to create variable binding for a and b, which will accept any value, regardless of shape. As a result, a is bound to an integer, while b is bound to a tuple.

Code Listing 15.1. Creating variable binding using patterns

```
let a=1;
let b=(1,2);
```

Here is a more complex example of pattern matching and variable binding:

```
let (a, b)=(1,2);
```

The pattern describes a tuple with two fields, which matches the value (i.e., (1,2)). Furthermore, the pattern is hierarchical and destructures not only the tuple, but also the tuple fields. *Field.0* is bound to variable a, while *field.1* is bound to variable b.

Listing 15.2 is similar to the previous example, except the pattern matches an array, not a tuple.

Code Listing 15.2. Creating variable binding for an array using patterns

```
let list=[1, 2, 3, 4];
let [a, b, c, d]=list;
println!("{} {} {} {}",a , b, c, d); // 1 2 3 4
```

The pattern here matches that of a four-element array. In the pattern, the square brackets indicate an array versus parentheses for tuples. The array elements are destructured in the pattern. The result is variable binding for a, b, c, and d. Each is assigned a value from the array, in order.

With a pattern, you can also destructure and bind to *existing* variables, not just create new variables. With existing variables, the variable type is the pattern and must be consistent with the value, as shown in Listing 15.3.

Code Listing 15.3. Updating variables by destructing a tuple

```
let mut a=0;
let mut b=0;
(a,b)=(1,2);  // pattern matching
println!("a: {} b: {}", a, b);    // a:1 b:2
```

Wildcards

You can ignore parts of a value using underscores (_) wildcards. In Listing 15.4, there is an underscore in the pattern for the second element of the array. Every other element in the array is bound to a variable. For this reason, the pattern will bind values to a, c, and d.

Code Listing 15.4. Destructing a pattern using a wildcard

```
let list=[1, 2, 3, 4];
let [a, _, c, d]=list;
println!("{} {} {}", a , c, d);    // 1, 3, 4
```

You can include multiple underscores within a pattern to ignore several parts of value, as shown in Listing 15.5:

Code Listing 15.5.   Destructing a pattern with multiple_wildcards

```
let list=[1, 2, 3, 4];
let [a, _, _, d]=list;
println!("{} {}", a, d);    // 1, 4

let list=[1, 2, 3, 4];
let [a, _, _, _]=list;
println!("{}", a);    // 1
```

The double dot (..) syntax can be used to ignore a portion of a value, such as from the beginning, until the end, or the middle portion of a value. The two patterns presented in Listing 15.6 achieve the same result; however, the .. syntax is more concise. Both patterns ignore the final portion of an array.

Code Listing 15.6.   Ignoring a portion of a pattern

```
let list=[1, 2, 3, 4];

let [a, _, _, _]=list;    // ignore individual elements
println!("{}", a);        // 1

let [a,..]=list;          // ignore to the end of the pattern
println!("{}", a);        // 1
```

Listing 15.7 includes additional examples of ignoring a portion of a value. For variable a, the pattern ignores the beginning of the array. The next pattern ignores the middle of the array to establish the binding for variables b and c.

Code Listing 15.7.   Ignoring portions of a pattern using the .. syntax

```
let list=[1, 2, 3, 4];
let [..,a]=list;    // ignore beginning
let [b,..,c]=list;  // ignore the middle
```

Complex Patterns

You can use more complex patterns to fully destructure complex values.

In Listing 15.8, the value is a nested tuple—a tuple that consists of two tuples. This requires a similar pattern that matches a nested tuple. Each inner tuple is destructured in the pattern and bound to variables a and b.

Code Listing 15.8.   With patterns, destructuring a nested tuple

```
let data=((1,2), (3,4));

let (a,b)=data;
println!("{:?}, {:?}", a, b);  // (1,2) (3,4)
```

We could destructure the tuple even further. In Listing 15.9, the individual fields of each nested tuple are also destructured. We create a variable binding for a, b, c, and d. In this example, the pattern describes a shape that is both nested and hierarchal.

Code Listing 15.9.   With patterns, destructuring fields of a nested tuple

```
let ((a,b),(c,d))=data;
println!("{}, {}, {}, {}", a, b, c, d);  // 1, 2, 3, 4
```

Sometimes it is beneficial to remove the refness from a value. This is sometimes done for practical reasons but also for convenience, such as simplifying the code. It may be counterintuitive; however, including an ampersand (&) in the pattern removes the refness of a value. What is remaining is simply the value. We could describe the transformation as &T to T.

In Listing 15.10, the refness is removed from a value.

Code Listing 15.10.   Removing reference semantics with a pattern

```
let ref1=&5;
let (&data)=ref1;
println!("{}", *data);
```

The ref1 variable is a reference to 5, a literal value. For ref1, the let pattern removes the reference and assigns the value to data. The transformation is confirmed in the println! macro. We try to dereference data (*data). However, you cannot dereference data—it is not reference. As expected, a compiler error occurs, as shown next.

```
error[E0614]: type '{integer}' cannot be dereferenced
 --> src\main.rs:4:20
  |
4 |     println!("{}", *data);
  |                    ^^^^^^
  |
```

Ownership

With patterns, ownership can be transferred when values are destructured. For values that implement copy semantics, this will not occur. However, for values that support move semantics, destructuring will transfer ownership to a new value. For example, String variables that are destructured during pattern matching lose ownership of their value, as shown in Listing 15.11. Strings have move semantics.

Code Listing 15.11. Destructuring a pattern that causes a side effect

```
fn main() {
    let tuple=("Bob".to_string(), 42);
    let (a, b)=tuple;  // destructures
    println!("{}", tuple.0);   // fail
    println!("{}", tuple.1);   // works
}
```

The tuple consists of a String and an integer field, which are destructured. Strings support move semantics, while integers implement copy semantics. For this reason, ownership of `tuple.0` is moved. But the ownership of `tuple.1` is not moved. As evidence of this, the first `println!` macro cannot display `tuple.0`. However, the second `println!` macro displays `tuple.1` without a problem.

The previous example would compile if the pattern created a reference to `tuple.0` and borrowed the field, not moved the value. For non-pattern syntax, the ampersand operator (&) creates a reference. However, the ampersand has a different meaning within the pattern syntax. For that reason, we need a different solution. The solution is the ref keyword. When a value is destructured within a pattern, the ref keyword creates a reference to the value. Therefore, the value will be borrowed.

If this change was made to the previous example, it would compile correctly. In the pattern, the `ref` keyword immediately precedes the binding for tuple.0. Now, the String value will be borrowed and not moved.

```
    let (ref a, b)=tuple;
```

The mut keyword can also appear in patterns. When destructuring a value, the mut keyword indicates a mutable binding. The default is immutable. In Listing 15.12, the tuple is destructured again. This time the pattern includes the mut keyword. As a result, variable a is mutable when tuple.0 is destructured. The push_str function is then called to modify variable a.

Code Listing 15.12. Destructuring to create a mutable value

```
fn main() {
    let tuple=("Bob".to_string(), 42);
    let (mut a, b)=tuple;
    a.push_str(" Wilson");
    println!("{}", a);         // Bob Wilson
}
```

You can combine the ref and mut keywords in a pattern to declare a mutable reference. When this is done, the rules of mutability are applicable, such as no more than one outstanding mutable reference at a time.

In Listing 15.13, when the pattern is applied, variable a is a mutable reference to tuple.0. Next, we modify variable a with the push_str function. As a mutable reference, both variable a and tuple.0 are changed. The subsequent println! macros display the result.

Code Listing 15.13.   **Creating a mutable reference when destructuring**

```
fn main() {
    let mut tuple=("Bob".to_string(), 42);
    let (ref mut a, b)=tuple;
    a.push_str(" Wilson");
    println!("{}", a);          // Bob Wilson
    println!("{}", tuple.0);    // Bob Wilson
}
```

We have shown examples where destructuring transfers ownership. This occurs when the value does not implement copy semantics. However, if the value is ignored (_) in the pattern, ownership is not moved. The behavior is different when the binding is ignored instead (_variable_name). Listing 15.14 will clarify the difference. In this example, we are destructuring our friendly tuple again. In the pattern, tuple.0 is ignored (_), no binding is established, and the value is *not moved*. For tuple.1, the value is bound to variable b, even though the binding is then ignored (_b). In this situation, ownership is still moved. The println! macros confirm where ownership was moved.

Code Listing 15.14.   **Showing the impact of ignoring a part of a pattern**

```
let tuple=("abc".to_string(), "def".to_string());
let (_, _b)=tuple;
println!("{}", tuple.0);   // not moved
println!("{}", tuple.1);   // moved - invalid
```

Irrefutable

There are refutable and irrefutable patterns. Irrefutable patterns are comprehensive and are a match for *anything*. As such, irrefutable patterns *always* match. Refutable patterns, in contrast, may match a subset of expressions, or even none at all. With irrefutable patterns, you must provide an alternative control flow for when a match is not found.

Irrefutable patterns are sometimes required. For example, the let statement only accepts irrefutable patterns, such as shown here. This is required because the let statement does not provide an alternative if the pattern does not match the value.

```
let a=1;
```

In the preceding `let` statement, variable a is a comprehensive pattern. Since it matches everything, the pattern is irrefutable.

However, the next example attempts to assign a refutable pattern in a let statement. The `Some(value)` pattern from the `Option` enum is refutable. The expression could evaluate to `None`, or any other value, to refute `Some(value)`. Unfortunately, with a `let` statement, there is no plan B. You must have a plan B to inform the compiler of the correct behavior if the match fails. Without this, the source code would not compile.

```
let Some(result)=option;     // Error
```

Here is the error message. Notice the mention of an irrefutable pattern, which the `let` statement requires. As usual, the Rust compiler provides a helpful message.

```
    = note: 'let' bindings require an "irrefutable pattern",
like a 'struct' or an 'enum' with only one variant
```

Ranges

Patterns can include ranges, which are limited to numerical and char values. This type of pattern is refutable, because the value may be outside the specified range. For this reason, you can only use pattern ranges where an alternative is available. Various syntaxes exist for describing inclusive ranges:

- `begin..=end` indicates "from beginning to ending value."
- `begin..` indicates "from beginning to maximum value."
- `..=end` indicates "from minimal to ending value."

In Listing 15.15, the pattern includes two ranges. The `if let` expression makes the pattern irrefutable. If the pattern matches, the if block is executed. Otherwise, the if block is skipped.

Code Listing 15.15.   Creating a pattern with ranges

```
fn get_value()->(i8, i8){
    // Implementation not shown
}

fn main() {
    let tuple=get_value();
    if let (1..=15, 1..=25)=tuple {
        println!("It matches!");
    }
}
```

The previous example displays a message when the pattern matches. It would also be helpful to know the specific value selected within the range. You can accomplish this by binding a variable to the pattern range using the @ syntax. This binds the selected value within the range to a variable:

```
binding@range
```

For Listing 15.16, we modify the if let expression to provide variable binding for both pattern ranges, variables a and b. We then display the variables to show the specific values that matched within the ranges.

Code Listing 15.16. Binding to the selected value within a range

```
if let (a@1..=15, b@1..=25)=tuple {
    println!("Match found ({}, {})", a, b);    // Match found (10, 20)
}
```

Multiple Patterns

You can combine multiple patterns with the pipe (|) operator. They are then evaluated from left to right. If any of the patterns match, the entire pattern matches.

We combine three patterns in Listing 15.17. If the pattern is either 5, 10, or 20, there is a match.

Code Listing 15.17. Combining patterns to find a match

```
fn get_value()->i8{
    // Not shown
}

fn main(){
    let value=get_value();
    if let 5|10|20= value {
        println!("Match found");  // Match found
    }
}
```

If a compound pattern matches a value, knowing the specific pattern that matches may be helpful. In the previous example, control is transferred to the if block when the value matches the pattern for 10, 20, or 30. As shown before, we can bind to the matching value within the range using the @ syntax.

Let's update the example to add variable binding to the pattern. The matching value is then displayed.

Code Listing 15.18. Combining patterns to find a match

```
if let a@(5|10|20)= value {
    println!("Match found {}", value); // Match found 10
}
```

Control Flow

You can use patterns to control the flow of execution within your application. Patterns that control flow must be refutable.

In the following example, the if let expression controls flow based on a pattern. If the pattern matches, the if block is executed. Destructured values are scoped to the if block. When the pattern doesn't match, the else block, if any, is executed. Listing 15.19 shows the syntax for the if let expression.

Code Listing 15.19. Syntax for if let expression

```
if let pattern=expression {
        // match
} else {
        // no match (optional)
}
```

An example of the if let expression is shown in Listing 15.20. The Some(result) pattern is matched to the option value. If option is a Some type, a match is found and the underlying value is bound to result. In addition, execution transfers to the if block, where the value is displayed. If a match is not found, execution branches to the else block.

Code Listing 15.20. Using a pattern to control branching within an if

```
if let Some(result)=option {
    println!("Found: {}", result);
} else {
    println!("Nothing found")
}
```

You can use a pattern with a while let expression. The while loop continues while the pattern matches the value, and it stops when the pattern no longer matches. Values destructured in the pattern are scoped to the while block.

In Listing 15.21, the while let expression iterates the vector while the pop function returns Some(element). At each iteration, the pattern is destructured to create binding to the current element, which is then displayed within the while loop.

Code Listing 15.21. Using a pattern within a while let expression

```
let mut data = vec![1, 2, 3, 4, 5];

while let Some(item) = data.pop() {
    println!("{}", item)
}
```

The for expression relies on iterators and patterns. At each iteration, the next method is called. The iteration continues for Some(item) and stops when *None* is returned. The for loop abstracts this detail.

In Listing 15.22, the for loop iterates the elements of a vector. The enumerate method returns an iterator that provides (index, item) tuples for each element of the vector. In this example, the pattern binds the tuple fields to the index and item variables. The values are then displayed.

Code Listing 15.22.   Using a pattern within a for

```
let data = vec![1, 2, 3, 4, 5];
for (index, item) in data.into_iter().enumerate() {
    println!("{} {}", index, item)
}
```

The match expression is another example of control flow, the most common for patterns. However, it is discussed later in its own section.

Structs

Patterns are often used to match structs. Destructuring can be particularly useful for structs. The result is source code that is more flexible, concise, and readable.

At a minimum, patterns for a struct must include the struct name and the proper field names, in any order. By default, struct fields are bound to variables of the same name.

An example of destructuring a struct is shown in Listing 15.23.

Code Listing 15.23.   Destructuring a struct

```
struct Rectangle {
    p1: (u32, u32),
    p2: (u32, u32),
}

fn main() {
    let r = Rectangle { p1: (10, 20), p2: (30, 40) };
    let Rectangle { p1, p2 } = r;   // destructuring
    println!("P1:{:?} P2:{:?}",
        p1, p2)   // P1:(10, 10) P2:(20, 20)
}
```

The Rectangle in this example has two fields, both tuples, providing the dimensions of the shape. We then create an instance of Rectangle. The value is then destructured using a pattern to create new variable bindings for p1 and p2. The pattern matches the shape of the Rectangle. Notice that the binding has the same names as field names.

A pattern can match the hierarchy of a struct at any level. In the previous example, Rectangle has two fields—both are tuples. Not only can we destructure the tuples within the struct, but also the individual fields of each tuple, as shown in Listing 15.24.

Code Listing 15.24.   Destructuring the hierarchy within a struct

```
let r = Rectangle { p1: (10, 20), p2: (30, 40) };
let Rectangle { p1:(a, b),
    p2:(c, d) } = r;  //  destructuring the fields
println!("[{}, {}] [{}, {}]",
       a, b, c, d)  // [10, 20] [30, 40]
```

Here, the pattern destructures the tuples, p1 and p2. In addition, the fields of each tuple are destructured: a, b, c, and d. Importantly, binding is only created for the innermost destructuring. Therefore, binding is *not* created for p1 and p2. Binding is created for a, b, c, and d.

When destructuring a struct, you don't have to adopt the current field names for the variable binding. Fields can be renamed, as variable bindings, with the field_name:binding_name specification in the pattern. This is useful when more descriptive names are helpful or provide additional context.

For the p1 and p2 fields, the pattern in Listing 15.25 creates the top_left and bottom_right variables, which are definitely more descriptive:

Code Listing 15.25.   Renaming a struct field as a variable

```
let r = Rectangle { p1: (10, 20), p2: (30, 40) };
let Rectangle { p1:top_left, p2:bottom_right } = r;   // destructure
println!("P1:{:?} P2:{:?}", top_left,
       bottom_right)   // P1:(10, 10) P2:(20, 20)
```

Patterns can include literals. Literals refine a pattern where only specific use cases can be matched. To match, the literal and value must be the same. In this manner, a literal becomes an additional condition that must be considered for a pattern matching.

In Listing 15.26, the pattern matches a Rectangle. However, the p2 tuple must also be (30, 50). The value (30, 50) is included in the pattern as a literal.

Code Listing 15.26.   Pattern matching with a literal

```
let r = Rectangle { p1: (10, 20), p2: (30, 40) };
let Rectangle { p1, p2: (30, 50) } = r;
```

The p2 tuple in the value, (30, 40) does not match the literal (30, 50) in the pattern. As an irrefutable pattern, this example will not compile. You will receive the following error message from the compiler:

```
error[E0005]: refutable pattern in local binding
  --> src\main.rs:8:9
   |
8 |     let Rectangle { p1, p2: (30, 50) } = r;
   |         ^^^^^^^^^^^^^^^^^^^^^^^^^^^^^^
               patterns 'Rectangle {
               p2: (0_u32..=29_u32, _), .. }' and
               'Rectangle { p2: (31_u32..=u32::MAX, _),
               .. }' not covered
```

Replacing the let statement with an if let expression removes the compiler error. The pattern is then refutable because of the else block. You now have control flow for when the pattern matches and does not match, as shown in Listing 15.27.

Code Listing 15.27. Showing a refutable pattern

```
let r = Rectangle { p1: (10, 20), p2: (30, 40) };
if let Rectangle { p1, p2: (30, 50) } = r {
    println!("P1: {:?}", p1);
}   else {
    println!("no match");
}
```

You can also use wildcards within patterns for destructuring. For fields, the underscore (_) wildcard ignores a value. The double dot (..) wildcard indicates that any remaining values will be ignored. It must be the last item in the pattern.

Listing 15.28 has various examples of using wildcards in patterns for structures. The patterns destructure a Triangle that consists of a tuple for the three corners. Explanations are provided in the comments.

Code Listing 15.28. Showing various examples of wildcards in patterns

```
struct Triangle {
    p1: (u32, u32),
    p2: (u32, u32),
    p3: (u32, u32),
}

fn main() {
    let tri = Triangle { p1: (10, 20),
        p2: (30, 40), p3: (0, 40) };

    /*  Create variable binding for p1, p2,
        and p3 but only if the literal
        values match.                           */

    let Triangle{p1, p2, p3}=tri;

    /*  Create binding for p1 and p3.
        Ignore p2.                              */

    let Triangle{p1, p2:_, p3}=tri;

    /*  Create variable binding for p1 and p3.
        Ignore p2.                              */

    let Triangle{p1, p3, ..}=tri;

    /*  Create variable binding for p2.
        Ignore p1 and p3.                       */
```

```
    let Triangle{p2, ..}=tri;

    /*  Destructure the tuple for p1. Create
        binding for tuple.0; but ignore tuple.1.
        In addition, ignore p2 and p3.          */

    let Triangle{p1:(a,_), ..}=tri;

    /*  Create variable binding for p1.  For p3,
        destructure the tuple; create variable
        binding a, b. However, b will not be
        used.  Finally, ignore p2.              */

    let Triangle{p1, p3:(a, _b), ..}=tri;

    /*  This is invalid. Having the ..
        wildcard on either side of the
        variable binding is ambiguous. More
        importantly, the .. wildcard cannot
        appear more than once within a
        pattern.                                */

    let Triangle(.., p2, ..);
}
```

Functions

Patterns can be applied to function parameters. The normal rules and syntax of patterns apply, just combined with the syntax of a function parameter. However, you can only use irrefutable patterns with function parameters.

The do_something function, shown in Listing 15.29, has a tuple parameter. It is destructured into variable bindings x and y. The ampersand (&) is part of the pattern and removes the "refness." Therefore, x and y are values, not references.

Code Listing 15.29.   A pattern that destructures function parameters

```
fn do_something(&(x, y): &(i8, i8)) {
    println!("{} {}", x, y);
}

fn main() {
    let values=(5, 6);
    do_something(&values);
}
```

Listing 15.30 is another example of using patterns with functions. The `combine` function combines the dimensions of two rectangles. The function parameters are rectangles. With patterns, each is destructured into their coordinates: x1, x2, y1, and y2. The coordinates are then combined to form a new rectangle, which is returned. In `main`, two rectangles are combined with the `combine` function. The result is then displayed.

Code Listing 15.30.   Patterns used with function parameters

```rust
#[derive(Debug)]
struct Rectangle { p1: (u32, u32), p2: (u32, u32),}

fn combine(Rectangle{p1:(x1_1, y1_1),
                     p2:(x2_1, y2_1)}:&Rectangle,
           Rectangle{p1:(x1_2, y1_2),
                     p2:(x2_2, y2_2)}:&Rectangle)
      ->Rectangle
{
    Rectangle{p1:(x1_1+x1_2, y1_1+y1_2),
       p2:(x2_1+x2_2, y2_1+y2_2)}
}

fn main() {
    let r1 = Rectangle {p1: (10, 10), p2: (20, 20)};
    let r2 = Rectangle {p1: (30, 30), p2: (40, 40)};
    let r3=combine(&r1, &r2);
    println!("Combined {:?}", r3);
}
```

Match Expressions

For control flow, match expressions are combined with patterns as a frequent solution. Each arm within a match is a pattern. When a match is found, you branch to that particular arm and execute its expression. In aggregate, the patterns of the match must exhaust the full range of the value. If not, add a default pattern (_) to exhaust the range. The default pattern is irrefutable. For that reason, it should be the final arm.

Here is the syntax of a match expression:

```
match expression {
    pattern¹=>expression,    // arm 1
    pattern²=>expression,    // arm 2
    patternⁿ=>expression,    // armⁿ
    _=>expression,           // default
}
```

Within a match expression, the patterns are evaluated in order. When there are duplicate or overlapping patterns, the first pattern that matches controls the flow.

A typical match expression is shown in Listing 15.31.

Code Listing 15.31.   Pattern matching within a match expression

```
let value=get_value();
match value {
    1=>println!("One"),
    2=>println!("Two"),
    _=>println!("Unknown, but not 1 or 2")
}
```

The patterns here consist of literals (1 and 2), which will match identical values. This does not exhaust the range of integers. Therefore, the default arm, with the underscore pattern (_), was necessary to encompass the remaining integer values.

We don't like mysteries. When a default pattern matches, the specific value is a mystery. Knowing the underlying value could be helpful. To obtain that value, you can replace the underscore pattern with variable binding.

In Listing 15.32, the other variable is bound to the value within the default range, whatever it is. You can then use other as the matching value for the default.

Code Listing 15.32.   Match expression with an irrefutable pattern for the default value

```
match value {
    1=>println!("One"),
    2=>println!("Two"),
    other=>println!("Default: {}", other)
}
```

Range patterns can be used within match expressions. In Listing 15.33, the match value falls within the range of the second pattern, which then displays a message:

Code Listing 15.33.   Using range patterns in a match expression

```
let value = 7;
match value {
    1..=5 => println!("1..=5"),
    6..=10=> println!("6..=10"),   // match found
    _ => println!("other value"),
}
```

For a range pattern, it is helpful to know the matching value within range. Precede a range pattern with the @ syntax to obtain that value. With the @ syntax, you create variable binding. In the next example, Listing 15.34, variable binding is created for both range patterns. The matching value is then displayed.

Code Listing 15.34.   Binding to the value within a range pattern

```
fn main() {
    let value = 7;
    match value {
        a@1..=5 => println!("Value is {}", a),  // Value is 7
        b@6..=10=> println!("Value is {}", b),
        _ => println!("other value"),
    }
}
```

The pattern for a match arm can combine multiple patterns with a pipe (|) operator, as shown before. The patterns are evaluated in order, left to right. If any of the patterns match, control is transferred to that arm's expression.

In Listing 15.35, we combine the patterns 25, 30, and 35. Control is transferred to that arm if the match value matches any of the patterns.

Code Listing 15.35.   Combining a pattern within a match

```
fn main() {
    let value = 25;
    match value {
        25 | 30 | 35 => println!("25 |30 | 35"),
        _ => println!("other"),
    }
    println!("{}", value);
}
```

Using patterns, enums are often handled within a match expression. The Option and Result enum are well-known examples. Listing 15.36 handles the variants of a Result, Ok and Err, within a match expression. The patterns for the match arms identify the variants and destructure the underlying value, which is then displayed.

Note
Enum variants that do not carry data cannot be destructured.

Code Listing 15.36.   Matching Result variants using patterns

```
let result=do_something();

    match result {
        Ok(result)=>println!("{}", result),
        Err(msg)=>println!("{}", msg)
    }
```

This is another example of destructuring an enum variant. It highlights again that destructuring can transfer ownership. As shown in Listing 15.37, the Name variant of Person carries a String. When destructuring that variant, to prevent moving ownership, we apply the ref keyword to borrow the value. The GovId variant carries an integer, with no special requirements.

Code Listing 15.37.   When destructuring, borrow instead of moving the value.

```
enum Person {
    Name(String),
    GovId(i32),s
}

fn main() {
    let bob: Person=Person::Name("Bob".to_string());

    match bob {
        Person::Name(ref name)=>println!(
            "Name: {}", name),        // borrow
        Person::GovId(id)=>println!(
            "Government Id: {}", id)    // copy
    }
}
```

In Listing 15.38, the match expression has patterns with literals. At each match arm, the pattern matches on Rectangles with specific dimensions. For example, the first arm matches on rectangles with a top corner at (10, 10). The next arm matches if the bottom corner is at (20, 20). If the Rectangle value contains neither of these corners, the default pattern matches.

Code Listing 15.38.   Match on specific use cases for Rectangles.

```
#[derive(Debug)]
struct Rectangle { p1: (u32, u32), p2: (u32, u32),}

fn main() {
    let r = Rectangle {p1: (10, 10), p2: (20, 20),};

    match r {
        Rectangle { p1: (10, 10), p2 } => println!(
            "Found: (10, 10), {:?}", p2),
        Rectangle { p1, p2: (20, 20) } => println!(
            "Found {:?}, (20, 20)", p1),
        _ => println!("No match"),
    }
}
```

In the previous example, patterns contained literals. You can bind to a literal in a pattern and then use the value elsewhere. Bind to literals with the @ syntax. For the purposes of matching, adding the @ syntax does not change the shape of the pattern. Here is an example:

```
Rectangle { p1: p1_lit@(10, 10), p2 } => println!(
"Found: {:?}, {:?}", p1_lit, p2),
```

We bind p1_lit to the literal with the @ syntax. We can now use p1_lit in the match arm and display the literal value. This is considerably more flexible than hardcoding the literal again.

Match Guards

Match guards are filters for pattern matching and a Boolean expression. If the match guard is false, the pattern is filtered and no match can occur. However, if the match guard is true, pattern matching occurs as usual.

Table 15.1 displays the possible outcomes of a match guard.

Table 15.1.   Result of a Match Guard

Pattern	Match Guard	Execute Match Arm
Matching	True	Yes
Nonmatching	True	No
Matching	False	No
Nonmatching	False	No

Listing 15.39 demonstrates match guards. The first two patterns have match guards that confirm whether a Rectangle is *not* properly shaped. This means the left side is left of the right side and the bottom is below the top.

Code Listing 15.39.   Matching if a Rectangle is not properly formed

```
#[derive(Debug)]
struct Rectangle { p1: (u32, u32), p2: (u32, u32),}

fn main() {
    let r = Rectangle {p1: (10, 10), p2: (20, 20),};

    match r {
        Rectangle { p1:(x1, _), p2:(x2,_ )}if x2 < x1
            => println!("Left invalid {} {}", x1, x2),
        Rectangle { p1:(_, y1), p2:(_, y2 )}if y2 < y1
            => println!("Bottom invalid {} {}", y1, y2),
        r => println!("Proper {:?}", r),
    }
}
```

The first pattern destructures the left side and right side of a rectangle, as variables x1 and x2. The top side and bottom side are ignored. The match guard confirms if the right side is less than the left side. If this is true, the rectangle is not normalized and a message is displayed. The second pattern performs the same analysis for y1 and y2, which is the top and bottom of the rectangle. The default pattern is selected when the rectangle is properly formed.

Here is a second example of match guards. For complex match guards, you can call functions. The function must return a Boolean value.

In the next example, we implement a match guard as a function. The function will accept a color, as either RGB or CMYK, and return true if the color is gray. RGB is gray when the primary colors, red, green, and blue, have the same intensity. For CMYK, gray is when cyan, magenta, and yellow are zero.

In Listing 15.40, we define a Colors enum with the RGB and CMYK variants. Both variants carry data: RgbColor and CmykColor structs respectively.

Code Listing 15.40.   Implementing the Color enum and related types

```
use Colors::RGB;
use Colors::CMYK;

#[derive(Debug, Copy, Clone)]
struct RgbColor {red: i32, blue: i32, green: i32,}

#[derive(Debug, Copy, Clone)]
struct CmykColor {cyan: i32, magenta: i32,
    yellow: i32, black: i32,}

enum Colors {
    RGB(RgbColor),
    CMYK(CmykColor),
}
```

For Colors, we implement the is_gray function to perform as a match guard. This is shown in Listing 15.41. The is_gray function returns either true or false indicating whether the current color is gray.

Code Listing 15.41.   Implementation of the is_gray function

```
impl Colors{
    fn is_gray(&self) -> bool {
        match self {
            RGB(color)=>(color.red==color.green)==
                (color.green==color.blue),
            CMYK(color)=>(color.cyan+color.magenta+
                color.yellow)==0,
        }
    }
}
```

In Listing 15.42, the `display_gray` function is implemented for `Colors`. The function will only display gray colors. In the match expression, the is_gray function is called as a match guard, preventing non-gray colors from being shown. At the bottom of the match expression, notice the RGB and CMYK arms *without* a match guard. These match the non-gray colors. The gray colors would have already been handled.

Code Listing 15.42.   Implementation of the display_gray function

```
fn display_gray(&self) {
    match *self {
        RGB(value)
            if self.is_gray()=>println!("RGB {:?} is gray",
                value),
        CMYK(value)
            if self.is_gray()=> println!("CMYK {:?} is gray",
                value),
        RGB(value)=>println!("RGB {:?} is not gray", value),
        CMYK(value)=> println!("CMYK {:?} is not gray", value),
    }
}
```

In `main`, as shown in Listing 15.43, we create an `RGB` and `CYMK` color and call the `display_gray` function on each to confirm if gray.

Code Listing 15.43.   Implementation of the display_gray function

```
fn main() {
    let rgb=RGB(RgbColor{red:100, green:155, blue:155});
    rgb.display_gray();

    let cmyk=CMYK(CmykColor{cyan: 0, magenta: 0,
        yellow: 0, black: 100});
    cmyk.display_gray();
}
```

This result is displayed:

```
RGB RgbColor { red: 100, blue: 155, green: 155 } is not gray
CMYK CmykColor { cyan: 0, magenta: 0, yellow: 0,
black: 100 } is gray
```

When multiple patterns are combined, the match guard is applied to all of them individually. In Listing 15.44, multiple literals are combined within a pattern. In this example, the match guard is a function that returns true only on Monday. Mondays are special! The match guard will be applied to each of the literals in the pattern. None of them can match unless it is Monday.

Code Listing 15.44.   Applying a match guard to combined patterns

```rust
fn is_monday()->bool {
    // determines whether Monday, or not
}

fn main() {
    match 1 {
        1 | 11 | 21 if is_monday()=>println!(
            "Value 1, 11, or 21"),
        _=>println!("Not Monday!")
    }
}
```

Summary

With patterns, you are only limited by your creativity. Rust supports both simple and complex patterns, used for advanced solutioning. This is accomplished with a rich pattern syntax. Starting with variable binding, patterns are virtually everywhere in Rust.

Patterns are used in three primary areas:

- Destructuring a value into its constituent parts
- Controlling the flow of your applications, including if let, while let, and match expressions.
- Filtering values with literals in patterns, refutable patterns, and match guards.

When destructuring values within a pattern, move semantics can apply. You can use the ref keyword within a pattern to borrow, not move. Speaking of references, you can remove the *refness* of a value by including an & in the pattern for a value.

For specific use cases, include literals in the patterns. This can be combined with other aspects of the pattern.

Wildcards can be used within patterns to skip or ignore one or more values. The underscore (_) pattern ignores a single value, while the double dot (..) pattern can ignore multiple values.

Match guards filter patterns. After a pattern, you add a match guard with the if keyword. For complicated match guards, you can call a function that returns a Boolean value. You can even apply match guards when multiple patterns are combined.

At this point in the book, traits, generics, and now patterns have been discussed. They are the major influencers on the *look and feel* of the Rust language.

16

Closures

A closure is an anonymous function that can "close over" variables from an outer function. This is the origin of the term *closure*. The closed-over variables are called free variables because they are free from the scope of the closure. Like any function, closures execute code, have parameters, and return values.

Closures are a popular feature in many languages, such as Java and C++. In other languages, such as Java, closures are called lambdas.

You may have to choose between using a closure or a standard function. Here are the advantages to closures.

- Closures are convenient when there is a single reference to the function.
- Closures are ideal as first-class citizens. You can treat closures as function parameters, return values, or even assign to a variable.
- Closures are often defined close to where the function is used, which makes the code more maintanable.

There are also many similarities between closures and standard functions. Indeed, there can be circumstances where a function and a closure are interchangeable.

Closures implement the Fn, FnMut, or FnOnce traits, each with a different behavior. The Fn trait is different from the fn keyword used when defining a function pointer type. Most of the time, the correct closure trait is inferred at compile time. If the desired trait is not available, you will receive a compiler error.

Unlike functions, closures have a flexible syntax. Most of the time a shorter syntax is preferred, when possible. For example, closures rarely state the return value type. It is simply implied.

Finally, closures are *not* nested functions. Nested functions do not have the capability to close over variables in the outer function. In addition, nested functions are named, while closures are anonymous.

"Hello, World"

We have shown a "Hello, World" program previously. Listing 16.1 shows a version using closures.

Code Listing 16.1. "Hello, World" program that uses a closure

```
fn main() {
    let hello=|| println!("Hello, world!");
    hello();
}
```

Closures start with the || syntax. Next is the implementation of the closure. As a value, the closure is assigned to the hello variable. You then execute the closure using the call operator, which is (). The closure will then display the greeting.

You can also call the closure directly. In Listing 16.2, the closure is immediately called with the call operator. It is not assigned to a variable first.

Code Listing 16.2. Calling the closure directly

```
fn main() {
    (|| println!("Hello, world!"))();
}
```

Closure Syntax

Some of the details of the previous closure were implied. That allowed the syntax to be shortened. Here is the complete syntax of a closure:

```
|parameter¹, parameter², ..., parameterⁿ|->return_type{
    // code block
}
```

Closures start with the distinctive || syntax. The function parameters are then placed between the pipes. If present, parameters are described in name:type pairs. The return_type sets the type of the return value. The closure block contains the expression to be executed when the closure is called.

In Listing 16.3, the cubed closure is described with the complete closure syntax.

Code Listing 16.3. Implementing a closure that cubes values

```
fn main() {
    let cubed=|number:usize|->usize{
        number*number*number
    };

    let value=5;
    let result=cubed(value);
    println!("{}", result);
}
```

When called, the closure here returns a cubed value. Both the parameter and return value of the closure are usize types. Within the closure, the parameter value is cubed and the result returned. The closure is assigned to the cubed variable. It is then called with the call operator, while accepting a local variable as the function parameter. The result is saved in a variable and displayed.

For the minimalist, the definition of the cubed closure can be shortened. Both the parameter and return types are optional and can be inferred. The closure block can also be removed. It is not required for a single expression. Here is the result.

```
let cubed=|number|number*number*number;
```

Closed Over

Closures can close over a free variable. The captured variable is then available within the closure. Most often, captured variables are borrowed from the outer function.

The closure in Listing 16.4 captures the value variable, which is a free variable. Within the closure, the captured variable is used to calculate the result.

Code Listing 16.4.   A closure that closes over a variable

```
fn main() {
    let value=5;
    let cubed=||value*value*value;
    let result=cubed();
    println!("{}", result);
}
```

As mentioned previously, the closed-over variables are borrowed within the closure.

The example shown in Listing 16.5 will not work! The values1 variable is a mutable tuple. When used within the closure, it performs a *mutable* borrow of values1. It will retain that mutable borrow until immediately after the closure is called. However, the values2 variable requests a second mutable borrow within that scope. Rust does not allow multiple mutable borrows on the same variable. Therefore, this will cause a compiler error.

Code Listing 16.5.   In closures, closed-over variables are borrowed.

```
fn main() {
    let mut values1=(5,10);

    // mutable borrow - starts
    let swap_values=||(values1.1, values1.0);
    let values2=&mut values1; // second mutable borrow
    let result=swap_values();
    // mutable borrow - ends

    println!("{:?}", result);                1
}
```

The error message shown next accurately describes the problem. It highlights the first and second mutable borrower.

```
3 |     let swap_values=||(values1.1, values1.0);
  |     --              --------- first borrow occurs
          due to use of `values1.0` in closure
  |                         |
  |                         immutable borrow occurs here
4 |     let values2=&mut values1; // does not work
  |                 ^^^^^^^^^^^^ mutable borrow occurs here
5 |     let result=swap_values();
  |                ----------- immutable borrow later used here
```

In Listing 16.6, `swap_values` is now called twice. This extends the scope of the initial mutable borrow to after the second swap_values call. Attempting a second mutable borrow within this scope will not compile, which is the same problem as before.

Code Listing 16.6.   Simultaneous mutable borrows are not allowed.

```
fn main() {

    let values1=(5,10);

    // mutable borrow - starts
    let swap_values=||(values1.1, values1.0);
    let mut result=swap_values();
    let values2=&mut values1;    // does not work
    result=swap_values();
    // mutable borrow - stops

    println!("{:?}", result);
}
```

Joy! The next version of the application works! There are no compiler errors. We initiate the second mutable borrow after the final swap_values call. For that reason, there is no overlap (see Listing 16.7).

Code Listing 16.7.   Mutable borrows, but not at the same time

```
fn main() {
    let mut values1=(5,10);

    // mutable borrow – starts
    let swap_values=||(values1.1, values1.0);
    let mut result=swap_values();
    result=swap_values();
    // mutable borrow – stops
```

```
        println!("{:?}", result);
        let values2=&mut values1;   // mutable borrow - works
}
```

Closures as Function Arguments

As first-class citizens, closures can be used as function arguments.

As previously mentioned, closures implement either the Fn, FnMut, or FnOnce trait. For now, we will focus on the Fn trait (more about the other function traits later). As a function parameter, select the Fn trait with the impl keyword. You must also provide the function definition.

In Listing 16.8, the do_closure function accepts a closure as the run parameter. The impl keyword identifies the closure type as Fn. The "()" after the trait name describes a function that has neither parameters nor a return value. Next, in the do_closure function, the closure bound to the run variable is executed.

Code Listing 16.8.   Accepting a closure as a function parameter

```
    fn do_closure(run:impl Fn()){
        run();
    }

    fn main() {
        let display=||println!("message");
        do_closure(display);
    }
```

Listing 16.9 is a more comprehensive example of closures as function parameters. It demonstrates the flexibility that closures provide.

Code Listing 16.9.   Closures bound to variables and as parameters

```
    enum Calculation {
        Cubed,
        Quad
    }

    fn get_result( run: impl Fn(i32)->i32, value:i32)->i32{
        run(value)
    }

    fn main() {
        let cubed=|value:i32|value*value*value;
        let quad=|value:i32|value*value*value*value;
```

```
        let calculation_type=Calculation::Cubed;
        let result=match calculation_type {
            Calculation::Cubed => get_result(cubed, 5),
            Calculation::Quad => get_result(quad, 5),
        };
        println!("{}", result);
    }
```

This example can either cube or quad a value. Both operations are implemented as closures and are Fn(i32)->i32 types. The get_result function has a parameter, run, that accepts closures of the same type. The run parameter is a Fn(i32)->i32 type, which is consistent with the cubed and quad closures. Within the function, the run closure is executed and the result returned.

In main, the Calculation enum indicates the chosen operation, Calculation::Cubed or Calculation::Quad. Based on the match value, the match expression then calls the get_result function with the proper closure as the function parameter.

Closures as Function Return Values

This section continues our conversation on closures as first-class citizens. Next, we'll explore closures as function return values. Returning a closure from a function can be done with the impl keyword. As with parameters, the impl keyword is used to select a closure trait such as the Fn trait.

Listing 16.10 is an example of a function that returns a closure.

Code Listing 16.10.   **Returning a closure from a function**

```
    fn get_closure()->impl Fn(i32)->i32 {
        |number|number*number*number
    }

    fn main() {
        let cubed=get_closure();
        let result=cubed(5);
        println!("{}", result);
    }
```

Based on the impl keyword, the get_closure function returns a closure of the Fn(i32)->i32 type, where Fn is the closure trait. The Fn(i32)->i32 type is compatible with the closure that is returned. In main, the get_closure function is called to return a closure, which is then assigned to the cubed variable. Afterwards, the cubed closure is called and the result displayed.

Implementation of Closures

Knowing the internal implementation of Rust closures can be helpful. This will provide clarity and remove some of the mystery about closures. In particular, the explanation will distinguish the differences between the Fn, FnMut, and FnOnce traits. The description omits some details to keep the explanation straightforward.

Rustc, the Rust compiler, implements closures at compile time. Closures are transformed into structs. The captured variables become the fields of the new struct.

There is no reference to the closure function within the closure struct. There is no need! The closure function is a method of the closure structure. The first parameter of any method, including a closure, is self. The attributes of the closure method, including self, are based on the closure trait selected at compile time.

In Listing 16.11, a typical closure is shown. For the adder closure, the Fn trait is implemented.

Code Listing 16.11.   **This is a typical closure.**

```
let a=1;
let b=2;
let adder=|prefix:String|println!("{} {}", prefix, a+b);
adder("Add Operation:".to_string());
```

Listing 16.12 depicts the internal struct created for the adder closure. The adder closure is converted to a struct with two fields, for the a and b captured variables. The closure function is implemented as a method, with &Self as the first parameter. The second parameter of the method is the initial parameter of the closure, which is the prefix. Remember, this is only an approximation of the implementation. Furthermore, the internal representation of a closure is subject to change at any time.

Code Listing 16.12.   **A representative struct created for a typical closure**

```
struct adder {
    a: i32,
    b: i32
}

impl Fn<(String)> for adder {
    type Output = ()
    fn call(&self, args: Args)->Self::Output {
        // details not provided
    }
}
```

The Fn Trait

For implementing closures, the Fn trait is preferred. The closure traits form a hierarchy of traits and supertraits, as shown in Figure 16.1.

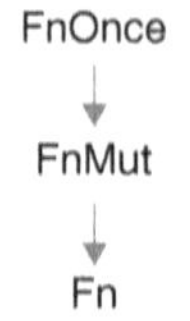

FnOnce

↓

FnMut

↓

Fn

Figure 16.1.   Hierarchy of closure traits

For example, the FnMut trait is a supertrait of Fn. This means the FnMut trait can be used wherever the Fn trait is requested. However, the reverse does not work for subtraits. You cannot substitute the FnMut with the Fn trait.

Closures that are immutable implement the Fn trait. This means the captured variables must be immutable also. For the Fn trait, `self` for the closure method is `&Self`. The captured variables are borrowed.

In Listing 16.13, the `hello` closure does not capture any variable. The closure is therefore self-contained and has no context. This also means the closure is immutable and implements the Fn trait. The do_closure function is called successfully with the hello closure as the function argument, which is a Fn type. This confirms the hello function implements the Fn trait. Otherwise, this would not compile.

Code Listing 16.13.   The `hello` closure implements the Fn trait.

```
fn do_closure(closure:impl Fn()){
    closure();
}

fn main() {
    let hello=||println!("Hello");
    do_closure(&hello);
}
```

Listing 16.14 is a slight modification of the previous example. The `hello` closure now captures the `hello_string` variable. The captured variable is immutable. For this reason, the compiler automatically implements the Fn trait for an immutable context. Once again, the do_closure function is called successfully to confirm the closure as Fn.

Code Listing 16.14.   The `hello` closure implements the Fn trait.

```
fn do_closure(closure:impl Fn()){
    closure();
}

fn main() {
```

```
    let hello_string="Hello".to_string();
    let hello=||println!("{}", hello_string);
    do_closure(&hello);
}
```

In this version, as shown in Listing 16.15, the hello_string is now mutable. The variable is still captured as a free variable in the hello closure. The closure now has a mutable state and will automatically implement the FnMut trait. The function parameter type for do_closure has been changed to FnMut type to confirm that the trait has been implemented for the closure.

Code Listing 16.15.   **The hello closure implements the FnMut trait.**

```
fn do_closure(closure:&mut impl FnMut()){
    closure();
}

fn main() {
    let mut hello_string="Hello".to_string();
    let mut hello=||println!("{}", hello_string);
    do_closure(&mut hello);
}
```

A rose by any other name.... A closure without context, no captured variables, is essentially a standard function. For this reason, standard functions and closures, without context, are interchangeable. Therefore, the Fn trait is compatible with standard functions.

In Listing 16.16, hello is a nested function, not a closure. Nonetheless, nested functions are standard functions. The do_something function is changed again—the parameter is a Fn type. The hello function is provided as a function argument to the do_closure function. This confirms whether the function is compatible with the Fn trait.

Code Listing 16.16.   **The nested function implements the Fn trait.**

```
fn do_closure(closure:impl Fn()){
    closure();
}

fn main() {
    fn hello(){
        println!("Hello");
    }

    do_closure(hello);
}
```

The FnMut Trait

As already mentioned, the FnMut trait is implemented for closures that have a mutable context. For the FnMut trait, the "self" for the closure method is &mut Self. Variables are captured with a mutable borrow.

In Listing 16.17, the increment closure implements the FnMut trait. Notice that the captured variables are mutable, giving the increment closure a mutable context. The do_closure function calls the closure successfully to confirm the FnMut trait is implemented.

Code Listing 16.17.   The increment closure implements the FnMut trait.

```
fn do_closure(mut closure:impl FnMut()){
    closure();
}

fn main() {
    let mut value=5;
    let increment=||value=value+1;
    do_closure(increment);
    println!("{}", value);   // 6
}
```

The FnOnce Trait

The FnOnce trait is implemented for closures that are allowed to execute once.

Enforcing safe coding patterns is a major advantage of Rust. Sometimes this means limiting a function to a single execution. Closures that implement the FnOnce trait can execute *only* once. Additional attempts to execute the closure will not compile. For the FnOnce trait, the "self" for the closure method is the Self type. For this reason, you are able to call the closure once.

Listing 16.18 is an example of the FnOnce trait.

Code Listing 16.18.   The hello closure implements the FnOnce trait.

```
fn do_closure(closure:impl FnOnce()->String){
    closure();
    closure();   // does not compile
}

fn main() {
    let value="hello".to_string();
    let hello=||value;   // value moved
    do_closure(hello);
}
```

Within the closure, the captured variable is returned. This is only possible if the closure owns the captured variable. For this reason, the Rustc compiler *moves* the value variable from the outer function into the closure, not *borrows*. This makes the value variable unavailable in the future. Therefore, the closure cannot be called again and the FnOnce trait implemented. For this reason, you cannot call the closure twice in the do_closure function.

Reasons for the FnOnce are not always readily apparent. Fortunately, you have a helpful compiler in Rust.

Listing 16.19 is another example where the FnOnce trait is required. In the dropper closure, the captured string is dropped. How often can the same String be dropped? Once! The Rustc compiler recognizes this and implements the FnOnce trait for the closure. The dropper closure is passed into the do_closure function, as a FnOnce type. It can only be called once in the function.

Code Listing 16.19.   **The dropper closure implements the FnOnce trait.**

```
fn do_closure_fn(closure:impl FnOnce()){
    closure();
    closure();  // not compile
}

fn main() {
    let value="data".to_string();
    let dropper=||drop(value);
    do_closure_fn(dropper);
}
```

The Fn and FnMut traits are subtraits of the FnOnce trait. Therefore, closures that implement either trait can be used as a FnOnce instance.

In Listing 16.20, the `hello` closure implements the Fn trait. This closure can be called multiple times. There is nothing about the implementation that prevents the closure from being called more than once. In the example, the `do_closure` function has a FnOnce parameter. In main, do_closure is called with the hello closure as the function argument, despite implementing the Fn trait. Within do_closure, the hello closure, as the closure variable, can be called just once.

Code Listing 16.20.   **The `hello` closure implements the FnOnce trait.**

```
fn do_closure(closure:impl FnOnce()){
    closure();
    closure();  // not compile
}

fn main() {
    let hello=||println!("hello");
    do_closure(hello);
}
```

The move Keyword

Every function has a stack frame for private memory storage. The stack frame contains function-specific information, such as local variables and register values. A closure can capture values from the outer function's stack frame, as free variables. Because of this, closures may not own their entire environment. This can create dependencies that cause problems, as shown in Listing 16.21.

Code Listing 16.21.   **Closure with a dependency**

```
fn get_closure()->impl Fn()->i32 {
    let number=1;
    ||number+2
}
```

The get_closure function returns a closure that relies upon a captured value (number), creating a dependency with the outer function. When the closure is returned, the stack frame for the outer function will no longer exist. As such, the dependency with the outer function cannot be maintained. For that reason, the following error is presented:

```
3 |      ||number+2
  |        ^^^^^^^^^^
help: to force the closure to take ownership of `number` (and any
other referenced variables), use the `move` keyword
  |
3 |      move ||number+2
  |        ++++
```

The error message indicates that the move keyword is the solution. Closures annotated with the move keyword take complete ownership of their environment and *do not* depend on the stack frame of the outer function. With the move keyword, captured values are transferred to the closure's environment. Based on the type of values, move or copy semantics is employed. This will remove any dependency with the outer function.

Except for the move annotation on the closure, the source code in Listing 16.22 is identical to the previous example. However, this version compiles without errors. Excellent!

Code Listing 16.22.   **Closure with its own environment**

```
fn get_closure()->impl Fn()->i32 {
    let number=1;
    move||number+2        // move closure
}

fn main() {
    let add_one=get_closure();
    let result=add_one();
    println!("{}", result);
}
```

In get_closure, the closure is adorned with the move keyword. For this reason, the number variable is transferred to the environment of the closure. We can now safely return the closure from the function. Back in main, the closure is assigned to the add_one variable. When add_one is called, the number value in the closure's environment will be updated and the result is returned.

The Impl Keyword

Traits are unsized. For that reason, you cannot create instances of a trait directly. Static dispatch and dynamic dispatch are solutions for managing concrete instances of a trait. The subject of traits, including static and dynamic dispatch, is reviewed in detail in Chapter 17, "Traits."

The closure traits have made several appearances already in this chapter. We created instances of the closure traits with the impl keyword. However, the impl keyword is not available in some use cases. It is available for function parameters and return values, as shown before. Most notably, however, the impl keyword is not supported for variable binding.

Here are two examples where the impl keyword is not accepted. First, we define a type alias for a tuple that contains two closures, using the Fn trait. This will not compile.

```
type closure_tuple=(impl Fn(),
    impl Fn())    // Does not compile
```

Next, we create a HashMap with Fn closures as the value for each entry. With the impl keyword, this will not compile.

```
let mut operation: HashMap<char, impl Fn()>=
                HashMap::new();         // Does not compile
```

When necessary, alternatives for the impl keyword include static dispatch or dynamic dispatch.

In Listing 16.23, AStruct is generic over type T. With the where clause, we constrain type T with the Fn trait bounds. This means the hello field, which is T, must be a Fn closure. All of this done without the impl keyword. In main, we then assign a closure to the hello field. Next, the closure is called.

Code Listing 16.23.   Assigning a closure without the impl keyword

```
struct AStruct<T>
where T: Fn() {
    hello: T,
}

fn main() {
    let value=AStruct{hello:||println!("Hello")};
    (value.hello)();
}
```

In Listing 16.24, we bind the hello variable to a closure. This cannot be done with the impl keyword. The dyn keyword provides dynamic dispatch. We can then assign a closure to the variable as a reference. The hello closure is then called.

Code Listing 16.24.   With dynamic dispatch, `hello` assigns a reference to a closure.

```
let hello:&dyn Fn()=&|| println!("hello");
hello();
```

Matrix Example

Let's look at an additional example that uses closures. The goal of this example is applying mathematical operations to each row of a matrix. Operations such as addition, subtraction, multiplication, and division are supported.

Here is the matrix:

Operation	LHS	RHS	Result
A	4	5	0
M	2	6	0
D	9	3	0
S	5	6	0

The first column of the matrix indicates the operation for that row, such as A for addition. The LHS and RHS columns are the left-hand side and right-hand side operands, respectively, for the binary operation. The result of the operation is placed in the Result column, the final column.

There are various possible solutions to applying a mathematical operation to each row of the matrix. You could use an enum to identify each operation. The enum variants would correlate to match arms, where the operations are performed. With this solution, the enum variant would carry the row data. Another solution is a vector of structures. Each struct would contain the relevant data to perform the operation for a particular row, including a reference to a closure.

We will use a third solution, with a `HashMap`. The benefit is a solution that is both dynamic and extensible. Listing 16.25 shows the complete application.

Code Listing 16.25.   The complete matrix program

```
use std::collections::HashMap;

type Row=(char, i32, i32, i32);
type OperationType<'a>=&'a dyn Fn(Row)->i32;

fn main() {
    let mut matrix=vec![('a', 4, 5, 0),
        ('m', 2, 6, 0),
        ('d', 9, 3, 0),
        ('s', 5, 6, 0),
    ];

    let mut operation: HashMap<char, OperationType>;
```

```
operation=HashMap::new();
operation.insert('a', &|row|row.1+row.2);
operation.insert('m', &|row|row.1*row.2);
operation.insert('d', &|row|row.1/row.2);
operation.insert('s', &|row|row.1-row.2);

for each_row in matrix.iter_mut() {
    each_row.3=(operation.get(&each_row.0)).
        unwrap()(*each_row);
}

println!("{:?}", matrix);
}
```

Let's examine each portion of the solution.

The program starts with two aliases. There is an alias for a tuple describing each row, including the operation, LHS, RHS, and result. OperationType is an alias defining the type of closures for the various binary operations. Dynamic dispatch is used to reference the Fn trait (see Listing 16.26).

Code Listing 16.26. Alias for the row type and mathematical operations

```
type Row=(char, i32, i32, i32);
type OperationType<'a>=&'a dyn Fn(row)->i32;
```

In main, we declare the matrix as a vector of tuples (see Listing 16.27).

Code Listing 16.27. Declaring the matrix

```
let mut matrix=vec![('a', 4, 5, 0),
    ('m', 2, 6, 0),
    ('d', 9, 3, 0),
    ('s', 5, 6, 0),
];
```

Next, the HashMap is declared (see Listing 16.28), and maps the mathematical operations, as closures, to characters. The HashMap key indicates the operation as a character, such as 'a' for addition. The values are the mathematical operations, as the OperationType type, which is a previously defined alias. Each operation, represented by a closure, is added to the HashMap with the insert method.

Code Listing 16.28. Adding operations, as closures, to a hash map

```
let mut operation: HashMap<char, OperationType>;
operation=HashMap::new();
operation.insert('a', &|row|row.1+row.2);
operation.insert('m', &|row|row.1*row.2);
operation.insert('d', &|row|row.1/row.2);
operation.insert('s', &|row|row.1-row.2);
```

The soup is now made. We can apply the various operations to the matrix, as shown in Listing 16.29. The `for` loop iterates the rows of the matrix. Each row is a Row type, which is a tuple. Within the loop, the key is the first field of the row. The `HashMap.get` method uses the key to return the operation (closure) for the current row. The closure is then called with the tuple as the parameters. We then assign the result to the last field of the row.

Code Listing 16.29.   **Iterating the matrix while executing the appropriate operation**

```
for each_row in matrix.iter_mut() {
    each_row.3=(operation.get(&each_row.0)).unwrap()(*each_row);
}
```

Finally, the result is displayed:

```
println!("{:?}", matrix);
```

We can now celebrate a job well done.

Summary

Closures are anonymous functions that can be used as first-class citizens. A closure can be used anywhere, including for a variable binding, function argument, function return, and so much more. There are a variety of benefits to closures, including convenience and flexibility.

Captured variables, also called free variables, are values in the outer function that are used within the closure. This is the primary difference between a closure and a standard function. For that reason, a closure without captured variables is similar to a standard function.

Closures are implemented with one of three traits:

- The Fn trait is implemented for closures that require an immutable context. The self for the closure is &Self.
- The FnMut trait is implemented for closures that require a mutable context. The self for the closure is &mut Self.
- The FnOnce trait is implemented for closures allowed to execute once. The self for the closure is Self.

The `impl` keyword is used to accept function traits, such as Fn, as function parameters and return values. This approach is not always supported. Static dispatch and dynamic dispatch are alternatives when the impl keyword is not available.

The `move` keyword creates a dedicated environment for the closure. The closure has ownership of this environment. Captured variables are transferred into the environment using either move or copy semantics. Move closures can extend the lifetime of the captured variables beyond the outer function, which is sometimes necessary.

17

Traits

Traits are abstract types that describe a behavior, which can consist of multiple functions. Traits are implemented by concrete types. Each implementation of a trait is a specialization for that type.

Traits create relationships between types. For example, the GasCar, ElectricCar, and HybridCar types could implement a Car trait. Each of them is a *kind of* Car. As such, they share a common interface and behavior, such as start, brake, accelerate, and turn functions. For these reasons, types that implement the same trait are related and interchangeable.

Types can implement more than one trait. An Amphibious type could implement both the Car and Boat traits. It would be a kind of Car and a kind of Boat. In Rust, some traits implement more than one trait. For example, the String type implements dozens of traits.

Fundamentally, traits are contracts. Types that expose a trait must fully implement it. The compiler enforces this contract. Partially implemented traits will cause compiler errors. This prevents an implementation of a trait missing an important behavior, such as brakes when implementing the Car trait.

Traits are also promises. A type that implements a trait is making a promise about its behavior. For example, a type that implements the Drop trait is droppable. Another example is the Clone and Copy trait. Types that implement both of those traits promise to support copy semantics.

Rust supports relationships between traits. A supertrait is a superset of another trait. Naturally, a trait that has a supertrait is a subtrait itself. Earlier, in Chapter 16, "Closures," we introduced the Fn and FnMut traits. FnMut is a supertrait of Fn. Therefore, Fn is a subtrait.

Trait Definition

Traits define a set of functions that must be implemented within a type. You declare a trait with the `trait` keyword, name, trait block, and a list of function definitions, separated with semicolons. Traits cannot have fields. You can have both instance and associated functions within the trait. For instance, methods—the first parameter will be either `self`, `&self`, or `&mut self`.

A Car trait is shown in Listing 17.1. Types that are a kind of car would implement this trait. It is an abstraction and includes the common functionality any car requires.

Code Listing 17.1.   Defining the car trait

```
trait Car {
    fn ignition(&mut self, drive:bool);
    fn turn(&mut self, angle:u8)->u8;
    fn brake(&mut self, amount:i8)->i8;
    fn accelerate(&mut self, new_speed:i8)->i8;
    fn stop(&mut self);
}
```

Types implement, or create a specialization, for traits. This is done within an impl block implemented for specific traits. Here is the syntax:

```
impl trait for type {
    // implementation
}
```

In the impl block for a trait, you need to implement *every* function defined in the trait. Otherwise, the source code will not compile. Fortunately, if that happens, the compiler will display an error message identifying the missing functions of the trait that are not implemented.

In Listing 17.2, the definition of the ElectricCar struct is presented.

Code Listing 17.2.   Definition of the ElectricCar

```
struct Battery {
    charge:i8
}

struct ElectricCar {
    battery:Battery,
    started:bool,
    speed:i8,
    direction:u8,
}
```

The Electric type has a get_charge_level function, as shown in Listing 17.3. It is implemented in the impl block for the type.

Code Listing 17.3.   Implementation of ElectricCar

```
impl ElectricCar {
    fn get_charge_level(&self)->i8 {
        self.battery.charge
    }
}
```

As a kind of car, the ElectricCar supports the Car trait. You must create a dedicated block that implements the trait for ElectricCar, as shown in Listing 17.4.

Code Listing 17.4.   **Implementing the Car trait for the ElectricCar**

```
impl Car for ElectricCar {
    fn ignition(&mut self, drive:bool){
        self.started=true;
    }

    fn turn(&mut self, angle:u8)->u8{
        self.direction+=angle;
        self.direction
    }

    fn brake(&mut self, amount:i8)->i8{
        self.speed-=amount;
        self.speed
    }

    fn accelerate(&mut self, new_speed:i8)->i8{
        self.speed+=new_speed;
        self.speed
    }

    fn stop(&mut self){
        self.speed=0;
    }
}
```

Implementing a trait for a type does not change how to create an instance or access its methods. In Listing 17.5, main creates an instance of ElectricCar. You are ready to drive! Various methods are then called to drive the car around. It is the standard Rust syntax.

Code Listing 17.5.   **Implementing the Car trait for the ElectricCar**

```
fn main() {
    let mut mycar=ElectricCar {
        battery:Battery{charge:0},
        started:false,
        speed:0,
        direction:0,
    };

    mycar.ignition(true);
    mycar.accelerate(25);
    mycar.brake(5);
    mycar.stop();
    mycar.ignition(false);
    mycar.get_charge_level();
}
```

Default Functions

As shown already, traits contain function definitions that types must implement. However, traits can also provide default functions that are implemented within the trait definition. The default function is shared with any type that implements the trait. Types that implement the trait have a choice—accept the default function or override with a specialization. This contributes to the extensibility of the language. Any future type that implements the trait will automatically gain the default function.

In Listing 17.6, the Shape trait defines behavior for geometric shapes, such as rectangles, ellipses, triangles, octagons, and others. In the definition, the trait implements draw as a default method. The other function, **erase**, is not implemented.

Code Listing 17.6.   **Defining the Shape trait**

```
trait Shape {
    fn draw(&self){println!("drawing...");}
    fn erase(&self);
}
```

The `Rectangle` and `Ellipse` types are kinds of geometric shapes and therefore implement the Shape trait. See Listing 17.7. `Rectangle` accepts the default `draw` method and only implements the erase method. However, `Ellipse` implements both methods, overriding the default method. Regardless, both `Rectangle` and `Ellipse` have two methods implemented.

Code Listing 17.7.   **Implementing the Shape type**

```
Struct Rectangle{}
struct Ellipse{}

impl Shape for Rectangle {
    // accepts Shape::draw
    fn erase(){}
}

impl Shape for Ellipse {
    fn draw(){}  // override Shape::draw
    fn erase(){}
}
```

Default functions can call other functions within the trait, whether implemented or not. This does not prevent you from overriding the default function, if desired.

In Listing 17.8, the Light trait is defined. The trait has `light_on` and `light_off` methods that confirm whether a light is on. The `light_off` method is implemented as a default function. It simply negates the result of the `light_on` method.

Code Listing 17.8.   Implementation of the Shape trait

```
Trait Light {
    fn light_on(&self)->bool;
    fn light_off(&self)->bool{
        !self.light_on()
    }
}
```

Marker Trait

A marker trait has no function definitions. It is an empty trait. However, marker traits are still quite useful. A marker trait typically indicates some sort of status. For example, Copy is a marker trait indicating that bitwise copying is supported for those that have that trait.

Marker traits are *adopted* but not implemented. There is nothing to implement!

Rust has several predefined marker traits, with many found in the std::marker module. The Copy trait is found in this module, for example. Other marker traits found in this module include the following:

- Send
- Sized
- Sync
- Unpin

The details of specific marker traits are explained, when relevant, in this book.

Associated Functions

Traits can have associated functions. These are functions without the self parameter. Without self, associated functions are called on the type, not a specific instance, using the :: operator. Associated functions were first discussed in Chapter 13, "Structures."

The following, Listing 17.9, is an implementation of a factory pattern. As a trait, the pattern can be applied to a variety of types. The trait has two associated functions. The new function abstracts the creation of the single instance, and the get_instance function returns the instance.

Code Listing 17.9.   Defining the Singleton trait

```
trait Singleton {
    fn new()->Self
        where Self:Sized;
    fn get_instance()->Self
        where Self:Sized;
}
```

In the previous example, Self for a trait is not sized because traits do not have a constant size. Traits can be implemented by various types, each potentially a different size. This is a problem because Rust does not allow instances of unsized types. However, the functions of the Singleton trait must return an instance. Fortunately, the trait functions are implemented for specific concrete types, which are sized. This mean self is sized when required. For that reason, in the where clause, we assign the Sized trait bounds to Self.

For a chess game, the chessboard could be implemented as a singleton, as shown in Listing 17.10. This is not a full implementation of a game. Notice there are two impl blocks: an impl block that implements a start function for Chessboard and a separate impl block that implements the associated functions for the Singleton trait.

Code Listing 17.10.   Defining the Singleton trait

```
struct Chessboard{
}

impl Chessboard {
    const INSTANCE:Chessboard=Chessboard{};
    fn start(&self) {
        println!("chess game started");
    }
}

impl Singleton for Chessboard {

    fn new()->Self {
        Chessboard::INSTANCE
    }

    fn get_instance()->Self {
        Chessboard::INSTANCE
    }
}
```

In Listing 17.11, the new function is called to create the Chessboard. As an associated function, the function is called with the :: syntax. The new instance is returned. You can then call the start function on the instance to start the game.

Code Listing 17.11.   Creating a singleton with the new constructor function

```
fn main() {
    let board=Chessboard::new();
    board.start();
}
```

Associated Types

Within a trait definition, an associated type is a type placeholder. Associated types resolve to a specific type when the trait is implemented. This allows you to integrate implementation-specific details into the trait. Associated types, as placeholders, can be used throughout the trait definition, such as a function parameter or return type.

Define associated types with the `type` keyword. When implemented, you assign the associated type an actual type. The syntax for using an associated type is shown next.

```
Self::associated_type
```

The Inventory trait defined in Listing 17.12 describes the behavior for managing an inventory. `StockItem` is an associated type and a placeholder for the type of inventory items. This means the trait can be implemented for different types of inventory items.

Code Listing 17.12.   Defining a trait with an associated type

```
trait Inventory {
    type StockItem;

    fn find(&self, stock_id:&String)->Self::StockItem;
    fn add(&mut self, item:Self::StockItem)->String;
}
```

Let us assume you are hired to create an inventory application for a reseller of chairs. For that reason, each stock item is a `Chair` type. In Listing 17.13, the Chairs type implements the Inventory trait with Chair as the associated type. In main, we create an instance of Chairs and call the inventory functions.

Code Listing 17.13.   Implementing a trait with an associated type

```
struct Chair{}

#[derive(Copy, Clone)]
struct Chairs{}

impl Inventory for Chairs {
    type StockItem=Chair;

    fn find(&self, stock_id:&String)->Self::StockItem{
        Chair{}
    }

    fn add(&mut self, item:Self::StockItem)->String {
        "ABC12345".to_string()
    }
}
```

```
fn main() {
    let mut catalog=Chairs{};
    let stock_id=catalog.add(Chair{});
    let item=catalog.find(&stock_id);
    println!("Stock id: {:?}", stock_id);
}
```

Traits can have multiple associated types. Consequently, you then have more than one type placeholder available within the trait.

In Listing 17.14, ATrait has two associated types. They are used to define the Result type for the do_something function. Each implementation of the trait can now decide what do_something should return.

Code Listing 17.14.   Defining a trait with two associated types

```
trait ATrait {
    type ValueType;
    type ErrorType;

    fn do_something(&self)->Result<Self::ValueType,
        Self::ErrorType>;
}
```

In Listing 17.15, we implement the ATrait trait for MyStruct. The associated types, ValueType and ErrorType, are set to i8 and String respectively. Consequently, the return value for do_something is Result<i8, String>:

Code Listing 17.15.   Implementation of a trait with two associated types

```
struct MyStruct {

}

impl ATrait for MyStruct {
    type ValueType=i8;
    type ErrorType=String;

    fn do_something(&self)->Result<Self::ValueType,
        Self::ErrorType> {
            Ok(42)
        }
}
```

Extension Methods

Until now, traits have been implemented by our types. With extension methods, you can also implement traits for *any* type with some limitations. This includes predefined types, such as primitives. Implement extension methods within an impl block for the target type. In this manner, you can augment any type with additional behavior. This provides extensibility across the language and the reason this feature is called extension methods.

In Listing 17.16, we implement extension methods. The Dump trait has the `write_dump` method, which dumps debugging information to a log file. This behavior could be useful for any type, making it an ideal choice for an extension method. Furthermore, the trait implements the `write_dump` method as a default function. With the impl keyword, we apply the Dump trait to the i8 type. Because of the default function, there is no implementation inside the impl block. We can simply start using the `write_dump` function. In main, we can now call `write_dump` on an i8 value. The `write_dump` method has been successfully added to its repertoire.

Code Listing 17.16.   Implementing extension methods with the Dump trait

```
trait Dump {
    fn write_dump(&self) {
        println!("{}", self);  // mock
    }
}

impl Dump for i8 {
}

fn main(){
    let num:i8=1;
    num.write_dump();
}
```

In the previous example, the Dump trait was applied to the i8 type, which is a primitive. Unfortunately, the application does not compile! In the `write_dump` method, the `println!` macro requires the `Display` trait because of the {} placeholder. However, the compiler is unsure whether `self` supports that trait. Why? In the trait definition, the type that ultimately implements the trait is unknown. This means the compiler does not have enough information to determine whether or not the `Display` trait is supported. Without this knowledge, the application cannot compile.

As the solution, apply `Display` as a trait bounds for `Self`. This assures that the target type for the extension method implements the `Display` trait. The compiler will now have the necessary assurance to accept the `println!` macro with { } placeholders, as shown in Listing 17.17.

Code Listing 17.17.   Implementing extension methods with the Dump trait

```
trait Dump {
    fn write_dump(&self) where Self: Display { // default
        println!("{}", self);
    }
}
```

You are not limited to a single constraint for an extension method. Multiple bounds can be added to the `where` clause with the + operator. This enforces additional conditions on the type.

Listing 17.18 is an updated version of the Dump trait. For this version of the Dump trait, the `where` clause requires that `Self` implement both the Display and Debug traits. This ensures support for both the {} and {:?} placeholders in the `println!` macro.

Code Listing 17.18.   Applying multiple constraints on an extension method

```
trait Dump {
    fn write_dump(&self) where Self: Display + Debug { // default
        println!("{:?}", self);
    }
}
```

There are limitations on when extension methods can be applied to avoid chaos. What would happen if an external library changed the behavior of types without the knowledge of an application? This is a possibility with extension methods. That would not be fun! To prevent this, there are two limitations:

- The trait must be within scope. If it's not within scope, you can bring the trait into scope with a `using` statement, if possible.
- Either the trait or the type for the extension method must be implemented within the application.

For example, the following would not compile in your application. Neither the trait nor the type, the Iterator trait or i8 type, is implemented within our application.

```
impl Iterator for i8 {
}
```

Fully Qualified Syntax

When you're implementing traits, it is possible to have ambiguous function calls. For example, a type implements separate traits that have identical function definitions. When the function is called on the type, which implementation is invoked? When there is ambiguity, the compiler will not guess. It is simpler and less risky not to compile. Therefore, it is your responsibility to resolve the ambiguity.

To avoid ambiguous function calls, it is helpful to know the various syntaxes for calling a function:

- **Implicit**: This is the *object.method()* syntax, where Self is implied. This is the most common syntax and preferred for calling methods.
- **Explicit**: This is the *type::function(Self)* syntax, where Self is the target type. It will call the function explicitly implemented for the target type and instance.
- **Fully qualified type**: This is the *<type as trait>::function(Self)* syntax used whenever everything requires context.

Listing 17.19 has examples of the various syntaxes:

Code Listing 17.19. Examples of function call syntaxes

```
// implied
 obj.do_something();

 // explicit
XStruct::do_something(&obj);

 // fully qualified syntax
<XStruct as Atrait>::do_something(&obj);
```

Let's review a practical example where the proper syntax is required, starting in Listing 17.20. Here, the Atrait and Btrait traits implement the get_name method. MyStruct implements both traits and accepts the default implementation of get_name for each. Finally, get_name is not specifically implemented on MyStruct. Therefore, the only versions of get_name come from the traits.

Code Listing 17.20. Ambiguous function call with the implicit syntax

```
Trait Atrait {
    fn get_name(&self){
        println!("Atrait");
    }
}

trait Btrait {
    fn get_name(&self){
        println!("Btrait");
    }
}

struct MyStruct{}

impl Atrait for MyStruct{}
impl Btrait for MyStruct{}

fn main() {
    let obj=MyStruct{};
    obj.get_name();  // implicit syntax - does not work
}
```

In main, the get_name function is called on a MyStruct instance using the implicit syntax. The compiler first looks for a direct implementation of **get_name**, which is not found. Next, the search continues to the traits. However, **get_name** is implemented for two traits. Therefore, the call is ambiguous and the program does not compile. The problem is fixable with the explicit syntax.

In Listing 17.21, we now use the explicit syntax to call get_name. Therefore, the trait name and instance are provided with function call. For that reason, it is no longer ambiguous and works spectacularly well.

Code Listing 17.21.   Successful function call with the explicit syntax

```
fn main() {
    let obj=MyStruct{};
    ATrait::get_name(&obj);   // explicit syntax
}
```

Listing 17.22 is another example where the explicit syntax for calling a function is required. The display_name function is an associated function. MyStruct has an implementation of the function. In addition, MyStruct implements ATrait including the display_name associated function *again*.

Code Listing 17.22.   Successful function call with the explicit syntax

```
trait ATrait {
    fn display_name();
}

struct MyStruct{}

impl ATrait for MyStruct{
    fn display_name() {
        println!("ITrait::MyStruct");
    }
}

impl MyStruct{
    fn display_name() {
        println!("MyStruct");
    }
}

fn main() {
    let obj=MyStruct{};
    // explicit
    MyStruct::display_name();
    // explicit
    ATrait::display_name();
}
```

In main, the `display_name` function is called twice using the explicit syntax. The first function call compiles successfully. However, the second does not compile: `ATrait::display_name()`. The reason is that functions cannot be called on traits. Function calls must be made on a concrete type or instance. What is needed is more context—something more than just the trait! The fully qualified syntax provides the additional information that is required. In addition to the trait, the fully qualified syntax also provides the concrete type.

The version of main, shown in Listing 17.23, uses the fully qualified syntax. For that reason, the application will compile successfully.

Code Listing 17.23. Example of the fully qualified syntax

```
fn main() {
    let obj=MyStruct{};

    // explicit
    MyStruct::display_name();

    // fully qualified syntax
    <MyStruct as ATrait>::display_name();
}
```

Supertraits

Traits can have a supertrait and subtrait relationship. The supertrait is the base trait, while the subtrait refines the supertrait. The relationship between traits can create cohesion. For example, a Shape trait could be the supertrait of the Rectangle trait. The Shape trait would contain the general behavior of all shapes. And the Rectangle trait would refine the Shape trait with methods specific to a rectangle shape. This allows you to create both a logical and technical hierarchy between traits, which provides transparency.

The supertrait and subtrait relationship may appear to be inheritance, as defined in object-oriented programming terms, but it is not. Rust does not support inheritance. The interfaces of the two traits are not combined and must be implemented separately. This is different from traditional inheritance, as it appears in C++ and Java.

Here is the syntax for creating a supertrait and subtrait relationship:

```
trait subtrait:supertrait {
    // subtrait functions
}
```

These are several examples of subtraits and supertraits in the standard library. Here are a few of them:

- `Copy: Clone`
- `Eq: PartialE`
- `FnMut<Args>:FnOnce<Args>`
- `Ord:Eq+PartialOrd`

The following example demonstrates a supertrait and subtrait, as shown in Listing 17.24.

Code Listing 17.24.   Implementing a supertrait and subtrait for fonts

```
struct Text {}



// traits
trait Font {
    fn set_font(&mut self,  font_name:String);
}

trait FontWithStyle: Font {
    fn set_style(&mut self, bold:bool, italics:bool);
}

// trait implementations
impl Font for Text  {
    fn set_font(&mut self, font_name:String) {}
}

impl FontWithStyle for Text  {
    fn set_style(&mut self, bold:bool, italics:bool){}
}

fn main() {
    let mut text=Text{};
    text.set_font("arial".to_string());
    text.set_style(true, false);
}
```

This example has two traits. Font is the supertrait and an abstraction of a font. FontWithStyle is the subtrait and refines the Font trait, adding support for bold and italics, which are font styles. The FontWithStyle trait is implemented for the Text struct in an impl block. Consequently, it must also implement the Font supertrait in a separate impl block. In main, a Text value is created that calls functions from both traits.

Subtraits can have multiple supertraits. Combine supertraits with the plus operator, as shown in Listing 17.25. Here we have added the Unicode trait as a second supertrait. It is a marker trait that indicates Unicode text. Because it is a marker trait, there is no need for a separate impl block. There is nothing to implement.

Code Listing 17.25.   Implementing multiple supertraits

```
struct Text {}

trait Font {
    fn set_font(&mut self,  font_name:String);
```

```
    }

    trait Unicode {
    }

    trait FontWithStyle: Font+Unicode {
        fn set_style(&mut self, bold:bool, italics:bool);
    }
```

Let's discuss the diamond problem. This is an infamous problem in programming lore and mostly associated with C++. Assume a struct implements two subtraits. Each of the subtraits has the same supertrait. That means the functions in the supertrait are found along two separate trait hierarchies. For this reason, calling those functions might be ambiguous. In C++, the virtual keyword is the solution. Fortunately, Rust is properly designed to prevent the diamond problem. Regardless of the number of times and places a supertrait appears in the trait hierachy, it is implemented only once! There is no ambiguity for this reason.

Listing 17.26 is an example of a shared supertrait. An amphibious vehicle is a kind of car and boat. Therefore, the Amphibious struct is based on both the Car and Boat traits. These traits share the same supertrait, which is the Vehicle trait. In other languages, this could pose a problem. For Rust, you simply implement the three traits in separate impl blocks. For brevity, the impl blocks are minimally implemented.

Code Listing 17.26.   **Implementation of a complex trait hierarchy**

```
struct Amphibious{
}

trait Vehicle {
    fn drive(&self){}
}

trait Car: Vehicle  {
}

trait Boat: Vehicle {
}

impl Car for Amphibious {
}

impl Boat for Amphibious {
}

impl Vehicle for Amphibious {
}
```

```
fn main() {
    let boat=Amphibious{};
    boat.drive();
}
```

Notice that the Vehicle trait, including the `drive` function, is implemented just once. When the function is called, there is no ambiguity.

Static Dispatch

Using traits instead of specific types can make your source code more extensible and concise, especially when used for function arguments and return values. Types that implement the same trait are interchangeable, within the context of that trait. You are not limited to a specific type. Treat traits as placeholders for any concrete type that implements the trait.

In this example, the function parameter is a trait:

Code Listing 17.27.   Function with a trait parameter

```
fn do_something(obj: ATrait) {
}
```

This example will not compile because traits are unsized, as mentioned earlier. You cannot create instances of unsized types—even traits. This problem can be resolved with either static or dynamic dispatch. We will start with static dispatch.

Static dispatch resolves a trait to a concrete type at compile time. The compiler then creates a specialization of the function for that specific type. This is called *monomorphization* and improves performance. However, it can lead to code bloat. The prerequisite to monomorphization is the ability to identify the concrete type at compile time.

For static dispatch, use the `impl` keyword. As shown in Listing 17.28, this version of the previous example compiles successfully:

Code Listing 17.28.   Function using static dispatch for a trait parameter

```
fn do_something(obj: impl ATrait) {
}
```

Note

The `impl` keyword can be used with function arguments and parameters. However, it cannot be used with variable binding.

In Listing 17.29, we define a Human and an Alien trait. The Human trait is an abstraction of Earth residents, while the Alien trait is for extraterrestrials. The Adult and Child types implement the Human trait. Martian implements the Alien trait. For brevity, most of the implementation in this example is hidden with ellipses.

Code Listing 17.29.   Function using static dispatch for a trait parameter

```
trait Human {
    fn get_name(&self)->String;
}

struct Adult(String);

impl Human for Adult {
    . . .
}

struct Child(String);

impl Human for Child {
    . . .
}

impl Child {
    . . .
}

trait Alien {
    fn get_name(&self)->String;
}

struct Martian (String);

impl Alien for Martian {
    . . .
}
```

Next, we have decided to throw a party for invited guests. This is a party reserved for human persons, however. For that reason, the invite_to_party function has the Human trait as the function parameter, via static dispatch. Because Martians do not implement the Human trait, they cannot attend the party. The Human trait will filter them – compile error. In this manner, traits imply membership. Every type that implements the trait receives member. Everyone else is not a member and cannot be used with that trait, as a parameter, return value, or elsewhere.

Code Listing 17.30. Function to invite humans to a party

```
fn invite_to_party(attendee: impl Human) {
...
}
```

In Listing 17.31, an Adult, Child, and Martian are created. All of them receive an invitation to the party. Both Bob and Janice implement the Human trait and can accept the invite. However, Fred the Martian does not implement the Human trait, only the Alien trait. For that reason, the invitation for Fred the Martian will incur a compile error.

Code Listing 17.31. Calling functions to invite humans to a party

```
fn main() {
    let bob=Adult("Bob".to_string());
    let janice=Child("Janice".to_string());
    let fred=Martian("Fred".to_string());
    invite_to_party(bob);
    invite_to_party(janice);
    invite_to_party(fred);  // not allowed
}
```

Dynamic Dispatch

Dynamic dispatch is available when the compiler cannot infer the concrete type, which is required for static dispatch. Instead, the concrete type must be identified at runtime. The same problem exists, however—we cannot create instances of unsized traits. For dynamic dispatch, the problem is resolved with references, which have a fixed size. However, more information is required than provided in a normal reference. For this reason, you combine the reference with the dyn keyword to create a trait object. The trait object is initialized at runtime with a pointer to the concrete type and to the implementation of the trait, which is a vtable.

There are a couple of ways to declare a trait object. The first is simply using the dyn keyword, like so:

&dyn *trait*

Alternatively, you can use Box to create the trait object:

Box<dyn *trait*>

Let's add another function to our ongoing example. For Listing 17.32, the create_person function can return either a new Adult or Child type. This is based on the first parameter, which is Boolean. Both types implement the Human trait. For that reason, it is the return type and applied with dynamic dispatch.

Code Listing 17.32.   Implementing dynamic dispatch for a function return

```
fn create_person(adult:bool, name:String)->Box<dyn Human> {
    if adult {
        Box::new(Adult(name))
    } else {
        Box::new(Child(name))
    }
}
```

Dynamic dispatch can also be used with variable binding. Let's revisit the Shapes example from earlier in this chapter. As a refresher, both `Ellipse` and `Rectangle` implement the Shape trait. In `main`, we want to create a vector of elements that implements the `Shape` trait. Otherwise, only values that implement the Shape trait will be allowed in this vector. In Listing 17.33, we define the vector of elements that implements the Shape trait, with dynamic dispatch. It is populated with Ellipse and Rectangle values, both members of the Shape trait. In the `for` loop, the trait objects in the vector are iterated. As Shape types, they are guaranteed to have the draw function, which is called at each iteration. This approach is more concise and extensible than other possible solutions.

Code Listing 17.33.   Calling functions to invite humans to a party

```
fn main() {
    let shapes: Vec<&dyn Shape>=vec![&Rectangle{},
        &Ellipse{}, &Rectangle{}];
    for shape in shapes {
        shape.draw();
    }
}
```

Enums and Traits

Enums can also implement traits. You can implement the trait in any manner. It is a free world! However, there is a best practice, which is shown in this chapter. When implementing the trait functions, you should provide a match for the enum variants to provide each a unique implementation of the trait.

The definition of the Scheme trait is provided in Listing 17.34. The methods of the trait return either a RGB or CMYK core color, such as red or cyan.

Code Listing 17.34.   This is the Schemes trait

```
trait Schemes {
    fn get_rgb(&self)->(u8, u8, u8);
    fn get_cmyk(&self)->(u8, u8, u8, u8);
}
```

In Listing 17.35, the CoreColor enum is defined with a list of the core RGB colors as variants, which are Red, Green, and Blue. Next, the Schemes trait is implemented for the CoreColor enum. We first implement the get_rgb function. Within the function, there is an arm for each core color, as a variant. Each arm returns the RGB color for that variant, for example, (255, 0, 0) is returned from Red. The get_cmyk function is also implemented. However, it returns a CMYK color for each core color.

Code Listing 17.35.   **This is the Schemes trait.**

```
enum CoreColor {
    Red,
    Green,
    Blue
}

impl Schemes for CoreColor {
    fn get_rgb(&self)->(u8, u8, u8) {
        match self {
            CoreColor::Red=>(255, 0, 0),
            CoreColor::Green=>(0, 255, 0),
            CoreColor::Blue=>(0, 0, 255)
        }
    }

    fn get_cmyk(&self)->(u8, u8, u8, u8) {
        match self {
            CoreColor::Red=>(0, 99, 100, 0),
            CoreColor::Green=>(100, 0, 100, 0),
            CoreColor::Blue=>(98, 59, 0, 1)
        }
    }
}
```

In main, we display the RGB and CYMK values for CoreColor::Green, as shown in Listing 17.36.

Code Listing 17.36.   **Using an enum that implements a trait.**

```
fn main() {
    let green=CoreColor::Green;
    let rgb=green.get_rgb();
    let cmyk=green.get_cmyk();
    println!("{:?} {:?}", rgb, cmyk);
}
```

Summary

Yes, traits are everywhere in Rust. Whether you're defining the expected behavior of a type, setting bounds for generics, dynamic typing, implementing default methods, and so much more, traits have an important role.

In Rust, traits are used in a variety of ways:

- To ensure a certain interface, consisting of function definitions
- To establish related types that are interchangeable
- To provide status with marker traits
- To extend the capabilities of any existing type with extension methods

Traits are also essential for operator overloading, as shown in Chapter 13, "Structures."

Traits are ultimately contracts. Types that implement a trait must fully implement the trait's interface. You can even set up relationships between traits, such as subtraits and supertraits. When you implement a subtrait, the contract is to implement both the subtrait and supertrait.

With all the traits floating around, ambiguous function calls are not unheard of. Either explicit or the fully qualified syntax should resolve any ambiguous function calls that may occur.

Traits are especially useful as function parameters and return types. As a function parameter or return type, traits make your application more extensible. You can resolve traits into concrete types using either static, impl keyword, or dynamic dispatch, dyn keyword. If the concrete type is known at compile, the preference should be static dispatch for better performance and improved readability.

Enums support traits. You implement traits for an enum in a dedicated impl block. Each function implemented for the trait should have a separate implementation for each enum variant.

18

Threads 1

Long ago in a faraway land, there were mainly single-processor computers and devices. Despite this, a process could have multiple paths of execution. Each path of execution in a process is known as a thread. In this environment, the threads share the processor. This is called *concurrency*. With this architecture, operating systems schedule threads onto the processor mainly in a round-robin fashion.

Multicore devices are now prevalent. We have true parallelization, where processes are decomposed into threads that run in parallel across multiple processors. Gaining the full benefit of the computing power of a multicore architecture is a worthy goal, especially for scalable applications. Unfortunately, it does not *just* happen. There is no wizard behind a curtain. You must write your applications to support parallelization. This is especially important when modeling applications that require scalability or increased performance. For example, parallel programming has helped usher in a new generation of artificial intelligence (AI) and machine learning (ML) applications.

A process initially has a single path of execution, known as the primary thread. With parallelization, additional threads can be added for parallel tasks or operations. In Rust, threads are implemented as physical or operating system threads. The `main` function is the primary thread. There is a 1:1 relationship between a Rust thread and an operating system thread. We do not have green threads, where multiple logical threads (M) can be scheduled onto a physical thread (N), for an M:N relationship. However, various implementations of green threads are available in crates.io.

Parallel programming and concurrency are the most important reasons for hosting multiple threads. Parallel programming decomposes a process into parallel operations for better performance. A server application with a thread for each client connection is a perfect example of parallel programming. The goal of concurrency is responsiveness; for example, maintaining a responsive user interface during an intensive operation such as sorting.

You would think that if two threads improve performance, then ten threads are even better. Sadly, this is not necessarily true. Many factors, some operating system specific, determine whether adding additional threads is beneficial. At some threshold, adding additional threads can actually reduce performance. The primary reasons are the inability to execute completely parallel because of dependences and thread overhead, such as context switches. Amdahl's law provides an algorithm for correlating performance with the number of threads. For these reasons, performance profiling is essential for multithreaded applications.

If a process were a house, threads are the people within the house performing specific tasks and often competing for shared resources. Process memory is the principal shared resource. Conflicts can occur when threads attempt to modify any shared resource at the same time. "Fearless concurrency" in Rust eliminates many of these concerns. Aspects of fearless concurrency are covered in this chapter, such as the ownership model.

Within the process "house," threads also own private assets. The most notable is the stack where locals, system information, and other information are maintained. In some environments, the default stack size is 2 mebibytes (MiB). For processes with dozens, even hundreds of threads, this can amount to a significant amount of memory. Fortunately, Rust allows you to manage stack sizes. The result is an application that is considerably more scalable.

Multithreading is a form of multitasking and, when present, adds complexity to any application. Naturally, managing multiple threads, each a separate path of execution, is more complicated than managing a single-threaded application. The most frequent challenges include the following:

- Race conditions where multiple threads compete for shared resources
- Deadlocks when a thread waits indefinitely for another thread or a resource to become available
- Multithreaded applications behave inconsistently if improperly implemented

Despite the additional complexity, multithreading is an important tool for creating scalable, responsive, and highly performant applications.

Synchronous Function Calls

Execution defaults to being synchronous. This is demonstrated in the next example.

In Listing 18.1, main is the entry point for the primary thread. The hello function is called in main. Keep in mind that main and hello share the same path of execution (i.e., the primary thread). For this reason, main will be suspended while hello is executing. After hello is done, main is resumed and continues until completion. When main exits, the primary thread and process also end.

Code Listing 18.1.   Defining the car trait

```
fn hello() {
    println!("Hello, world!");
}

fn main() {
    println!("In main")
    hello();
    println!("Back in Main")
}
```

This is the result of the application:

```
In main
Hello, world!
Back in Main
```

In Listing 18.2, there is an example of another synchronous function call, where main calls the display function. Both functions have local variables that are place on the stack, which is thread state.

Code Listing 18.2.   Displaying functions that have thread state

```
fn display() {
    let b=2;
    let c=3.4;
    println!("{} {}", b, c);
}

fn main() {
    let a=1;
    println!("{}", a);
    display();
}
```

Functions receive a carve out, called a stack frame, to store their private data. The stack continues to grow with each synchronous function call as additional stack frames are added. As functions exit, stack frames are removed from the stack.

In the preceding example, main and display each own a stack frame that contains their local variables (see Table 18.1).

Table 18.1.   Stack Frame and Local Variables

Function	Local	Stack Frame
main	vara	0
display	varb and varc	1

Threads

Details related to threads are found in the thread module. This includes the thread::spawn function that creates and then executes a thread. The only parameter is the entry point for the thread, either a function name or a closure, which is executed asynchronously. Here is the syntax for the spawn function:

```
pub fn spawn<F, T>(f: F) -> JoinHandle<T> where
    F: FnOnce() -> T + Send + 'static,
    T: Send + 'static,
```

As the return value, the JoinHandle is used for thread synchronization and accessing the underlying return value of the thread function. Type parameter F is for the entry point function, while type parameter T is for the thread's return value. The Send constraint means the value can safely be transferred to another thread. The lifetime 'static is required. You do not know when a thread will start or end. This means the new thread can outlive the parent thread. For that reason, both the function and return value must be static.

The term "parent thread" is used figuratively. When thread a spawns thread b, logically thread a is the parent thread. However, technically there is no relationship between the two threads.

In Listing 18.2, the spawn function is called to create a new thread with a closure as the entry point. The closure then displays a hello message.

Code Listing 18.2.   Spawning a closure as a new thread

```
use std::thread;

fn main() {  // primary thread
    thread::spawn(|| println!(
        "Hello, world!"));  // another thread
    println!("In Main")
}
```

The preceding example will exhibit inconsistent behavior. The main function and the closure run in parallel on different threads. If main finishes first, the process will exit before the closure displays the hello message. The reason is that both functions, as threads, are racing to their end. This is considered a race condition. Worst of all, running the program several times may result in different outcomes. The hello message may or may not be displayed, depending on whether main or the closure finishes first.

When the primary thread exits, the program is terminated. This includes terminating other threads still running. However, the behavior is different for nonprimary threads. When they exit, other threads are not affected and merrily continue running.

The fork/join model prevents race conditions that can occur when parallel threads are racing for the exit. The spawn function implements the fork/join model. The spawn function returns a JoinHandle, which is a specialized thread handle. JoinHandle is used to serialize the execution of two threads. The JoinHandle::join method blocks the current thread until the associated thread exits.

The lock remains in place until the associated thread is detached, such as being dropped.

In Listing 18.3, the join method prevents a race condition. Here, the JoinHandle is assigned to the handle variable. We then call the join function to block main until the new thread exits. This means main will wait for the thread to exit before continuing.

Code Listing 18.3.   Spawning and waiting on a thread to complete

```
use std::thread;

fn main() {
    let handle=thread::spawn(|| println!("Hello, world!"));
```

```
    let result = handle.join();    // wait for other thread
    println!("In Main");
}
```

You may want to capture the result of a thread. This can be done with the JoinHandle. The Join function blocks until the thread completes. At that time, the function also returns the thread's underlying result.

In Listing 18.4, we spawn a thread, using a closure, that returns 1. With the `JoinHandle`, we call the `Join` method to wait for the thread to complete. Afterwards, the thread result is found in Ok(value). We unwrap the Result to display the underlying value, which is 1.

Code Listing 18.4.   Display the result of a thread

```
use std::thread;

fn main() {
    let handle=thread::spawn(|| 1);

    // wait and get return value
    let result = handle.join().unwrap();
    println!("Return value {}", result);
}
```

What if a running thread does not complete successfully, such as having an unhandled panic? If this is the primary thread, usually main, the program terminates. For other threads, the thread will simply terminate after the stack unwinds, but the other threads in the application will continue to execute. If joined, the Join function returns an Err result, as notification of the panic.

In Listing 18.5, we forced an unhandled panic in the new thread. In main, the thread is joined, as shown before. The result of the join method is handled in the match expression. Because of the unhandled panic, the Err arm is chosen and the error message displayed.

Code Listing 18.5.   Capturing the result of a thread

```
use std::thread;

fn main() {
    let handle=thread::spawn(|| panic!("kaboom"));
    let result = handle.join();    // wait for other thread
    match result {
        Ok(value)=>println!("Thread return value: {:?}", value),
        Err(msg)=>println!("{:?}", msg)
    }
}
```

The application will display the following information indicating that the panic occurred!

```
thread '<unnamed>' panicked at 'kaboom', src\main.rs:4:37
note: run with `RUST_BACKTRACE=1` environment variable
to display a backtrace
Any { .. }
```

When the thread is a closure, you can pass data into a thread as captured variables. That is the most common input source for a thread. However, threads run asynchronously and are not bound by the scope of the parent thread. The new thread could even outlive the parent thread. For that reason, ownership of the captured data must be moved into the thread with the move keyword.

As shown in Listing 18.6, the variables a and b are moved into the thread, where the total is calculated and displayed:

Code Listing 18.6.   Capturing input data for a thread

```
use std::thread;

fn main() {
    let a=1;
    let b=2;
    let handle=thread::spawn(move || {
        let c=a+b;
        println!("Sum {} + {}: {}", a, b, c);
    });
    let result = handle.join();
}
```

Scoped threads remove some of the limitations of normal threads with captured variables. Most notably, scoped threads have a deterministic lifetime. A scoped thread does not outlive a designated scope, which eliminates the need for the move keyword. Because of this, you can capture variables with the normal syntax.

To create scoped threads, call the thread::scope function. This function accepts a scope object, which sets the boundary (i.e., scope) of the scoped threads. The scope object is a function itself and will contain the scoped threads. Within the function, the scoped threads are spawned as normal. The scoped threads are then automatically joined at the end of the scope object.

Here is the function definition for the thread::scope function:

```
fn scope<'env, F, T>(f: F) -> T
where
    F: for<'scope> FnOnce(&'scope Scope<'scope, 'env>) -> T,
```

Type parameter F describes the scope object as a function, while type parameter T describes its return type. The 'scope lifetime refers to the lifetime of the scope object. The 'env lifetime is for any borrowed values. For that reason, the lifetime of 'scope cannot outlive 'env.

Scoped threads are shown in Listing 18.7. The scoped thread borrows the count value as a mutable reference. This can be done directly with a scoped thread—no move keyword is necessary.

Code Listing 18.7.   Creating scoped threads

```
fn main() {
    let mut count = 0;       // 'env
    thread::scope(|s| {      // 'scope
        s.spawn(|| {
            count+=1;
        });
        println!("{}", count);
}
```

The Thread Type

The Thread type is a handle to a thread. In addition, it is also an obfuscated type and managed via functions. As such, thread objects are not created directly but rather with either the thread::spawn or Builder::spawn function. More about the Builder type shortly.

Quite often a thread does not have a handle to itself. Having that handle would allow the thread to manage itself. Fortunately, the Thread::current function returns a handle to the current thread. You can then use the handle to call various functions that manipulate or get the status of the thread.

In this example, we get a handle to the current thread. The handle is then used to display information about the thread.

Code Listing 18.8.   Getting the current thread to display information

```
use std::thread;

fn main() {
    let current_thread=thread::current();
    println!("{:?}", current_thread.id()); // ThreadId(1)
    println!("{:?}", current_thread.name()); // Some("main")
}
```

The thread::id function returns a ThreadId, which is an opaque type. It is the unique identifier for a thread for the entirety of the process. The ThreadId is not reused when the thread expires. The name function returns the thread name as a string, within a Result type. For unnamed threads, the default is the name of the entry-point function. If initiated with a closure, the thread starts unnamed.

Processor Time

Running threads share processor time. Different operating environments have various scheduling algorithms. Most modern operating systems use preemptive scheduling where running threads are preempted after a time slice. Threads can also voluntarily yield their remaining time slice, with the `thread::yield_now` function, in order to be more cooperative. That may allow a different thread an opportunity to receive processor time.

In addition, a thread can be asked to sleep for a designated duration. While sleeping, a thread will not receive processor time. This is often done to synchronize or otherwise coordinate the execution of a thread. Alternatively, maybe the thread simply has nothing to do. The `thread::sleep` function forces a thread to sleep for at least the designated duration. The Duration type has the following functions to specify time with different granularity:

- `duration::as_micros`: microseconds
- `duration::as_millis`: milliseconds
- `duration::as_nanos`: nanoseconds
- `duration::as_secs`: seconds

For the next example, Listing 18.9, we demonstrate the `sleep` function. In the `for`, two threads are created using information provide in an array of tuples. Each `tuple` provides the thread name and a sleep duration. For each thread, we count from 1 to 4 while displaying the result and the current count. At the end of each loop, the thread sleeps the sleep duration, as identified in the duration field of the tuple. The final `sleep` function, outside the `while`, mitigates any race condition.

Code Listing 18.9.   Pausing threads using the sleep function

```
use std::thread;
use std::time::Duration;

fn main() {

    for (name, duration) in [("T2", 50), ("T3", 20) ]{
        thread::spawn(move ||{
            let mut n=1;
            while n < 5 {
                println!("{} {}", name, n);
                n=n+1;
                thread::sleep(Duration::from_millis(duration));
            }
        });
    }

    thread::sleep(Duration::from_secs(3));

}
```

Various operating systems provide lower-level support for blocking, called a spinlock. Spinlocks, a thread continuously "spins" the thread, while wasting time, until the synchronization resource is available. This is typically more efficient when there is low contention. Synchronization with other components, such as mutexes and semaphores, can be more expensive than a spinlock.

The Thread::park function initiates a spinlock and effectively blocks the current thread. There is a token associated with each thread. The park function blocks until the token is available or otherwise released, such as a timeout. The unpark method unparks the parked thread (releases the spinlock). The park_timeout parks a thread for an indicated duration. If the thread is not unparked before the timeout, it is awakened.

In Listing 18.10, we model a retail store. The store_open function has a thread that emulates handling customers. However, some setup must occur, such as disabling the alarm and unlocking the registers, before the store can open. For that reason, the thread for opening the store is parked initially. In main, after the setup is completed, the store_open thread is unparked to begin handling customers.

Code Listing 18.10. Demonstrating how to park threads using a store analogy

```rust
use std::thread;
use std::time::Duration;
use std::thread::Thread;

fn store_open()-> Thread {
    thread::spawn(|| {
        thread::park();
        loop {
            println!("open and handling customers");
            //  hopefully, lots of sales
        }
    }).thread().clone()
}

fn main() {
    let open=store_open();

    // Do setup
    disable_alarm();
    open_registers();

    open.unpark();

    thread::sleep(Duration::from_secs(2));  // arbitrary wait
}
```

Builder

At the moment, threads have two configurable attributes: the thread name and the stack size. The thread name is a String type. For the stack size, you specify the number of bytes. You may configure these attributes using the Builder type. Afterwards, you can spawn the thread with the `Builder::spawn` method, which returns a `Result<JoinHandle<T>>`. You have to unwrap the Result to obtain the JoinHandle for the new thread.

The `Builder::name` function sets the name of the thread. This can be especially helpful when you're debugging an application. Thread IDs are not consistent across processes, making them less than ideal for debugging.

The initial stack size for a thread is operating system specific. Managing the stack size can improve performance and reduce the memory footprint of a process. In addition, this can increase scalability. For Rust, you can set the stack size for any thread, except the primary thread, which is dependent on the operating environment. If desired, you can set the default stack size for every thread using the RUST_MIN_STACK environment variable. This can also be done programmatically, for a single thread, with the `Builder::stack_size` function.

Both the `Builder::name` and `Builder::stack_size` functions return a Builder. This allows for the daisy chaining of these function calls.

In Listing 18.11, a Builder is used to set the thread name and stack size. Afterwards, the builder is used to spawn a new thread. Within the thread, the thread name is displayed.

Code Listing 18.11.   Setting the thread name and stack size

```
use std::thread;
use std::thread::Builder;

fn main() {
    let builder = Builder::new()
        .name("Thread1".to_string())
        .stack_size(4096);
    let result = builder.spawn(|| {
        let thread = thread::current();
        println!("{}", thread.name().unwrap());
    });

    let handle=result.unwrap();
    let result=handle.join();
}
```

Communicating Sequential Process

The Communicating Sequential Process (CSP) defines a threading model where threads communicate through a synchronous message-passing object that implements a FIFO queue. In 1978, Charles Antony Richard Hoare wrote a seminal article on communicating sequential processes (CSP) for the ACM (Association for Computing Machinery), aptly name *Communicating Sequential Processes*. CSP defines a threading model where threads exchange messages through a message-passing object. In addition to Rust, several modern languages, such as Golang and Scala, also implement the CSP model as channels.

In Rust, a channel is a conduit between threads, with two halves. There is a sender half and a receiver half. The sender sends information through a channel. Conversely, a receiver receives information from the channel. The sender and receiver are opposite halves of the same channel. If either becomes invalid, communication through the channel will fail. Finally, channels adhere to a multiple producers and single consumer model. Every channel has a single receiver but can have multiple senders.

Support for thread synchronization is found at the `std::sync` module in the standard library, including mutexes, locks, and channels. There are various types of channels, including:

- `Sender`: this is an asynchronous channel
- `SyncSender`: this is a synchronous channel

Asynchronous Channel

Asynchronous channels are unbounded, with theoretically an infinite queue. Senders never block when sending data to the channel. For this reason, you never know when a receiver actually receives data from a channel. It could be immediately, or even never. The channel will only block if the receiver attempts to receive data from an empty channel.

The `mpsc::channel` function creates an asynchronous channel:

```
fn channel<T>() -> (Sender<T>, Receiver<T>)
```

The function returns both halves of the channel as a tuple: (`Sender<T>`, `Receiver<T>`). Type parameter `T` indicates the kind of data allowed into the channel. The `Sender` inserts data into the channel. This is done with the `Sender::send` function. For multiple senders, you clone the `Sender`. The `Receiver` type represents the receiver. The `Receiver::recv` function receives data from the channel.

Here are the important methods for an asynchronous channel.

```
fn Receiver::recv(&self) -> Result<T, RecvError>
fn Sender::send(&self, t: T) -> Result<(), SendError<T>>
```

Listing 18.12 is a simple example of a working asynchronous channel. First, an asynchronous channel is created with the `mpsc::channel` function. The function returns a tuple that can be destructured into a `Sender` and `Receiver` value, both sides of the channel. In separate threads, send is called to insert an integer into the channel, while recv is called to receive data from the channel. The `recv` function will block until data is inserted into the channel.

Code Listing 18.12. Inserting and reading an asynchronous channel

```
use std::sync::mpsc;
use std::thread;

fn main() {
    let (sender, receiver) = mpsc::channel();
    thread::spawn(move || {
        sender.send(1);
```

```
    });

    let data=receiver.recv().unwrap();
    println!("{}", data);
}
```

Next is another example of an asynchronous channel but with multiple producers. In Listing 18.13, we create an asynchronous channel with the channel function. The return value is destructured to obtain handles to both sides of the channel. For multiple producers, the Sender side is then cloned. In separate threads, the senders write into the same channel. In an additional thread, the Receiver reads data from the channel using a while let expression. The while let will end when both Senders are dropped.

Code Listing 18.13. Inserting and receiving data from an asynchronous channel

```
use std::sync::mpsc::channel;
use std::thread;

fn main() {
    let (sender1, receiver) = channel();
    let sender2=sender1.clone();

    thread::spawn(move || {
        for i in 0..=5 {
            sender1.send(i);
        }
    });

    thread::spawn(move || {
        for i in 10..=15 {
            sender2.send(i);
        }
    });

    let handle = thread::spawn(move || {
        while let Ok(n) = receiver.recv() {
            println!("{}", n);
        }
    });

    handle.join();
}
```

If either half of a channel becomes disconnected, the channel becomes unusable. This can occur when either the Sender or Receiver is dropped for a channel. When that occurs, you will be unable to insert data until the channel. However, you are still allowed to read any remaining data from the channel.

In Listing 18.14, we create an asynchronous channel, with the requisite Sender and Receiver. After inserting an integer in the channel, the Sender is quickly dropped. The channel immediately becomes unusable. You are allowed to receive the item inserted into the channel. However, the next attempt (second) to receive data from the channel creates a panic. This is because the channel is unusable and empty.

Code Listing 18.14. **Attempting to use an unusable channel**

```
use std::sync::mpsc;
use std::thread;
use std::time::Duration;

fn main() {
    let (sender, receiver) = mpsc::channel();
    thread::spawn(move || {
        sender.send(1);
    }); // sender dropped

    let data = receiver.recv().unwrap();
    println!("Received {}", data);

    thread::sleep(Duration::from_secs(1));
    let data = receiver.recv().unwrap(); // panic on error
}
```

Here is the error message from the panic:

```
thread 'main' panicked at 'called
    `Result::unwrap()` on an `Err` value: RecvError',
    src\main.rs:15:30
note: run with `RUST_BACKTRACE=1`
    environment variable to display a backtrace
error: process didn't exit successfully:
    `target\debug\sync_channel3.exe` (exit code: 101)
```

Synchronous Channel

Synchronous channels are bounded per a size limit. This is unlike asynchronous channels, which are unbounded and infinite in size. Synchronous channels are preferred in scenarios where a specific capacity is beneficial. For example, if implementing a message pump, you may want to limit the number of messages in the message queue as an efficiency.

The `mpsc::sync_channel` function creates a synchronous channel:

```
fn sync_channel<T>(bound: usize) -> (SyncSender<T>, Receiver<T>)
```

The bound parameter sets the maximum size of the channel. You cannot have more than that number of items in the channel. The return value is a tuple that provides both halves of the synchronous channel: sender and receiver. The sender is `SyncSender` and the `SyncSender::send` function inserts data into the channel. For a synchronous channel, the send function blocks if the channel is at capacity. It remains blocked until another thread receives from the channel, reducing the number of items in the channel. The receiver half of the channel is `Receiver`. This is the same `Receiver` used with asynchronous channels. `Receiver::recv` receives data from the channel and blocks if the channel is empty.

Here is the syntax for `SyncSender::send`:

```
fn send(&self, t: T) -> Result<(), SendError<T>>
```

In Listing 18.15, we create a synchronous channel. A new thread is created to write into the channel. The main thread reads from the channel.

Code Listing 18.15.   Inserting and receiving data from a synchronous channel

```
use std::sync::mpsc;
use std::thread;
use std::time::Duration;

fn main() {
    let (sender, receiver) = mpsc::sync_channel(1);
    let handle=thread::spawn(move || {
        sender.send(1);
        println!("Sent 1");
        sender.send(2);
        println!("Sent 2");
    });

    let data=receiver.recv().unwrap();
    println!("Received {}", data);
    handle.join();
}
```

The sync_channel function is called to create a synchronous channel, with a capacity of one item. Both halves of the channel are returned as a tuple and bound to sender (SyncSender) and receiver (Receiver) respectively. Next, a new thread is spawned. The spawned thread captures sender and calls the send function to insert a couple of items into the channel. Because of the bound size, only the first item is initially delivered. Back in main, the recv function is called on the receiver. This removes an item from the channel and allows the other thread to insert the second item into the channel. The join function is called to allow the spawned thread an opportunity to finish.

Note that a second item was placed into the channel but never delivered. For some applications, this could be a problem.

Rendezvous Channel

Rendezvous channels have guaranteed delivery. This resolves the problem just described—knowing when an item in a channel has been delivered. A rendezvous channel is a synchronous channel with a bound size of 0. For a rendezvous channel, the SyncSender::send function is blocking. The function will unblock after the inserted item has been received. That is considered your notification of guaranteed delivery.

In Listing 18.16, we create a rendezvous channel. We then spawn a thread. In that thread, the send method is called to insert an item into the channel. The send function will block and wait for that item to be received. In main, after an arbitrary time, the recv function is called to remove the item from the channel. This will unblock the currently blocked send function as confirmation of guaranteed delivery. The Instant type is not required but used to confirm the wait time.

Code Listing 18.16. Using a rendezvous channel

```
use std::sync::mpsc;
use std::thread;
use std::time::{Duration, Instant};

fn main() {
    let (sender, receiver) = mpsc::sync_channel(0);
    let handle = thread::spawn(move || {
        println!("SyncSender - before send");
        let start = Instant::now();
        sender.send(1);
        let elapsed = start.elapsed();
        println!("After send - waited {} seconds",
            elapsed.as_secs());
    });

    thread::sleep(Duration::from_secs(10));
    receiver.recv();
    handle.join();
}
```

Here is the result of the application:

```
SyncSender - before send
After send - waited 10 seconds
```

The try Methods

Senders can block! This occurs when there is an attempt to insert data into a channel that is at capacity. As an alternative, you might prefer a notification. This is the behavior of the try_send method. The method returns a TrySendError, as a form of notification, if the channel is full. This allows the thread to do something else, instead of blocking, while a channel is at capacity. Here is the definition of the try_send method:

```
fn try_send(&self, t: T) -> Result<(), TrySendError<T>>
```

Listing 18.17 demonstrates the `try_send` function. We create a synchronous channel with a capacity of two items. The `send` function is then called twice to put the channel to capacity. The `try_send` attempts to add a third item to the full channel. Instead of blocking, the function returns an Err result and continues execution. The unwrap_err function is called to check for an error. You will get an error message indicating the channel is full.

Code Listing 18.17.   Responding to a full synchronous channel

```
use std::sync::mpsc;
use std::thread;

fn main() {
    let (sender, receiver) = mpsc::sync_channel(2);
    sender.send(1);
    sender.send(2);
    let result=sender.try_send(3).unwrap_err();
    println!("{:?}", result);  // Full(..)
    println!("Continuing ...")
}
```

The receiver can block also! This occurs when the channel is empty and the `recv` function is called. It will remain blocked until a `Sender` inserts an item into the channel. At that time, recv unblocks and receives the item from the channel. The `try_recv` function, shown next, is a nonblocking alternative. When the channel is empty, the `try_recv` function receives an Err result. This allows the receiver thread to continue executing when it would otherwise be blocked.

```
fn try_recv(&self) -> Result<T, TryRecvError>
```

Performing *idle work* is a valid use case for the `try_recv` method. The thread has an opportunity to perform work when it would normally be idle (i.e., blocked).

There are two common scenarios for idle work:

- Completing work in stages. Resource cleanup is an excellent example. You might perform resource cleanup at the end of an application, which is time-consuming. However, you can begin resource cleanup during idle time. That reduces the effort required at the end of the program.
- Conversely, idle work is useful for low-priority or optional tasks. This work can be done when there is nothing better to do, such as executing user interface handlers.

Next is an example of the `try_recv` method. For this example, the channel is a message queue. The sender inserts messages into the message queue. In the message pump, the receiver receives and handles messages from the message queue. When the message queue is empty, the receiver can perform idle work.

The sender portion of the application is shown in Listing 18.18. We create the message queue as a synchronous channel, which is limited to ten messages. A separate thread is created for sending messages. To name the thread ("Messages"), a `Builder` type is used to spawn the thread. The thread captures the sender for the message queue (channel). Lastly, in a for, a few messages are inserted in the message queue.

Code Listing 18.18. Using a synchronous channel as a message queue

```
let (sender, receiver) = mpsc::sync_channel(10);
let builder = Builder::new()
    .name("Messages".to_string())
    .stack_size(4096);
let result = builder.spawn(move || {
    let messages=["message 1".to_string(),
                  "message 2".to_string(),
                  "message 3".to_string(),
                  "".to_string()];
    for message in messages {
        sender.send(message);
    }
});
```

Next, Listing 18.19 implements a thread for the message pump. It receives and handles messages placed into the message. Remember, the message queue is implemented as a channel. Another thread, named "Message Pump," is required to accept messages from the message queue. It is created using a Builder. The receiver is then captured in this thread. Within loop, the try_recv function is called to receive the next message in the message queue. The match expression interprets the result. In the Ok arm, the next message is handled. An empty message instructs the application to exit. When the message queue is empty, the Err arm is chosen. It will call the idle_work function, where idle work is performed.

Code Listing 18.19. Implementing an idle loop using try_recv

```
let builder = Builder::new()
    .name("Message Pump".to_string())
    .stack_size(4096);
let result = builder.spawn(move || ->i8 {
    loop {
        match receiver.try_recv() {
            Ok(msg)=>{
                if msg.len()==0 {
                    break 0;
                }
                println!("Handling {}", msg);
            }
            Err(_)=>idle_work(),

        }
    }
});
```

Listing 18.20 is the full application:

Code Listing 18.20.   **Complete message pump example**

```rust
use std::sync::mpsc;
use std::thread;
use std::time::Duration;
use std::thread::Builder;

fn idle_work() {
    println!("Doing something else...")
}

fn main(){
    let (sender, receiver) = mpsc::sync_channel(10);
    let builder = Builder::new()
        .name("Messages".to_string())
        .stack_size(4096);
    let result = builder.spawn(move || {
        let messages=["message 1".to_string(),
                      "message 2".to_string(),
                      "message 3".to_string(),
                      "".to_string()];
        for message in messages {
            sender.send(message);
                thread::sleep(Duration::from_millis(2));
        }
    });

    let builder = Builder::new()
        .name("Message Pump".to_string())
        .stack_size(4096);
    let result = builder.spawn(move || ->i8 {
        loop {
            match receiver.try_recv() {
                Ok(msg)=>{
                    if msg.len()==0 {
                        break 0;
                    }
                    println!("Handling {}", msg);
                }
                Err(_)=>idle_work(),

            }
        }
    });

    let handle=result.unwrap();
    handle.join();
}
```

The recv_timeout function is another alternative to the recv. Both recv_timeout and recv functions block if a channel is empty. However, the recv_timeout function will awaken when a specified timeout is exceeded. When this occurs, recv_timeout returns RecvTimeoutError as the Err result. Here is the function definition:

```
fn recv_timeout(&self, timeout: Duration) ->
Result<T, RecvTimeoutError>
```

The example in Listing 18.21 has a RecvTimeoutError error. We create a new channel and thread, as the sender. The thread sleeps for 200 milliseconds before inserting an item into the channel, with the send function. The main thread is the receiver. It receives items from the channel using the recv_timeout method, and sets the timeout to 100 milliseconds. This is less than the wait in the sender thread, before inserting an item in the channel. Because of this, the recv_timeout method will eventually time out and unblock the receiver thread. The subsequent match expression handles the Err return, displaying the timeout message.

Code Listing 18.21.   Handing a timeout for the recv_timeout function

```
use std::sync::mpsc;
use std::time::Duration;
use std::thread;

fn main() {
    let (sender, receiver) = mpsc::sync_channel(1);
    thread::spawn(move || {
        thread::sleep(Duration::from_millis(200));
        sender.send(1);
    });

    let data = receiver.recv_timeout(
        Duration::from_millis(100)); // wait
    match data {
        Ok(value)=>println!("Data received: {}", value),
        Err(_)=>println!("Timed out: no data received")
    }
}
```

You can also receive items from a channel, as an iterator. This gives you the convenience of a well-known interface. In addition, as an iterator, channels are more extensible, thus expanding the use cases where channels are available. With the iter method, Receiver can request an iterator for a channel. The functions of the iterator, such as next, can then be used to access items in the channel.

Listing 18.22 is a simple example of accessing a channel using an iterator. Using the receiver, the iter function is called to obtain the iterator for the channel. The next function is then called repeatedly to iterate the items in the channel.

Code Listing 18.22.   Accessing a channel using an iterator

```
use std::sync::mpsc;
use std::thread;

fn main() {
    let (sender, receiver) = mpsc::sync_channel(4);

    sender.send(1);
    sender.send(2);
    sender.send(3);

    let mut iter=receiver.iter();
    println!("{}", iter.next().unwrap());
    println!("{}", iter.next().unwrap());
    println!("{}", iter.next().unwrap());
}
```

As mentioned, as an iterator, channels are more extensible. You can even iterate a channel using a for as an example.

In Listing 18.23, a new thread is created that inserts two items into a channel. In main, the for iterates the Receiver to get the items in the channel. This is possible because Receiver implements the Iterator interface. The for loop stops iterating when there are no remaining items and the channel is unusable. For the next example, this occurs when the sender is dropped.

Code Listing 18.23.   Iterating a channel in a for loop

```
use std::sync::mpsc;
use std::thread;

fn main() {
    let (sender, receiver) = mpsc::channel();

    thread::spawn(||{
        sender.send(1);
        sender.send(2);
    });   // sender dropped

    for item in receiver {
        println!("{}", item);
    }
}
```

Store Example

Earlier in the chapter, an example was presented that emulated a store opening. The updated version, presented here, both opens and closes the store. This example demonstrates many of the threading features introduced in this chapter.

Let's start with a review of each portion of the revised program, beginning with `main`, in Listing 18.24. In `main`, we create an asynchronous channel with the `channel` function. The channel is used as a notification that the store is closing. When an item is sent to the channel, the store should close. For that reason, the receiver is named *closing*.

Code Listing 18.24.   Main function for the store application

```
fn main() {
    let (sender, closing) = channel::<()>();

    store_open(closing);

    thread::sleep(Duration::from_secs(2));

    store_closing(sender);
}
```

The `store_open` function manages opening the store, as presented in Listing 18.25. The closing channel is provided as the function argument. Within the function, a separate thread is created to handle this operation. Within the thread, prepping for opening the store, turning off the alarm system, and opening the registers can be done in parallel. For that reason, these tasks are spawned as separate threads. With the `join` method, we wait for the prepping to complete. After the prepping, the store is finally opened! Afterwards, the loop represents the continuous handling of customers. Inside the loop is a match expression that checks if the store should close, per closing channel. The `try_recv` method checks the closing channel. If data is received from the closing channel, that is an indication to begin closing the store, which is done at the `Ok` arm. Otherwise, the default arm is chosen and the store remains open and handling customers.

Code Listing 18.25.   Showing the store_open function

```
fn store_open(closing:Receiver<()>) {
    thread::spawn(move || {
        // Opening setup
        let alarms=thread::spawn(
            || println!("turning off alarm"));
        let registers=thread::spawn(
            || println!("open registers"));
        alarms.join();
        registers.join();

        // Store fully open - handling customers
        loop {
            match closing.try_recv() {
                Ok(_)=> {
                    println!("cleaning up and exiting...");
                    break;
                },
```

```
                      _=>{
                          println!("open and handling customers");
                          thread::sleep(Duration::from_secs(1));
                      }
                  }
              }
          });
      }
```

In Listing 18.26, the store_closing function is presented. The function accepts a Sender as the function argument. This is the sender half of the closing channel. The first step is sending a value to the closing channel. It could be anything. However, the empty tuple is chosen here. This notifies the open thread, implemented in the store_open function, to exit (i.e., stop handling customers). The sleep function gives the open thread an opportunity to clean up and then exit. Next, the alarms are reenabled and the registers are closed as separate threads. We wait for them to complete. Now the store is closed!

Code Listing 18.26.   Showing the store_closing function

```
fn store_closing(sender:Sender<()>){
    sender.send(());  // notification of the store closing
    thread::sleep(Duration::from_millis(300));
    let alarms=thread::spawn(|| {
        println!("turning on alarms");
    });
    let registers=thread::spawn(|| {
        println!("closing registers");
    });

    alarms.join();
    registers.join();
    println!("Store closed!");
}
```

The entire application is presented in Listing 18.27.

Code Listing 18.27.   Entire store application

```
use std::thread;
use std::time::Duration;
use std::sync::mpsc::{channel, Receiver,
Sender, TryRecvError};

fn store_open(closing:Receiver<()>) {
    thread::spawn(move || {
        // Opening setup
        let alarms=thread::spawn(
        || println!("turning off alarm"));
```

```
            let registers=thread::spawn(
                || println!("open registers"));
            alarms.join();
            registers.join();

            // Store fully open - handling customers
            loop {
                match closing.try_recv() {
                    Ok(_)=> {
                        println!("cleaning up and exiting...");
                        break;
                    },
                    _=>{
                        println!("open and handling customers");
                        thread::sleep(Duration::from_secs(1));
                    }
                }
            }
        });
}

fn store_closing(sender:Sender<()>){
    sender.send(());
    thread::sleep(Duration::from_millis(300));
    let alarms=thread::spawn(|| {
        println!("turning on alarms");
    });
    let registers=thread::spawn(|| {
        println!("closing registers");
    });

    alarms.join();
    registers.join();
    println!("Store closed!");
}

fn main() {
    let (sender, closing) = channel::<()>();

    store_open(closing);

    thread::sleep(Duration::from_secs(2));

    store_closing(sender);
}
```

Summary

Threads are unique paths of execution within a process. With threads, you can decompose a process into parallel operations. Threads have become an essential feature because of the prevalence of multicore architecture processors and the demand for scalable and responsive applications.

Fearless concurrency helps mitigate the added complexity that parallel threading undoubtedly will introduce. Despite this, as a best practice, you should only add threads when needed.

In Rust, most of the ingredients for threads are found in the thread module. In that module, you will find the Thread type, which is a handle to a thread. In addition, the `thread::spawn` function creates new threads. Alternatively, you can use the Builder type and the `Builder::spawn` method. With Builder, you can configure the thread, such as setting the stack size, before starting it.

The `JoinHandle::join` function helps coordinate the actions of two threads, where a thread can wait for another to complete. Both the `thread::spawn` and `builder::spawn` functions return a JoinHandle. For `builder::spawn`, the JoinHandle is returned within the Result value.

Lambdas are the most common type of function for a thread. You pass data into the thread as a captured variable. Since the lifetime of threads is unknown, the ownership of captured variables should be transferred into the lambda with the `move` keyword.

Channels are one-way conduits between threads for exchanging data, such as the result of an operation. There are different kinds of channels:

- Asynchronous channels are unbounded. They can hold an unlimited number of items and are created with the `channel` function.
- Synchronous channels are bounded and limited to a specific size. They are created with the `sync_channel` function.
- Rendezvous channels are synchronous channels with guaranteed delivery. For this type of channel, the bound size is zero.

Channels have a sender half and a receiver half. The sender sends data to the channel. The receiver receives data from the channel. Here are the related types:

- **Sender** sends data to the asynchronous channel.
- **SyncSender** sends data to a synchronous channel.
- **Receiver** receives data from either type of channel.

`Receiver` has various recv methods that support different use cases. For example, `try_recv` does not block if a channel is empty.

We concluded the chapter with the store application. In that application, the channel is used also as a notification event. Some may consider that an inelegant solution. Other synchronization objects, such as a `CondVar`, may offer a more elegant solution and are discussed in the next chapter.

19

Threads 2

Parallel programming with threads was introduced in the previous chapter. In many ways, the threads within a process are similar to multiple family members living in a house. They must share and often inadvertently compete for resources within the home. This can lead to conflicts and unpredictable behavior if not properly coordinated. Similarly, there is sometimes a need for thread synchronization. The conversation of thread synchronization began in the previous chapter with the discussion of the `join` function and channels. Both of these provide coordination between threads.

Adding essential synchronization contributes to a safe environment that promotes increased parallelization. You can confidently add layers of parallelization without the worry of threads literally crashing into each other. However, over-synchronization can increase the complexity of an application and lessen performance.

Parallel programming is inherently more complex than sequential programming. When problems occur, there is the tendency to add synchronization for more predictable results. When this is repeated, resolving problems by synchronization creates significant technical debt. Eventually, you will have essentially a sequential program running under the guise of a parallel application. Synchronization is often justified and sometimes required. However, remember to keep parallel programs *parallel*.

Starting with your first application, typically a "Hello, World"–style application, you may have already experienced thread synchronization. The `println!` macro is often used to display the greeting. The macro is made safe with an internal mutex. Without this synchronization, multiple threads could use `println!` macro at the same time, causing unpredictable results.

Mutex

Mutex is the most well-known synchronization primitive. It provides mutually exclusive access to data that has shared ownership. As such, "mutex" is an abbreviation of *mutual exclusion*. By using mutexes, you can prevent threads from accessing shared data at the same time. Without synchronization, shared access may cause unpredictable results especially with mutable data. With the Mutex, access to the data is serialized to eliminate these sorts of problems. In this manner, a Mutex guards shared data.

Mutexes can be locked or unlocked. When locked, a Mutex enforces the mutual exclusion concurrency policy. The thread that owns the lock can exclusively access the data, providing thread safeness. At the same time, another thread (or threads) will block when attempting to acquire a lock for the already locked Mutex. When the Mutex is unlocked, a waiting thread may acquire the lock. If it's successful, the blocked thread is awakened and can access the shared data.

The Mutex lock has thread affinity. When locked, it must be unlocked from the same thread. This prevents another thread from stealing access to the Mutex. Imagine the chaos! Any thread, wanting the Mutex, could simply unlock it and access the guarded value. Fortunately, this is prevented in Rust because there is no unlock function! More about this later.

In many languages, mutexes are about the proper placement of functions in source code. When accessing guarded data, you must bracket that data with a lock and unlock from a Mutex. The correctness of the synchronization is therefore based solely on programmer discipline—placing the Mutex in the correct location. This can be a greater problem during refactoring when the guarded data or any Mutex can be inadvertently moved or even removed. For these reasons, Rust takes a different approach and directly associates the guarded data with a Mutex. This direct correlation prevents the sort of problems that occur in other languages.

The `Mutex<T>` type is an implementation of a mutex. It is found in the `std::sync` module, as with other synchronization components. Mutex is generic over type T, where T represents the guarded data.

You create a new Mutex with the `Mutex::new` constructor, which is also generic over type T. The sole parameter is the data being guarded. Here is the function definition:

```
fn new(t: T) -> Mutex<T>
```

The `Mutex::lock` function locks the Mutex for exclusive access to the guarded data. If the Mutex is unlocked, you can acquire the lock and continue execution. When the Mutex is already locked, the current thread will block until the lock can be acquired.

```
    fn lock(&self) -> LockResult<MutexGuard<'_, T>>
```

The `lock` function returns a MutexGuard. It implements the Deref trait that provides access to the inner value, the guarded data. The MutexGuard is the guaranty that the current thread can access the data safely. Importantly, when the MutexGuard is dropped, the Mutex is automatically unlocked. This is the reason an unlock function is not necessary.

Listing 19.1 is a single-threaded example of locking, accessing the guarded data, and unlocking a Mutex. The Mutex is created in an inner block and guards an integer value, initialized to zero. After locking the Mutex, we dereference the MutexGuard, with the * operator, to access the guarded data, an integer in this example.. The data is incremented and then displayed. The MutexGuard is dropped at the end of the inner block. This causes the Mutex to be unlocked.

Code Listing 19.1.   Locking and unlocking a Mutex

```
use std::sync::{Mutex};

fn main() {
    {
        let mutex=Mutex::new(0);
        let mut guard=mutex.lock().unwrap();
```

```
            *guard+=1;
            println!("{}", *guard);
        }  // mutex unlocked
    }
```

Listing 19.2 is an example of using a Mutex with multiple threads. To easily share the Mutex, scoped threads are used, which were introduced in the previous chapter. We spawn two threads that share the same code base. The Mutex protects access to an integer value across them. The goal is to safely increment and display the guarded value.

Code Listing 19.2.   With a Mutex, guarding a value across multiple threads

```
use std::thread;
use std::sync::Mutex;

fn main() {
    let m=Mutex::new(0);
    thread::scope(|scope|{
        for count in 1..=2 {
            scope.spawn(||{
                let mut guard=mutex1.lock().unwrap();
                *guard+=1;
                 println!("{:?} Data {}",
                     thread::current().id(), *guard )[]
            });
        }
    });
}
```

You can inadvertently leak a Mutex. A Mutex remains locked for the lifetime of the MutexGuard. If the MutexGuard is never dropped, or simply delayed, the Mutex remains unavailable to other threads, which can cause deadlocks. When this occurs, the Mutex is considered leaked. This may occur for a variety of reasons, including poor management of the MutexGuard. In Listing 19.3, the Mutex is locked potentially for an extended period of time.

Code Listing 19.3.   Lifetime of a MutexGuard controls the Mutex

```
    let mut hello=String::from("Hello");
    let mutex=Mutex::new(&mut hello);
    {
        let mut guard=mutex.lock().unwrap();
        guard.push_str(", world!");
        // something time-consuming, pending threads waiting
    }  // mutex unlocked
```

The example in Listing 19.4 is practically the same code. However, the MutexGuard is not bound to a variable. This means the MutexGuard is temporary and dropped immediately at the next source line. At that time, the Mutex is unlocked. We are no longer waiting until the end of the block to unlock the Mutex.

Code Listing 19.4.   Dropping a MutexGuard almost immediately

```
let mut hello=String::from("Hello");
let mutex=Mutex::new(&mut hello);
{
    (*mutex.lock().unwrap()).push_str(", world!");
    // guard dropped - mutex unlocked
    // something time-consuming

}
```

Finally, you can explicitly drop the MutexGuard to unlock the Mutex.

In Listing 19.5, the MutexGuard is dropped explicitly and the Mutex unlocked prior to starting an extended task. This means other waiting threads, if any, resume execution sooner. This could result in a major performance gain.

Code Listing 19.5.   Explicitly dropping a MutexGuard and unlocking a Mutex

```
{
    let mutex=Mutex::new(0);
    let mut guard=mutex.lock().unwrap();
    *guard+=1;
    drop(guard);   // mutex unlocked
    do_something_extended();
}
```

Nonscoped Mutex

You can share a Mutex with nonscoped threads as well. The Arc type is the best solution for sharing mutexes in this manner.

Ownership is a frequent and important topic in this book. Multithreaded applications often require *shared* ownership, where multiple threads share the ownership of data. The Arc type supports shared ownership where the number of owners is tracked with reference counting. When the final shared owner (i.e., thread) exits, the count drops to zero. At that time, the shared data is dropped. The reference counting is performed atomically to protect against race conditions or corruption of the reference count.

The Arc type is found in the std::sync module. You create a new Arc with the Arc::new constructor. The only parameter is the shared data. Here is the function definition:

```
fn new(data: T) -> Arc<T>
```

You clone the Arc to share with other threads. The reference count increases with every clone. In addition, Arc implements the Deref trait to provide access to the inner value.

Listing 19.6 is an example of the Arc type.

Code Listing 19.6.   Shared ownership using an Arc

```
use std::sync::Arc;
use std::thread;

fn main() {
    let arc_orig=Arc::new(1);
    let arc_clone=arc_orig.clone();
    let handle=thread::spawn(move || {
        println!("{}", arc_clone);  // Deref
    });

    println!("{}", arc_orig);  // Deref

    handle.join();
}
```

In the preceding example, the primary thread creates a new Arc for an integer value. The Arc is then cloned and the reference count incremented. The cloned Arc is then moved to another thread. Now both threads share the data. The `println!` macro for both threads automatically dereferences the Arc to display the underlying value. Because the value is shared, the threads display the same result.

The last example had two Arcs: `arc_orig` and `arc_clone`. Naming can become a problem as the number of threads sharing the Arc increases. This can lead to Arcs named arc1, arc2, arc3, arc4, and so on. A better solution is sharing the same name for the Arc across threads. This can be done by shadowing the name, as shown in Listing 19.7.

Code Listing 19.7.   Shadowing an Arc name

```
let arc=Arc::new(1);
{  // new block
    let arc=arc.clone();
    let handle=thread::spawn(move || {
        println!("{}", arc);  // Deref
    });
    handle.join();
}  // end block

println!("{}", arc);
```

It's important to realize that the Arc provides referencing counting for shared ownership, but it is not a `Mutex`. Arc does not synchronize access to data. However, Arcs are great for sharing mutexes with nonscoped threads. The Arc shares the Mutex, while the Mutex protects the data.

The example in Listing 19.8 demonstrates sharing a Mutex via an Arc.

Code Listing 19.8.   Sharing a Mutex using an Arc

```
use std::thread;
use std::sync::{Mutex, Arc};

fn main() {
    let arc_mutex = Arc::new(Mutex::new(0));
    let mut handles=vec![];

    for i in 0..=2 {
        let arc_mutex=Arc::clone(&arc_mutex);
        let handle=thread::spawn(move || {
            let mut guard=arc_mutex.lock().unwrap();
            *guard+=1;
            println!("{}", *guard);              });
        handles.push(handle);
    }

    for i in handles {
        i.join();
    }
}
```

In this example, the Mutex guards an integer value. The Mutex is shared using an Arc, arc_mutex. In addition, a vector is created to store the JoinHandles from the spawned threads.

New threads are spawned in the for. Each thread captures a cloned version of the Arc, arc_mutex. The arc_mutex is then locked to synchronize access to the integer value. If the lock is acquired, the MutexGuard is returned. It is dereferenced to access the inner value, which is then incremented. After the for, in a subsequent for loop, Join is called on each JoinHandle to prevent any race conditions.

Mutex Poisoning

A Mutex becomes poisoned when a panic is raised on the thread where the Mutex is locked, and the MutexGuard is dropped. At that time, the state of the underlying data is undetermined. For this reason, attempts to lock the Mutex will return an error. Poisoning the Mutex forces the application to recognize the potential problem. However, you can decide how to handle the problem, even ignoring the problem, but the status is "buyer beware."

As mentioned, locking a poisoned Mutex returns an Err for the Result. Specifically, it returns PoisonError. The PoisonError::into_inner function returns the MutexGuard for the poisoned Mutex. You can then access the underlying data as usual, if desired.

In Listing 19.9, the first spawned thread will panic and drop the MutexGuard. Consequently, the second thread receives an error when locking the Mutex. We handle the result within a match expression. If there is an error, the into_inner function is used to access the underlying value, which is potentially corrupted. In this example, we simply display the value.

Code Listing 19.9.   Handling a poisoned Mutex

```
use std::thread;
use std::sync::{Mutex, Arc};
use std::time::Duration;

fn main() {

    let arc_mutex = Arc::new(Mutex::new(0));

    let arc_mutex1=Arc::clone(&arc_mutex);
    let handle1=thread::spawn(move || {
        let mut guard=arc_mutex1.lock().unwrap();
        *guard+=1;
        panic!("panic on mutex");
    });

    let arc_mutex2=Arc::clone(&arc_mutex);
    let handle2=thread::spawn(move || {
        thread::sleep(Duration::from_millis(20000));
        let mut guard=arc_mutex2.lock();
        match guard {
            Ok(value)=>println!("Guarded {}", value),
            Err(error)=>println!("Error: Guarded {}",
                *error.into_inner())
        }
    });

    handle1.join();
    handle2.join();
}
```

Mutex also has a `try_lock` function. Unlike the `lock` function, `try_lock` does not block when the Mutex is already locked. Instead, execution continues and the function returns an Err as the Result. This allows your application to do something else while the Mutex is locked.

Reader-Writer Lock

The reader-writer lock, similar to a mutex, guards data. It allows multiple readers to access the data at the same time. Alternatively, a writer has exclusive access to the data. Naturally, readers have read-only access, while writers can modify the data.

RwLock implements the reader-writer lock. It contains the implementation for both the readers and writers, as follows:

- Readers call the `read` function to acquire the reader lock. If successful, the function returns a RwLockReadGuard as the underlying value. The lock remains valid until the RwLockReadGuard is dropped. The `read` function will block if there is an active writer lock. Here is an example:

```
fn read(&self) -> LockResult<RwLockReadGuard<'_, T>>
```

- Writers acquire a writer lock with the RwLock::write function. If successful, the function returns a RwLockWriteGuard within the Result type. If acquired, the lock is released when the RwLockWriteGuard is dropped. The write function blocks if there are outstanding reader locks or another active writer lock.

Here is the function definition:

```
fn write(&self) -> LockResult<RwLockWriteGuard<'_, T>>
```

RwLock can become poisoned, but only for writer threads. When the RwLockWriteGuard is dropped during a panic, the RwLock becomes poisoned, in which case both the read and write functions will return an error.

If there are multiple pending writer locks, the ordering for acquiring the lock is nondeterministic.

In Listing 19.10, we create a RwLock to guard an integer. The RwLock is then shared across threads using an Arc. The writer thread, which is the primary thread, increments the integer. The reader threads display the integer.

Code Listing 19.10.   Example of the RwLock

```
use std::thread;
use std::sync::{Arc, RwLock};
use std::time::Duration;

fn main() {
    let mut handles=Vec::new();
    let rwlock = RwLock::new(0);
    let arc=Arc::new(rwlock);

    for reader in 1..=3 {
        let arc =arc.clone();
        let handle=thread::spawn(move || {
            let mut guard=arc.read().unwrap();
            println!("Reader Lock {} Data {:?}", reader, guard);
            thread::sleep(Duration::from_millis(400));
            println!("Reader UnLock");
        });
        handles.push(handle);
    }

    for writer in 1..=3 {
        let mut guard=arc.write().unwrap();
        thread::sleep(Duration::from_millis(600));
        println!("Writer lock");
        *guard+=1;
    }

    for item in handles {
        item.join();
    }
}
```

A RwLock is created for an integer. To share the RwLock, it is encapsulated within an Arc. Next, we create a vector to hold the JoinHandle for each reader thread, as shown in the previous example. In the subsequent for loop, the reader threads are spawned. Each reader thread captures a clone of the Arc. With the cloned Arc the RwLock is read and the proper guard is returned. The guard is then used to display the value of the integer.

We need a writer to update the guarded integer. To obtain the writer, the RwLock is accessed via the original Arc. This is done in a for loop. The write function is called to get a write guard for the RwLock. The write guard is then dereferenced to increment the guarded integer.

The various sleep statements were added to emulate a running program.

Here is the result of the application.

```
Writer lock
Reader Lock 1 Data 1
Reader Lock 3 Data 1
Reader UnLock
Reader UnLock
Writer lock
Writer lock
Reader Lock 2 Data 3
Reader UnLock
```

As shown, the reader and writer threads are interleaved with RwLock providing thread synchronization. The read and write functions will block when necessary. The output also demonstrates simultaneous reader locks and nondeterministic ordering.

The RwLock type also has try_read and try_write functions. These functions are nonblocking. If the lock is not available, an Err result is returned with both functions but execution continues.

Condition Variables

Condition variables provide thread synchronization based on custom events. Accordingly, other languages refer to condition variables as *events*. You define the semantics of the conditional variable, which makes each unique. For this reason, conditional variables are also considered custom synchronization. When no other synchronization type works, a condition variable is often the best solution because it can be customized.

Mutexes are paired with conditional variables to provide a locking mechanism. They are often combined within a tuple. This prevents inadvertent decoupling of a conditional variable from its associated mutex, where the wrong mutex is used. In addition, a conditional variable has an associated Boolean value that confirms the status of the event. The Boolean value should be guarded by the Mutex.

Condition variables are the Condvar type. You create a Condvar with the Condvar::new constructor function. It takes no parameters. Here is the function definition:

```
fn new() -> Condvar
```

To wait for an event, the Condvar::wait function blocks the current thread until an event notification is received. The only parameter is the MutexGuard from the associated Mutex. Therefore, the Mutex must be locked before the wait function is called. Note that the wait function will unlock the Mutex. Here is the function definition:

```
pub fn wait<'a, T>(
    &self,
    guard: MutexGuard<'a, T>
) -> LockResult<MutexGuard<'a, T>>
```

The Condvar::notify_one and Condvar::notify_all functions will notify waiting threads that the event has occurred or completed. The notify_one function wakens a single waiting thread, even if several are pending. To notify all waiting threads, call the notify_all function. Here are the function definitions for notify_one and notify_all:

```
fn notify_one(&self)
fn notify_all(&self)
```

The example in Listing 19.11 presents a typical scenario where a Condvar is useful. For a program that requires upfront setup, parts of the program may need to wait until the setup is completed.

Code Listing 19.11.   **Managing application setup using a Condvar**

```
use std::sync::{Arc, Mutex, Condvar};
use std::thread;
use std::time::Duration;

fn main() {
    let setup_event=Arc::new((Mutex::new(false),
        Condvar::new()));
    let setup_event2=setup_event.clone();

    thread::spawn(move || {
        let mutex=&setup_event2.0;
        let cond=&setup_event2.1;

        let mut setup=mutex.lock().unwrap();
        println!("Doing setup...");
        thread::sleep(Duration::from_secs(2));
        *setup=true;
        cond.notify_one();
    });

    let mutex=&setup_event.0;
    let cond=&setup_event.1;

    let mut setup=mutex.lock().unwrap();
    while !(*setup) {
```

```
        println!("Wait for setup to complete.");
        setup=cond.wait(setup).unwrap();
    }
    println!("Main program started");
}
```

Here are the steps:

- Within an Arc, the application declares a tuple, setup_event, that pairs a Condvar with a Mutex. The Mutex guards a Boolean value that indicates whether the setup has been completed.
- Next, we create a dedicated thread to perform the setup. It receives a clone of the setup_event tuple, containing the paired Condvar and Mutex. Before performing the setup, we lock the Mutex and receive the related match guard (setup status).
- When the setup is finished, using the match guard, the setup_status is updated to true. With the notify_one function, we then notify other threads that the setup has completed.

Back in main, we want to block until setup is completed.

- Lock the Mutex to retrieve the MatchGuard containing the setup status.
- The wait function blocks the thread and releases the lock from the Mutex.
- The thread remains blocked until there is notification that the event occurred. In this example, the event is that the setup is completed.

Notice that the wait function is called in a while loop. When awakened from a wait, the thread rechecks the condition to make sure a spurious awake has not happened. If that occurs, the condition is unchanged and the thread should resume waiting for the proper event. This check is probably not necessary for the setup event. The event status is unlikely to ever change from false (setup not completed) to true (setup completed) and then back to false. However, in general, we have shown the best pattern for a CondVar.

Atomic Operations

Rust includes a full complement of atomic types for the primitives. These types are closely related to C++20 atomics. The exact list of atomic types depends on the operating system.

An atomic operation is performed in a single uninterruptable step, despite the number of assembly level steps involved. This prevents data corruption or other problems that can occur when sharing an operation across threads. With atomic types, you can perform certain operations, such as read and write, as a unit. Importantly, the implementation of atomic types does employ include locks, which improves performance.

We have already used atomics in this chapter, at least indirectly. For example, the Arc type atomically increments the reference count. This is done to safely modify the reference count.

Atomic types are found in the std::sync::atomic module and include the following:

- AtomicBool
- AtomicI8, AtomicI16, and so on
- AtomicU8, AtomicU16, and so on
- AtomicPtr
- AtomicIsize and AtomicUsize

Store and Load

Atomic types have a consistent interface for storing and loading data. In addition, they can be modified through a shared reference.

Atomic operations have an ordering parameter that provides guarantees on the ordering of operations. The least restrictive ordering is Relaxed, which guarantees the atomicity of a single variable. However, no assurances are made about the relative ordering of multiple variables, such as provided with memory barriers.

The load and store functions are the core functions of atomic types. The store function updates the value, while load gets the value.

The next example calculates the percentage completion of a lengthy operation. Users typically appreciate updates when lengthy operations are running. This is best done with a concurrent thread. For example, if reading a large file, most users expect feedback as the file is being loaded, such as the percentage of load completion. For the percent complete, we could use an AtomicU8 type, with the store and load functions. This is done to prevent receiving a percent completion that is in transition.

Here is the signature for the AtomicU8::load and AtomicU8::store functions. This is also representative of the load and store methods of other atomic types.

```
fn load(&self, order: Ordering) -> u8
fn store(&self, val: u8, order: Ordering)
```

Listing 19.12 provides the example.

Code Listing 19.12.   Using an AtomicU8 value to provide a status update

```
use std::sync::atomic::AtomicU8;
use std::sync::atomic::Ordering::Relaxed;
use std::thread;

fn do_something(value:u8) {
    // performing operation
}

fn main() {

    static STATUS:AtomicU8=AtomicU8::new(0);
    let handle=thread::spawn(||{
        for n in 0..100 {
            do_something(n);
            STATUS.store(n, Relaxed);
        }
    });

    thread::spawn(||{
        loop {
            thread::sleep(Duration::from_millis(2000));
            let value=STATUS.load(Relaxed);
```

```
            println!("Pct done {}", value);
        }
    });

    handle.join();
}
```

The AtomicU8 type, for the percentage of completion, is created with a static lifetime. That makes it easier to share across multiple threads. The first new thread performs a lengthy operation within a for loop. With the store function, the percentage complete is updated at the end of each iteration. In a companion thread, the percentage complete is periodically checked with the load function. The result is then displayed to the user.

Fetch and Modify

The fetch and modify operations are more complicated than the load and store operations. There are several functions that support fetch (load) and modify (store) operations. The functions include fetch_add, fetch_sub, fetch_or, fetch_and, and more.

The following program calculates a running total using two threads. The AtomicU32::fetch_add function is used to calculate a running total.

Here is the definition of the AtomicU32::fetch_add function:

```
fn fetch_add(&self, val: u32, order: Ordering) -> u32
```

Atomically, the function adds to the current value and returns the previous value. This function definition is representative of other fetch and modify functions.

Listing 19.13 is the example of calculating a running total. An AtomicU32 variable is created to track the running total. Two threads are then spawned. With the fetch_add function, each thread contributes to the running total. At the end, the final total is obtained using the load function. If the operation was not atomic, the add operation in parallel threads could corrupt the data.

Code Listing 19.13.   **Maintaining a running total using the fetch_add function**

```
use std::sync::atomic::AtomicU32;
use std::sync::atomic::Ordering::Relaxed;
use std::thread;

fn main() {

    static TOTAL:AtomicU32=AtomicU32::new(0);

    let handle1=thread::spawn(||{
        for n in 1..=100 {
            let a=TOTAL.fetch_add(n, Relaxed);
        }
```

```
    });

    let handle2=thread::spawn(||{
        for n in 101..=200 {
            TOTAL.fetch_add(n, Relaxed);
        }
    });

    handle1.join();
    handle2.join();

    println!("Total is {}", TOTAL.load(Relaxed));
}
```

Compare and Exchange

Envision multiple threads racing toward the same value, where the first to arrive changes the value atomically. A later thread arriving at the scene should notice the change and not modify the value *again*. This scenario is relatively common with parallel programming and is the basis of the compare and exchange operation.

With the compare and exchange operation, you indicate an expected value. If the expected value is found, the current value is updated with a new value. This is the exchange. However, if the expected value is not found, it is assumed a *different thread* already modified the value. When this occurs, another exchange should not happen.

In the next example, two threads attempt to update an AtomicU32 type. The compare_ exchange function is called to update the value. Here is the function definition:

```
pub fn compare_exchange( &self, current: u32, new: u32,
    success: Ordering, failure: Ordering) -> Result<u32, u32>
```

The current parameter is the expected value. If the current parameter matches the present value, the AtomicU32 value is updated with the new parameter. The final parameters are the separate Ordering parameters. The first Ordering is for the exchange operation. The second Ordering parameter is used when the operation does not exchange the value. In addition, if the exchange does not occur, an Err is returned.

Listing 19.14 is an example where we create a static AtomicU32 value. The first thread that calls the compare_exchange function updates the value.

Code Listing 19.14. Using the compare_exchange function

```
use std::sync::atomic::AtomicU32;
use std::sync::atomic::Ordering::Relaxed;
use std::thread;

fn main() {

    static A:AtomicU32=AtomicU32::new(0);
```

```
    let handle1=thread::spawn(|||{
        A.compare_exchange(0, 1, Relaxed, Relaxed);
    });

    let handle2=thread::spawn(|||{
        A.compare_exchange(0, 2, Relaxed, Relaxed);
    });

    handle1.join();
    handle2.join();

    println!("Value is {}", A.load(Relaxed));
}
```

In this example, the result of compare_exchange is not checked. To handle an error, you should bind to the result.

Summary

Thread synchronization, or the coordination of threads, is sometimes required for the correctness of an application. There are several reasons this may be necessary, including preventing race conditions, performing setup before core activities, or performing operations atomically. This often results in a thread being blocked at least temporarily.

Rust has a complement of synchronization types, including common types such as Mutex, RwLock, Condvar, and atomic types. Here are some key points to note concerning these types:

- Mutexes are for mutual exclusion.
- RwLocks are for reader-writer locks. With the RwLock, you can have multiple concurrent readers but only a single writer at a time.
- Condvar is used for conditional variables and events. This typically pairs a Condvar and a Mutex. You will also need a Boolean condition for the status of the event. The Condvar provides custom synchronization where the meaning of the event is determined by the application. Implementing the Condvar requires several steps.
- Atomic types exist for the primitive types to perform essential operations atomically. Various atomic operations include store and load, fetch and add, and compare and exchange.

Shared ownership of synchronization components is sometimes necessary. The Arc type encapsulates shared ownership through reference counting. You can use the Arc type to share the synchronization components across non-scoped threads. Other solutions to sharing synchronization components are scoped threads and static variables.

20

Memory

Without memory, there is no data. Most applications, whether they are a server, blockchain, artificial intelligence, game, or something else, require data. Consequently, understanding the intricacies of memory is essential.

With memory, you have a variety of options. The various categories of memory all have unique characteristics and benefits, and sometimes limitations. The correct choice of memory is often dependent on several factors, including data size, ownership, lifetime, mutability, and persistence. These factors, taken together, will help you make an informed decision. Helping you make this decision is the goal of this chapter.

The three main areas of memory are stack, static, and heap memory. You can place data in any of these locations. At times, Rust provides some direction, such as placing the elements of a vector on the heap. However, it is primarily your decision where data is located.

It should be noted that Rust does not have a formal memory model. There is no wizard behind a curtain who magically handles memory issues, such as organizing memory efficiently, reducing memory pressure as needed, or moving memory around to improve performance. Rust does provide *some* help, though. Aspects of Rust, such as default immutability, smart pointers, ownership, and lifetimes, form an informal memory model.

Stacks

Every thread owns a stack for dedicated memory. The stack grows when a thread calls a function. Conversely, the stack shrinks as a thread returns from a function. Each function has a stack frame, which reserves memory for it. The memory in the stack frame is used for the local variables, parameters, return values, and system data. This data is automatically freed by the system.

The stack is implemented as a LIFO (last-in/first-out) queue. It is similar to a stack of plates, where additional plates are added at the top and removed in order, starting at the top. This approach means data is stored efficiently in consecutive memory. Stacks have a predictable behavior. For that reason, the system can manage the stack effectively.

For Rust, except for the primary thread, the default stack size is 2 kilobytes. When a thread is spawned, you can explicitly set the minimum stack size with the Builder type and the `stack_size` function. Alternatively, you can change the default stack size with the RUST_MIN_STACK environment variable. However, neither approach places a ceiling on the stack size. Stacks are growable and will expand as needed, within the available memory.

The let statement creates a local variable using memory within the current stack frame. In Listing 20.1, we create several local variables on the stack.

Code Listing 20.1.   Declaring variables on the stack

```
let a:i32=1;
let b:i32=2;
let c:i32=do_something();

println!("{:p} + {} (i32) = {:p} + {} (i32) = {:p}",
        &a, &b-&a, &b, &b-&a, &c)
```

The locals, a, b, and c, are in consecutive memory locations on the stack. Each requires 32 bits of memory, or 4 bytes. The println! macro displays the memory addresses of each variable, confirming they are in contiguous memory on the stack. Here's an example:

```
0x5e552ff7bc + 1 (i32) = 0x5e552ff7c0 + 1 (i32) = 0x5e552ff7c4
```

The example shown in Listing 20.2 will not compile. In the inner block, the variable c is pushed onto the stack. It is then removed from the stack at the end of the same block, thus demonstrating that even within a function, data can be added and removed from the stack. Therefore, c is no longer on the stack to be displayed with the println! macro.

Code Listing 20.2.   Declaring variables in an inner block

```
let a:i32=1;
let b:i32=2;

{
    let c:i32=3;
}

println!("{a} {b} {c}");
```

Unsized types cannot be placed on the stack. You are limited to fixed-sized types. For example, traits are not fixed sized. Therefore, the example in Listing 20.3 also will not compile. We are using the Copy trait, which is unsized, as a parameter. This prevents the parameter from being placed on the stack.

Code Listing 20.3.   The Copy trait as a parameter

```
fn do_something(a:Copy){

}
```

You could combine the dyn or impl keywords with a trait parameter to successfully compile the function. These keywords replace the trait with a concrete value, which is a fixed size.

Stacks can consume an enormous amount of memory. For that reason, be careful about placing large objects on the stack. Another problem can be recursive functions. Inadvertently creating runaway recursive functions can quickly erode available memory.

Some data types, such as vectors and strings, are smart pointers. When declared with the let statement, the value for these types is allocated on the heap, as discussed later in this chapter. A pointer to the value is placed on the stack. In the following example, the value [1,2,3,4] is placed on the heap. The vp variable, which is a fat pointer, is placed on the stack.

```
let vp=vec![1,2,3,4];
```

Static Values

Static values are persistent for the lifetime of the application. This is accomplished by storing the static values in the binary itself, which makes the values always available. This also means that an abundance of static values can cause binary bloat, which can impact performance. In addition, static values are rarely mutable to maintain thread safeness.

Static binding is created with the static keyword. By convention, variable names for static values are entirely uppercase. In addition, the type for static variables cannot be inferred. Instead, it must be explicitly indicated.

In Listing 20.4, we use the golden ratio number, which is 1.618. Many ratios in nature adhere to the golden ratio, even for honeybees. In a hive, the ratio of female to male honeybees is typically the golden ratio.

Code Listing 20.4.   Defining a static variable for the golden ratio

```
static GOLDEN_RATIO:f64=1.618;
let male_bees=100.0;
let female_bees:f64=male_bees*GOLDEN_RATIO;
println!("{}", female_bees as i32);
```

The address of static variables when compared to stack variables should clearly identify different areas of memory. The example in Listing 20.5 displays the memory addresses of both static and stack-based variables.

Code Listing 20.5.   Showing memory addresses for stack and static regions

```
static A:i8=1;
static B:i8=2;
let c:i8=3;
let d:i8=4;
```

```
println!(
    "[ Global A: {:p}  B: {:p} ]\n[ Stack c: {:p}  d: {:p}]",
    &A, &B, &c, &d);
```

Based on their addresses, the result shows the global and stack variables grouped in different regions of memory:

```
[ Global A: 0x7ff6339ee3e8  B: 0x7ff6339ee3e9 ]
[ Stack c:  0x5e9c6ff5ae    d: 0x5e9c6ff5af]
```

The Heap

The heap is process memory available to an application at runtime. This is often the biggest pool of available memory for an application, and it is where large objects should be placed. At runtime, applications allocate memory on the heap as needed. This is frequently referred to as dynamic memory allocation. When no longer required, the heap memory can be deallocated and released back to the available pool.

Heap memory is taken from the virtual memory of an application. A process shares the physical memory of a device with other running processes. For that reason, an application does not own all the memory on a computer, for example. Instead, applications are assigned a virtual address space, called *virtual memory*, that the operating system then maps to physical memory.

When there is a request for memory on the heap, the operating system must first locate enough contiguous memory to accommodate the request. The memory is then allocated at that location and a pointer to the address is returned. The process of locating and allocating memory can be time-consuming. In addition, the heap can become fragmented from a series of allocations, especially of different-sized data. This can prevent future allocations from being successful even when there is enough available memory, but not in a single location. Some operating systems provide a system API to defragment the heap to help mitigate this problem.

Unlike the stack, the heap is shared memory that's available to all the threads within a process. For that reason, data on the heap may not be thread-safe. Types, such as RwLock, exist to manage shared memory.

In Rust, Box is used to allocate memory on the heap. When the Box is dropped, typically at the end of the current block, the heap memory is freed. However, you can leak memory in situations where the boxed value is never dropped. Alternatively, boxed values can be dropped explicitly, and the related memory freed, with the drop statement.

Here is the description of the Box type:

```
pub struct Box<T, A = Global>(_, _)
    where A: Allocator, T: ?Sized;
```

The Box struct is generic over type T, where T is the type being dynamically allocated. Type parameter A is a reference to the memory allocator. Global is the default allocator used to allocate memory on the heap. You can replace it with a custom allocator, if desired. For example, a custom allocator could take memory from preallocated memory pools. You create a Box with the new constructor. Here is the function definition:

```
fn new(x: T) -> Box<T, Global>
```

The Box::new function creates a value on the heap and returns a Box value, not a pointer, to the heap. To access the boxed value, which is on the heap, dereference the Box. However, this is not always necessary. At times, automatic dereferencing can occur. The println! macro is a prime example where automatic dereferencing occurs for boxed values.

Listing 20.6 shows how to dereference a Box both directly and automatically. The Box::new function creates an integer value (1) on the heap. The result is a Box that is bound to boxa. Next, we want to add 1 to the boxed value. For that reason, boxa is dereferenced with the * operator. This provides the expression access to the boxed value. The println! macro then displays both the result of the expression and the boxed value. Because the println! macro automatically dereferences a Box, the * operator is not required here.

Code Listing 20.6.   Accessing boxed values on the heap

```
fn main() {
    let boxa=Box::new(1);
    let stackb=*boxa+1;-
    println!("{} {}", boxa, stackb);   // 1 2
}
```

The purpose of Listing 20.7 is comparing pointers to values and boxed values. This will show where locals are placed on the stack, and where the boxed values are placed on the heap.

Code Listing 20.7.   Boxing integers and accessing their raw pointers

```
fn main() {
    let boxa=Box::new(1);
    let boxb=Box::new(2);

    let c=1;
    let d=2;

    println!("boxa:{:p} boxb:{:p} c:{:p} d:{:p}",
        &boxa, &boxb, &c, &d);

    let rawa=Box::into_raw(boxa);
    let rawb=Box::into_raw(boxb);

    println!("{:p} {:p} {:p} {:p}", rawa, rawb, &c, &d);

    let boxc;
    let boxd;
```

```
    unsafe {
        boxc=Box::from_raw(rawa);
        boxd=Box::from_raw(rawb);
    }

    println!("boxc value: {}", *boxc);
    println!("boxd value: {}", *boxd);
}
```

With the Box::new function, memory is allocated for integers on the heap. This results in boxa and boxb, both a Box. Regular integer variable are also declared on the stack, c and d. The println! macro lists the memory addresses of the variables: boxa, boxb, c, and d. This confirms that the variables are in the same area of memory: the stack. Even though a Box references data on the heap, the Box itself is often found on the stack.

```
    boxa:0x498aaff958 boxb:0x498aaff960 c:0x498aaff968 d:0x498aaff96c
```

Next, we use the into_raw function to obtain *raw* pointers to the boxed values: rawa and rawb. The raw pointer directly refers to the heap and is unsafe. When it is dropped, the heap memory is *not* removed. Instead, you accept the responsibility to free the memory sometime in the future. The second println! macro in the application displays the memory addresses of the boxed values. In addition, the memory addresses of c and d are displayed. This confirms that the boxed values and local variables c and d reside in different areas of memory.

```
    rawa:0x237291bff90 rawb:0x237291bffb0 c:0x55a6eff328 d:0x55a6eff32c
```

Alternatively, you can place the raw pointer back into a Box with the from_raw function. Afterwards, Rust will resume responsibility for the item on the heap. The from_raw function must be called as unsafe.

You can also move values from the stack to the heap. The result depends on whether the value supports move or copy semantics. For example, when boxing a String variable, ownership is transferred to the heap with the value. In Listing 20.8, an integer variable is boxed. Integers implement copy semantics. Therefore, a copy of the integer is placed on the heap. When the Box is dereferenced and the value is incremented, only the value on the heap is changed.

Code Listing 20.8.   **Moving a value from the stack to the heap**

```
let a=1.234;
let mut pa=Box::new(a);
*pa+=1.0;
println!("{} {}", a, *pa);   // a:1.234 pa:2.234
```

Interior Mutability

Interior mutability is best described with a scenario.

You manage a grocery store within a large chain. At checkout, the customer's items in the cart are totaled and recorded on a receipt. The store ID and transaction ID on the receipt are constant, while the total field is mutable. Listing 20.9 shows the Transaction type.

Code Listing 20.9.   The Transaction type for a grocery store

```
struct Transaction {
    storeid: i8,
    txid: i32,
    mut total:f64,
}
```

Unfortunately, the Transaction struct will not compile. Why? Individual fields within a struct cannot be mutable. Mutability is defined at the struct level.

Listing 20.10 is a workable solution with the struct defined as mutable when declared as a variable. However, this solution is semantically incorrect and allows improper changes, as shown. We should not be able to change the storeid field, but the application does modify this field.

Code Listing 20.10.   Updated Transaction and sample code

```
struct Transaction {
    storeid: i8,
    txid: i32,
    total:f64,
}

fn main() {
    let mut tx=Transaction{storeid: 100, txid: 213,
        total:0.0};

    tx.storeid=101 // oops
}
```

Interior mutability exists to provide a solution to challenges, as described with the Transaction type. Types that support interior mutability are wrappers of an interior value. The wrapper can remain immutable while the interior is mutable. That's correct! The wrapper presents an immutable façade while indirectly allowing changes to the interior value.

Cell is a type that supports interior mutability. It is generic over type T, where T describes the interior value. Cell is found in the std::cell module.

Cell can remain immutable while the interior value is modified using functions, such as the Cell::get and Cell::set functions. The set function modifies the interior value, and the get function returns a *copy* of the interior value. Because it's a copy, there is no dependency between the copy and the interior value. Here are the definitions of the get and set functions:

```
fn get(&self) -> T
fn set(&self, val: T)
```

You can create a Cell with the `Cell::new` constructor, like so:

```
fn new(value: T) -> Cell<T>
```

Next, a Cell is created for an interior integer value, initialized to 1. Notice that the Cell is immutable but the interior value is modified with the set function. Prior to modifying, we get a copy of the interior value. Both the updated interior value and the copy of the original value are displayed to demonstrate their independence (see Listing 20.11).

Code Listing 20.11.   Getting and setting a Cell's interior value

```
use std::cell::Cell;

fn main() {
    let a=Cell::new(1);
    let b=a.get();
    a.set(2);
    println!("a={} b={}", a.get(), b); // a=2 b=1
}
```

Cell resolves the mutability dilemma with Transaction. Let's modify Transaction, changing the total field to a Cell for a float (see Listing 20.12). This means the total field is mutable even when the remainder of the struct is immutable. Therefore, the integrity of the other fields is maintained.

Code Listing 20.12.   Updating Transaction for Cell type

```
use std::cell::Cell;

struct Transaction {
    storeid: i8,
    txid: i32,
    total:Cell<f64>,
}

fn main() {
    let item_prices=[11.21, 25.45, 8.24, 9.87];
    let tx=Transaction{storeid: 100, txid: 213,
        total:Cell::new(0.0)};

    for price in item_prices {
        let total=tx.total.get()+price;
        tx.total.set(total);
    }

    println!("Store {}\nReceipt {}\nTotal ${:.2}",
        tx.storeid, tx.txid, tx.total.get());
}
```

Here is another benefit of the Cell type. In Rust, you are allowed immutable and mutable references (borrows) to the *same* value, but there are limitations. You can have simultaneous immutable references. However, more than one mutable reference to a value is not allowed. Listing 20.13 is a brief example with mutable and immutable references to the same value.

Code Listing 20.13.   Invalid multiple mutable references

```
let mut a=1;

let ref1=&a;  // immutable reference
let ref2=&a;  // immutable reference

let mut ref3=&mut a;  // mutable reference
let mut ref4=&mut a;  // mutable reference
*ref3=2;

println!("{ref3}");
```

In the preceding example, there are two immutable and mutable references to the same value. The immutable references are allowed, but the multiple mutable references are not. The compiler generates the following error, which correctly identifies the problem.

```
7 |      let mut ref3=&mut a;
  |                   ------ first mutable borrow occurs here
8 |      let mut ref4=&mut a;
  |                   ^^^^^^ second mutable borrow occurs here
9 |      *ref3=2;
  |      ------- first borrow later used here
```

There could be circumstances where limiting the number of mutable references is overly restrictive. This is another scenario where interior mutability could be helpful, as shown in Listing 20.14.

Code Listing 20.14.   Modifying an interior value from separate RefCells

```
let a=1;

let cell=Cell::new(a);
let ref1=&cell;
let ref2=&cell;

ref1.set(2);
ref2.set(3);
println!("{}", ref1.get());   // 3
```

At the start, Cell is initialized with an integer value. Two references are created to the immutable Cell. We then use functions to modify the interior value from different references, similar to multiple mutable references.

Other useful Cell functions include the following:

- `replace`: Replaces the interior value with a new value and then returns the replaced interior (old) value.
- `swap`: Swaps the interior values of two Cells.
- `take`: Get the interior value and then replace it with the default value.

RefCell

RefCell is similar to Cell. It is also located in the `std::cell` module. However, RefCell provides references to the interior value, not copies. You obtain a reference to the interior value with either the `RefCell::borrow` function or the `RefCell::borrow_mut` function. The `borrow` and `borrow_mut` functions provide an immutable and mutable borrow, respectively. Here are the function definitions:

```
fn borrow(&self) -> Ref<'_, T>
fn borrow_mut(&self) -> RefMut<'_, T>
```

You create a RefCell with the `new` constructor:

```
fn new(value: T) -> RefCell<T>
```

The example in Listing 20.15 uses RefCell with both `borrow` and `borrow_mut`. With dereferencing, we use `borrow_mut` to change the interior value. `borrow` is then used to display the interior value, where mutability is not required.

Code Listing 20.15.   Example of `borrow` and `borrow_mut`

```
let refcell=RefCell::new(1);
*refcell.borrow_mut()+=10;
println!("refcell {}", refcell.borrow());
```

For RefCell, the rules of mutability fully apply. However, the rules are enforced at runtime instead of compile time. For this reason, be extra careful not to break these rules. For example, more than one mutable reference is not allowed, as previously discussed. This is one of the most important rules of mutability.

In Listing 20.16, two mutable references are created to the same: a and b. Consequently, the program will panic when one of the references is used.

Code Listing 20.16.   Multiple mutable borrows are not supported

```
let refcell=RefCell::new(1);
let mut a=refcell.borrow_mut();  // mutable borrow
let mut b=refcell.borrow_mut();  // mutable borrow
*a+=10;  // panic
```

With the `borrow` function, you can have multiple immutable borrows at the same time. However, you cannot call `borrow` if there is currently a mutable borrow. Requesting a `borrow` at that time will cause a panic, which is demonstrated in Listing 20.17.

Code Listing 20.17.   The `borrow` panics because of the preceding `borrow_mut`

```
let refcell=RefCell::new(1);
let mut a=refcell.borrow_mut();  // mutable borrow
let mut b=refcell.borrow();      // immutable borrow - panic
*a+=10;
```

The `try_borrow` function is an alternative to the `borrow` function. The function returns a Result. Instead of panicking, when there is an outstanding mutable reference (borrow), the `try_borrow` function returns an Err for the Result. If it is successful, `Ok(reference)` is returned. Listing 20.18 is an example.

Code Listing 20.18.   The `try_borrow` avoids a panic when there is a current `borrow_mut`

```
let refcell=RefCell::new(1);
let mut a=refcell.borrow_mut();
let result=refcell.try_borrow();

match result {
    Ok(b)=>println!("Interior value: {}", b),
    Err(_)=>println!("Do something else")
}
```

Listing 20.19 is an updated version of the latest Transaction application. Cell has been replaced with RefCell. For adding to the interior value, the `borrow_mut` function obtains a mutable reference. Later, the `borrow` function is called to get the final total.

Code Listing 20.19.   Updating the Transaction struct for the RefCell type

```
use std::cell::RefCell;

struct Transaction {
    storeid: i8,
    txid: i32,
    total:RefCell<f64>,
}

fn main() {
    let item_prices=[11.21, 25.45, 8.24, 9.87];
    let tx=Transaction{storeid: 100, txid: 213,
        total:RefCell::new(0.0)};

    for price in item_prices {
        *tx.total.borrow_mut()+=price;
```

```
    }

    println!("Store {}\nReceipt {}\nTotal ${:.2}",
        tx.storeid, tx.txid, tx.total.borrow());
}
```

Other useful functions include the following:

- **replace**: Replaces the interior value with another value, returning the current value
- **swap**: Swaps the interior value of two RefCells

OnceCell

Similar to Cell and RefCell, OnceCell supports interior mutability. However, you are limited to modifying the interior value once. Additional attempts to modify the interior value will result in an error. You create a OnceCell with the new constructor. The **set** function initializes the interior value. If it is already initialized, the Result is an Err. The **get** function returns the interior value. Of course, you can get the interior value as many times as necessary. Here are the function definitions for the new, set, and get functions:

```
fn new() -> OnceCell<T>
fn set(&self, value: T) -> Result<(), T>
fn get(&self) -> Option<&T>
```

In Listing 20.20, we attempt to update the OnceCell value more than once in a for loop. First time through the loop, the **set** function successfully modifies the interior value. In later iterations, the set function will return an Err value—the interior value can only be modified once. At the end of the application, the interior value is 1 from the first set function.

Code Listing 20.20. Using OnceCell to update the interior value

```
let once=OnceCell::new();
let mut result;
for i in 1..=3 {
    result=once.set(i);
    match result {
        Ok(_)=>println!("Updated"),
        Err(_)=>println!("Not updated")
    }
}
println!("Final value: {:?}", once.get().unwrap());
```

Here is the result:

```
Updated
Not updated
Not updated
Final value: 1
```

Other helpful functions include the following:

- `get_mut`: Gets a mutable reference to the interior value.
- `get_or_init`: Gets the interior value and, if not initialized, sets it with a closure.
- `take`: Gets the interior value and then resets to the default value.

Summary

Mastering the memory profile of your application is important for developing successful applications. This includes understanding the different areas of memory and respective benefits. The three primary areas of memory are static, stack, and heap memory.

- The stack is the memory assigned to each thread for local variables. It resides in contiguous memory. The `let` statement, parameters, and return values are your locals.
- Static memory is for global memory and exists for the lifetime of the application. The `static` keyword creates values in static memory.
- At runtime, memory can be allocated from the heap. When no longer required, the memory should be dropped. You can allocate memory on the heap with the Box type. The memory is deallocated when the Box is dropped.

Certain types, such as String and Vec types, also have a presence on both the stack and heap. With these types, the value is allocated on the heap while a reference resides on the stack. When it is dropped, the value on the heap is deallocated.

We introduced Cell, RefCell, and OnceCell for interior mutability. These types are wrappers for an interior value. The wrapper can be immutable while the interior value is changed through functions. Interior mutability is helpful for structs where all the fields are not exclusively mutable.

21

Macros

Never limit yourself because of others' limited imagination.

— Mae Jemison

The use of macros allows you to reimagine Rust within the context of your own aspirations. Rust's support of macros is a powerful feature that provides almost unlimited capabilities. You can provide new features, implement default behavior, or simply avoid redundancy.

The `println!` macro is probably the most well-known macro in the Rust universe. It provides the *capability* of a variadic function. This is because Rust does not support variadic functions. Therefore, the `println!` macro provides a feature not available in the standard language. A close second in popularity is the `derive` attribute. The `derive` attribute for the Clone and Copy traits, for example, is actually a macro that implements a default behavior of those traits.

Fundamentally, a macro is code that generates code—otherwise known as metaprogramming. Macros are evaluated (expanded) at compile time. For that reason, errors in a macro, especially due to malformed code, are often found at compile time.

Macros are literally found everywhere in Rust. For many languages, macros are an add-on for developers, but not with Rust. Macros play an important role even in the core language. Some elements of the language, such as `println!`, `format!`, `vec!`, `assert!`, `hash_map!`, and many more, are macros.

Rust does not support robust reflection, such as `any::type_name`. Macros provide limited reflection. This increases the importance of macros within the language.

You may presume that macros are simply fancy functions. However, macros have the following features that are distinct from functions:

- Macros support variadic parameters.
- Macros are expanded at compile time.
- Macro variables (metavariables) are untyped.
- Macros have a different error-handling model.
- Macro logistics can be different, such as where a macro can reside.

There are two flavors of macros: declarative and procedural macros. The `println!` macro is the most common declarative macro, while the `derive` attribute is the most common example of a procedural macro.

Macros in Rust are quite versatile; unfortunately, that versatility may come with additional complexity, particularly when compared with functions. In addition, macros can be less than transparent or readable. For these reasons, if a task can be accomplished adequately with a function, you should choose a function!

Because macros can be complex, this chapter showcases many examples that can be used as templates for your adventures with macros.

Tokens

When compiled, Rust programs are first converted into a sequence of tokens. This stage of compilation is called tokenization. You are probably familiar with some of the tokens, such as literals and keywords, created at this stage.

After tokenization, the next stage of compilation is the transformation of the token stream into an abstract syntax tree (AST), which is a hierarchical structure consisting of tokens, trees, and leaves that describe the behavior of your application.

Macros are evaluated after the AST creation stage. For this reason, macros must contain valid syntax; otherwise, the program will not compile. At this stage, a macro can *read* the tokens in the AST to understand an application or code fragment and plan a response. The response could be replacing existing tokens or inserting additional tokens into the token stream.

The token stream uses the following different types of tokens:

- Keywords
- Identifiers
- Literals
- Lifetimes
- Punctuation
- Delimiters

Figure 21.1 shows a mapping of tokens, and their types, to specific elements in the example code.

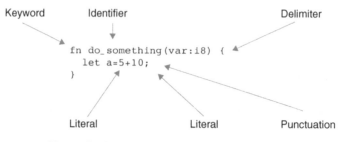

Figure 21.1.   Example annotated with token types

Declarative Macros

As mentioned, there are two types of macros: declarative and procedural. Since declarative macros are more straightforward, we will start there.

A declarative macro is similar to a match expression but for code, not values. For a declarative macro, a pattern is called a macro matcher. You will match on a type of code fragment, such as an expression. The equivalent of a match arm used in a match expression is the macro transcriber used in a declarative macro. If matched, the macro transcriber is the replacement code inserted into the token stream. The declarative macro is evaluated top-down. At the first matching pattern, the transcription is expanded into the token stream.

Declaring a declarative macro with the `macro_rules!` macro is an example of dogfooding, macros creating macros. Here is the syntax for declaring a declarative macro:

```
macro_rules!identifier {
        (macro_matcher¹)=>{ macro_transcriber } ;
        (macro_matcher²)=>{ macro_transcriber } ;
        (macro_matcherⁿ)=>{ macro_transcriber }
}
```

The `identifier` names the macro. You can then call the macro with the macro operator (!).

We create the `hello!` macro in Listing 21.1. The macro displays the celebrated "Hello, world!" greeting. The `macro_rules` macro is used to declare the macro. This macro has an empty macro matcher, which is all-inclusive. The macro is replaced with a `println!` at compile time that displays the greeting. In `main`, the `hello!` macro is called. The resulting `println!` displays the greeting.

Code Listing 21.1. Implementing the hello! declarative macro

```
macro_rules!hello{
    ()=>{    // empty macro matcher
        println!("Hello, world!")
    };
}
fn main() {
    hello!()    // replaced with println!...
}
```

In non-macro code, values are assigned types, such as i8, f64, or even String. Macros also have a set of types. However, macros manipulate code instead of values. These types relate to code, instead of values, for that reason. The "types" for a macro are called fragment specifiers.

Here is the list of fragment specifiers:

- **block**: A block
- **expr**: An expression
- **ident**: The name of the item or keyword
- **item**: A code item
- **lifetime**: A lifetime annotation

- **literal**: A literal or label identifier
- **meta**: The content of an attribute
- **pat**: A pattern
- **pat_param**: A pat that allows the or (|) token
- **path**: The TypePath
- **stmt**: A statement
- **tt**: A TokenTree
- **ty**: A type
- **vis**: The visibility

You can declare variables that bind to code, which is similar to declaring a variable that binds to a value. Variables that bind to code fragments are called metavariables and are preceded with a dollar sign ($).

Listing 21.2 is a more flexible version of the hello! macro. You can change the greeting with this version. Consequently, this macro accepts a parameter for the name within the greeting. It uses both a fragment specifier (expr) and a metavariable (name).

Code Listing 21.2.   The hello! macro with variable input

```
macro_rules!hello{
    ($name:expr)=>{
        println!("Hello, {}!", $name);
    };
}
fn main() {
    hello!("Douglas");
}
```

Within the macro, expr is the fragment specifier, for expressions, and the only acceptable pattern. The name metavariable is bound to the macro input. If name is an expression, the there is a match and the greeting is displayed using the metavariable.

In main, when the hello! macro is invoked, "Douglas" is provided as the expression. For that reason, the macro finds a match and displays the name.

Let's explore another fragment specifier. In Listing 21.3, the talk! macro accepts only literals. Therefore, the macro matcher is the literal fragment specifier. The transcriber is simple and inserts code that displays the literal. In main, the macro is called successfully for separate literal values. However, the macro does not compile when called with the input expression. Expressions are not literals.

Code Listing 21.3.   Macro using the literal fragment specifier

```
#[derive(Debug)]
struct Test;

macro_rules!talk{
    ($lit:literal)=>{
        println!("Literal: {:?}!", $lit);
    };
```

```
}
fn main() {
    let input=42;

    talk!("Douglas");
    talk!("Adams");
    talk!(input);    // Does not work
}
```

Repetition

Repetition is a construct that can repeat a transformation on a code fragment. It can be done within either a macro matcher or transcriber. This capability is important because it provides support for variadic macros, which the core language does not support.

Here is the syntax for a repetition:

```
($(code fragment), * |+|? )
```

Figure 21.2 shows the annotated version of the syntax.

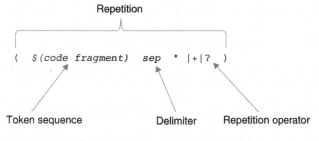

Figure 21.2. Example annotated with token types

Here are the possible repetition operators:

- **Asterisk (*)**: Zero or more
- **Plus sign (+)**: One or more
- **Question mark (?)**: Zero or one

Let's create a macro that uses a repetition. The vec_evens! macro will be similar to the vec! macro, but the vec_evens! macro will only append even-numbered integer values to a vector. Odd-numbered integers will be ignored. The macro is variadic, accepting a variable number of values. Listing 21.4 shows the macro being used to create a vector of even-numbered integers.

Code Listing 21.4. Invoking the vec_evens! variadic macro

```
use evens_macro;

fn main() {
    let answer=evens_macro::vec_evens![2,4,5,9,12];
    println!("{:?}", answer);    // 2, 4, 12
}
```

Listing 21.5 is the `vec_evens!` macro. The macro matcher has a repetition that matches on expr patterns. Within the transcriber, a new vector is created. Afterwards there is another repetition. This repetition generates code to add each expression to the vector. Before adding to the vector, the macro checks whether the expression is even.

In this circumstance, the macro is placed in a separate crate. The `macro_export!` attribute makes the macro visible outside its crate.

Code Listing 21.5.   Implementing the `vec_evens!` macro

```
#[macro_export]
macro_rules! vec_evens {
    ( $( $item:expr ),* ) => { // repetition
        {
            let mut result = Vec::new();
            $(   // repetition
                if ($item % 2) == 0 {
                    result.push($item);
                }
            )*
            result
        }
    };
}
```

As already shown, you can even refer to a declarative macro from within a macro. Listing 21.6 is a more elaborate version of the macro that displays the "Hello, world!" greeting. The `hello_world` macro, shown next, relies on the `hello` macro and `world` macro to display the greeting. All three macros are declarative and reside within the same crate.

Code Listing 21.6.   A macro that invokes macros from within the same crate

```
#[macro_export]
macro_rules! hello_world {

    () => {
        println!("{} {}", hello!(), name!());
    }

#[macro_export]
macro_rules! hello {
    () => {"Hello"}
}

#[macro_export]
macro_rules! name {
    () => {"Bob"}
}
```

However, this `macro_world` macro will not compile. The reason is that declarative macros, `hello` and `world`, expand at their invocation site. This does not include macros that are not presently in scope, such as the println! macro. For that reason, the hello_world macro contains references to invalid macros. Prefixing the macro invocation with the $crate metavariable prevents this behavior. As a separator, you must also add the :: operator. The version of the hello_world macro shown in Listing 21.7 compiles successfully when using the $crate metavariable.

Code Listing 21.7. Version of the hello_word macro that uses the $crate metavariable

```
#[macro_export]
macro_rules! hello_world {
    () => {
        println!("{} {}", $crate::hello!(),
            $crate::name!());
    }
}
```

Listing 21.8 is the application that calls the hello_world macro.

Code Listing 21.8. Application that uses the hello_world declarative macro

```
use say::hello_world;

fn main() {
    hello_world!();
}
```

Multiple Macro Matchers

A macro can have multiple macro matchers, as shown in Listing 21.9. With two macro matchers, the product macro accepts code fragments with either two or three expressions. The transcriber for each inserts the proper code in the token stream for that pattern.

Code Listing 21.9. A declarative macro that has multiple macro matchers

```
macro_rules! product{
    ($a:expr,$b:expr)=>{
        {
            $a*$b
        }
    };

    ($a:expr, $b:expr, $c:expr)=>{
        {
            $a*$b*$c
        }
    };
}

fn main() {
```

```
    let result=product!(1, 2);
    let result2=product!(3, 4, 5);

    println!("{} {}", result, result2);
}
```

We have now completed our conversation on declarative macros. It's time to discuss procedural macros, which have additional capabilities. Fortunately, many of the concepts, such as tokens, remain the same. Therefore, you already have a start at learning procedural macros.

Procedural Macros

Procedural macros receive a stream of tokens as input that describes some portion of the application. Normally, the macro evaluates the input and returns a different token stream as a response. The response is then inserted into the overall token stream of the application at the site of the macro. Procedural macros do not have pattern matching. The macro instead interprets an input stream and returns an output stream.

There are three flavors of procedural macros:

- Derive macros
- Attribute macros
- Function-like macros

TokenStreams are the essential ingredient of all procedural macros. A TokenStream is an abstraction of a sequence of tokens, or a code fragment. The input and output of a procedural macro are a TokenStream. The TokenStream type is found in the proc_macro crate.

You will need a convenient method to convert source code to a TokenStream. This is necessary to create a response to the input token. The TokenStream::FromStr function is the solution. It converts a source code fragment, as a str, to a TokenStream. If the code fragment is malformed, the conversion to a TokenStream will result in an error.

Here is the definition of the from_str function:

```
fn from_str(src: &str) -> Result<TokenStream, LexError>
```

Unlike declarative macros, procedural macros must reside in a separate crate marked as a procedural macro crate. For this purpose, add the proc-macro key within the lib section of the cargo.toml file, as follows:

```
[lib]
proc-macro=true
```

The syn and quote crates are optional helper crates for procedural macros:

- The syn crate has functionality to convert between TokenStream and DeriveInput types. DeriveInput represents the AST. It is a hierarchal token structure that is more convenient to iterate than the TokenStream, which is a String. The parse_macro_input! macro converts a TokenStream directly to a DeriveInput. As another option, the parse_derive_input function provides the same behavior. If the conversion is successful, the function returns a DeriveInput within the Result.

Here is the definition of the parse_derive_function:

```
pub fn parse_derive_input(input: &str) ->
       Result<DeriveInput, String>
```

- The quote crate contains the quote! macro, which can convert source code, as a string, into a sequence of tokens. You can call the into function to convert the tokens to a TokenStream. Alternatively, the TokenStream::from function converts tokens to a TokenStream.

Derive Macros

As the derive attribute, derive macros are the most identifiable of the procedural macros. Derive macros frequently implement a trait, such as the Debug or Clone trait. This is the syntax for applying a derive macro:

```
[derive(macro_name)]
type
```

The derive attribute is available for these types:

- Structs
- Unions
- Enums

When declaring a derive macro, you must adorn the macro function with the proc_macro_derive attribute. The only parameter is the name of the macro. For the macro function, the TokenStream is the sole parameter.

In Listing 21.10, Hello is a derive macro that displays the "Hello, world!" greeting. Let us assume that the macro is in a dedicated crate, as required. In addition, the proc-macro entry has been added to the lib section in the cargo.toml file.

The macro is implemented in the hello function, which has the proc_macro_derive attribute. The TokenStream is not required for this macro. For that reason, it is ignored. As a string, we next implement a hello_world function. The parse function converts the string to a TokenStream, which the macro returns. It is then inserted into the TokenStream for the application.

Code Listing 21.10. The Hello macro as a procedural and derive macro

```
use proc_macro::TokenStream;

#[proc_macro_derive(Hello)]
pub fn hello(input: TokenStream) -> TokenStream {
    r##"fn hello_world(){ println!("Hello, world!")}"##
        .parse().unwrap()
}
```

In Listing 21.11, the `Hello` macro is used. We apply the derive macro to the `Bob` struct. The macro inserts the `hello_world` function into the TokenStream. You can then call the hello_world function, as shown in `main`.

Code Listing 21.11.   Using the `Hello` macro, which is a derive macro

```
use hello::Hello;

#[derive(Hello)]
struct Bob;

fn main() {
    hello_world();
}
```

Let's create a new version of the `Hello` derive macro. This version of the macro integrates the target type, which is more realistic! The previous version of the macro ignored the TokenStream as an input parameter. The TokenStream represents the partial code for the struct, enum, or whatever is the target of the macro. In this example, the macro implements the Hello trait for the target type. The greeting will now be "Hello *type*." Listing 21.12 shows the macro.

Code Listing 21.12.   Version of the `Hello` macro that accepts variable input

```
#[proc_macro_derive(Hello)]
pub fn hello(input: TokenStream) -> TokenStream {
    let token_string = input.to_string();

    let derive_input =
        syn::parse_derive_input(&token_string).unwrap();
    let name=&derive_input.ident;
    let code=format!(r##"impl Hello for {name} {{
            fn hello_world() {{
                println!("Hello {name}");
            }}
    }}"##);

    code.parse().unwrap()
}
```

In this version of the macro, the `parse_derive_input` function transforms the input `TokenString` to `DeriveInput`. The `DeriveInput::ident` field then returns the name of the target, which is then bound to the `name` variable. The name is then integrated into the code fragment that implements the Hello trait (see the `println!` macro). At the end, the `parse` function converts the code fragment back to the `TokenStream`, which is returned from the macro.

In the main application, the Hello trait is defined, including the `hello_world` function. Next, we apply the Hello macro to the `Bob` struct, which implements the Hello trait for that type. The `hello_function` is then called on `Bob` to display the greeting (see Listing 21.13).

Code Listing 21.13.   Using the revised `Hello` macro

```
use hello_world::Hello;

trait Hello {
    fn hello_world();
}

#[derive(Hello)]
struct Bob;
fn main() {
    Bob::hello_world();   // Hello Bob
}
```

Listing 21.14 shows the final version of the `Hello` macro. The result is the same as the previous version—it implements the hello trait. In this version, we convert the `TokenStream` to a `DeriveInput` using the `parse_macro_input!` macro. In addition, the hello_world function is implemented within the `quote!` macro, instead of using a string. Precede the variable with a #, such as *#variable*, to include a variable from the macro function within the quote! macro. The result of the quote! macro can be converted to a TokenStream with the TokenStream::from function. The quote! macro is more transparent for writing extended or complex macros.

Code Listing 21.14.   Final version of the `Hello` macro

```
use proc_macro::TokenStream;
use quote::quote;
use syn;

#[proc_macro_derive(Hello)]
pub fn hello(input: TokenStream) -> TokenStream {
    let syn::DeriveInput { ident, .. } =
        syn::parse_macro_input!{input};

    let tokens = quote! {
        impl Hello for #ident {
            fn hello_world() {
                println!("Hello from {}", stringify!(#ident));
            }
        }
    };
    TokenStream::from(tokens)
}
```

Another practical example would be helpful. In this example, the Type trait presents an interface for runtime type information (RTTI). The `get` function of the trait returns the type of a value. The `Type` macro implements the trait. In the get function, the `any::type_name` function is called to obtain the name of the current type (see Listing 21.15).

Code Listing 21.15.   Implementation of the Type macro

```
use proc_macro::TokenStream;
use quote::quote;
use syn;

#[proc_macro_derive(Type)]
pub fn get_type(input: TokenStream) -> TokenStream {
    let syn::DeriveInput { ident, .. } =
        syn::parse_macro_input!{input};
    let tokens = quote! {
        impl Type for #ident {
            fn get(&self)->String {
                std::any::type_name::<#ident>().to_string()
            }
        }
    };
    TokenStream::from(tokens)
}
```

In Listing 21.16, we use the Type trait. It is applied to the MyStruct type. The get function is then called to return the type name, MyStruct.

Code Listing 21.16.   Using the `Type` macro to display the type name

```
use get_type_macro::Type;

trait Type {
    fn get(&self)->String;
}

#[derive(Type)]
struct MyStruct;

fn main() {
    let my=MyStruct;
    println!("{}", my.get()); //MyStruct
}
```

Attribute Macros

Attribute macros are invoked as custom attributes. This is different from a derive macro, which is presented in a `derive` attribute. There are several differences between an attribute macro and a derive macro:

- Attribute macros are adorned with the `proc_macro_attribute`.
- Attribute macros define new attributes, not the `derive` attribute.
- Attribute macros can also be applied to structs, enums, unions, as well as functions.
- Attribute macros replace the target.
- Attribute macros have two `TokenStream`s as parameters.

Here is the definition of an attribute macro:

```
#[proc_macro_attribute]
pub fn macro_name( parameter1: TokenStream,
    parameter1: TokenStream) -> TokenStream
```

Attribute macros have two TokenStreams. The first describes the parameters of the macro. When there are no parameters, the TokenStream is empty. The second TokenStream describes the target of the attribute macro, such as a struct or function. And, of course, the macro returns a TokenStream. Unlike a derive macro, the TokenStream replaces the target. For example, if you apply an attribute macro to a struct, the macro completely replaces the struct in the token stream.

Listing 21.17 is an example of an attribute macro. The info macro simply displays the contents of both TokenStream parameters. This will help convey the purpose and the role of each TokenStream parameter. This will provide a description of each parameter. Understanding this information will help in your planning for the attribute macro.

Code Listing 21.17. Implementing an attribute macro that displays the TokenStreams

```
use proc_macro::TokenStream;
use quote::quote;

#[proc_macro_attribute]
pub fn info( parameters: TokenStream, target: TokenStream)
        -> TokenStream {
  let args=parameters.to_string();
  let current=target.to_string();
  let syn::DeriveInput { ident, .. } =
        syn::parse_macro_input!{target};
  quote!{
    struct #ident{}

    impl #ident {
      fn describe(){
        println!("Token 1: {}", #args);
        println!("Token 2: {}", #current);
      }
    }
  }.into()
}
```

In the info macro, both TokenStreams parameters are converted to Strings: args and current. The parse_macro_input! macro converts the target into DeriveInput. We can then destructure the ident field, for the type name. Within the quote macro, a struct is created with the type name (#ident). For the type, we implement the describe function that displays the contents of both `TokenStreams`.

Listing 21.18 is an application that uses the `info` macro. We apply the macro to the `sample` struct. In `main`, the `describe` function is called to display both `TokenStreams`.

Code Listing 21.18.   Using the `info` attribute macro

```
use example_macro::info;

#[info(a,b)]
struct sample{}

fn main(){
    sample::describe();
}
```

The result is:

```
Token 1: a, b
Token 2: struct sample {}
```

Function-Like Macros

The final procedural macro to discuss is the function-like macro. Function-like macros are declared with the `#[proc_macro]` attribute and invoked directly using the macro operator (!). Here is the definition of a function-like macro:

```
#[proc_macro]
pub fn macro_name( parameter1: TokenStream
                        -> TokenStream
```

Listing 21.19 is an example of a function-like macro. The `create_hello` macro creates the `hello_world` function. This is similar to the code shown earlier in the chapter.

Code Listing 21.19.   The `create_hello` macro is a function-like macro.

```
use proc_macro::TokenStream;

#[proc_macro]
pub fn create_hello(_item: TokenStream) -> TokenStream {
    r##"fn hello_world(){ println!("Hello,
     world!");}"##.parse().unwrap()
}
```

In Listing 21.20, the `create_hello` macro is used within an application. It implements the `hello_world` function, which is subsequently called in `main`.

Code Listing 21.20.   Using the `create_hello` function-like macro

```
use hello_macro::create_hello;

create_hello!();

fn main() {
    hello_world();
}
```

Summary

Macros, such as the `println!` and `vec!` macros, provide extra capabilities to the Rust language. You can extend the language capabilities further by creating your own macros.

A macro is a code generator. It is metaprogramming where the macro is code for creating other code. At compile time, the result of the macro replaces the macro itself. It is inserted into the TokenStream of the application.

More specifically, macros accept a sequence of tokens that describes a portion of your application. There are different types of tokens for keywords, literals, statements, and other language artifacts. The `TokenStream` type is an abstraction of a stream of these tokens.

There are two types of macros: declarative and procedural. Declarative macros are similar to a match expression, but for code, not values. The println! macro is an example of a declarative macro. For a declarative macro, the patterns for code are expressed as fragment specifiers, such as `expr` and `ident`. Within the macro, you can create metavariables with the dollar ($) prefix. These metavariables can be used in the output code. In addition, within a declarative macro, you can create a variadic macro using a repetition. Use the macro_rules! macro to create declarative macros.

For procedural macros, there are `TokenStream`s for input parameters and return values. The macro inspects an input TokenStream, applies some transformation, and returns the result as an output TokenStream. You can convert an input `TokenStream` into a `DeriveInput`, which is an abstract syntax tree (AST). With the `DeriveInput`, it is often easier to interpret and decompose specific data in the TokenStream.

There are three types of procedural macros, each associated with a specific attribute:

Derive	`#[proc_macro_derive(Name)]`
Attribute	`#[proc_macro_attribute]`
Function-like	`#[proc_macro]`

Each of the procedural macros is applied differently. The derive macro is invoked as a derive macro. The attribute macro is invoked as a custom attribute, and, finally, the function-like macro is invoked with the macro operator (!).

The only limit to the capabilities of a macro is your imagination, so start exploring!

22

Interoperability

"No man is an island, entire of itself; every man is a piece of the continent, a part of the main" is a renowned adage from English poet John Donne. It also applies to most programming languages, especially system programming languages, including Rust.

At times, Rust needs to communicate with applications and libraries written with other programming languages. This includes the ability to call operating system APIs. Even though crates.io and the Rust ecosystem offer a lot of capabilities, there are occasions when more is needed. This means you may need to leave the comfort of Rust, on occasion, to interface with another programming language or the operating environment itself. Interoperability provides the ability to communicate with foreign languages.

Rust supports the C application binary interface (ABI). Despite some limitations, the C ABI is the preferred public interface of many programming languages and operating systems. In addition, C has been around, in some variation, for more than 50 years. For this reason, the catalog of applications written in C/C++ is extensive. It encompasses virtually every computing need, and more. Interoperability provides Rust developers access to this exhaustive repository of capabilities.

Exchanging data safely between different languages is a major challenge, especially with strings. For example, C strings are null-terminated, while Rust strings are not null-terminated. Pascal strings are different also, with length-prefixed strings. The different type systems between those languages can cause difficulties. Another potential problem is how pointers are managed, which can also vary between languages. The solution to these problems is the Foreign Function Interface (FFI), which provides the ability to marshal data between Rust and other (foreign) languages, in order to handle these differences. Marshaling is the capability of transfer data back and forth between different type models and standards.

In this chapter, we focus on Rust-to-C/C++ interoperability.

Foreign Function Interface

The Foreign Function Interface (FFI) is the glue that assures interoperability is successful. It creates a translation layer between Rust and C. Appropriately, the ingredients of FFI are naturally found in the `std::FFI` module. There you will find the scalars, enums, and structs necessary to marshal data from Rust to C in most circumstances.

Strings are the hardest type to correctly marshal. This is understood when considering the differences between Rust and C/C++ strings:

- C strings are null-terminated. Rust strings are not null-terminated.
- C strings cannot contain nulls, while Rust strings allow nulls.
- C strings are directly accessible with raw pointers. Rust strings are accessed via a fat pointer, which has additional metadata.
- Rust strings primarily use Unicode and UTF-8 encoding. For C, the use of Unicode can be vary.

Even the Rust char is different from the C char. The Rust char is a Unicode scalar value, while the char for C supports Unicode code points. A Unicode scalar value spans the core Unicode character sequence. Conversely, Unicode code points are limited to the seven classifications of Unicode values. For this reason, you can use characters in C that are not available in Rust.

In the FFI, the CString type is available for marshaling strings between Rust and C. The CStr type is for transforming a C string to a Rust &str. There are also the OsString and OsStr types for reading operating system strings, such as command-line arguments and environment variables.

The std::ffi module also offers types for marshaling primitive values (see Table 22.1).

Table 22.1. List of Types for Marshaling Primitive Types

Rust	C/C++
c_char	char (i8)
c_char	char (u8)
c_schar	signed char
c_uchar	unsigned char
c_short	short
c_ushort	unsigned short
c_int	int
c_uint	unsigned nut
c_long	long
c_ulong	unsigned long
c_longlong	long long
c_ulonglong	unsigned long long
c_float	float
c_double	double
c_void	void

In addition, some Rust types are fully compatible "as is." This includes floats, integers, and basic enums. Conversely, dynamically sized types are not supported, such as traits and slices.

For a limited number of items, creating the proper interfaces for marshaling is manageable. However, this can quickly become unsustainable when there are hundreds of items to marshal. Marshaling portions of the C standard library is a good example. You would not want to marshal the entire stdlib.h header file, for example. Fortunately, the libc crate provides binding to marshal portions of the C standard library.

Basic Example

As our first example, we begin with "Hello, World." Surprise, surprise! We plan to call a C function from Rust.

Listing 22.1 shows the C source file. It offers a single function that displays the greeting. We want to export this function and call it from Rust.

Code Listing 22.1.   **C program with `hello` function**

```
// Hello.c
#include <stdio.h>

void hello () {
    printf("Hello, world!");
}
```

We compile the C source and create a static library using the clang compiler and the LLVM tool, as shown next. The library will be used to bind the `hello` function implementation to our Rust program.

```
clang hello.c -c
llvm-lib hello.o
```

Important

Various C compiler and helper tools exist. Any traditional C compiler should work with the examples in this chapter, not just clang. I would recommend using whatever compiler you are most comfortable with. There's no reason to learn a new tool.

In the Rust program, place function definitions for functions exported from C within an `extern "C"` block, which will function as a Rust-style header. You can now call the function. However, you must call the function within an `unsafe` block. Rust cannot vouch for the safeness of a foreign function.

The `hello` function has neither parameters nor a return value. Therefore, you can simply call the function, as shown in Listing 22.2.

Code Listing 22.2.   Rust program that calls a C function

```
// greeter.rs
extern "C" {
    fn hello();
}

fn main() {
    unsafe {
        hello();
    }
}
```

It's time to build the application. With the rustc compiler, you can build an executable crate from a Rust source file while linking to an external library. For the current example, here is the rustc command that creates the executable crate:

```
rustc "greeter.rs" -l "hello.o" -L .
```

The command compiles greeter.rs. The -l option links to the hello.o library. In addition, the -L option identifies where the library can be found. The "." indicates the library is in the current directory. The command will create an executable crate, greeter.exe, for this example.

When you run greeter, the following greeting is displayed:

```
Hello, world!
```

You can automate the build process, including linking the library. This can be done within the build.rs script, which is similar to a makefile in other languages. This is convenient when the build includes multiple steps, managing a build pipeline, or when you just want to automate the process. The build.rs file is automatically detected and executed by Cargo during the build process. Fortunately, unlike a makefile, which can appear to be written in an alien language, the build.rs file looks like normal Rust code with build instructions as function calls.

Listing 22.3 is the build.rs file for the previous hello program.

Code Listing 22.3.   Build.rs file that builds a Rust binary linked to a C library

```
extern crate cc;

fn main() {
    cc::Build::new().file("src/hello.c").compile("hello");
}
```

As with most Rust applications, main is the entry point for the build application. The first step is to create a Build type using the Build::new constructor. The Build::file function identifies the input file, a C source file, to be compiled. The file::compile function performs the actual compilation and links to the library (.lib) file. These functions are found in the cc crate.

You must add cc, which is found in crates.io, to the build-dependencies section in the cargo. toml file, as shown here:

```
[build-dependencies]
cc = "1.0"1
```

The hierarchical file listed for the greeter package is shown in Figure 22.1, including the build.rs file, which is highlighted.

Figure 22.1.   File hierarchy when automating the build process

With the build process scripted within build.rs, you can call *cargo build* to build the executable crate. Alternatively, you can call *cargo run* to build and run it.

Libc Crate

As mentioned, the libc crate contains FFI bindings to marshal data with portions of the C Standard Library. This includes FFI bindings for stdlib.h. In an extern block, you list items from the C Standard Library that will be used within your application. Nothing else is required. That is the benefit of the libc crate. You can now use the selected items wherever needed.

The application shown in Listing 22.4 uses the atof and atoi functions, both found in stdlb, to convert numbers stored as strings into normal numbers. The atof function converts a string to a float, while atoi converts a string to an integer.

Code Listing 22.4.   Rust application that uses libc to access the C Standard Library

```rust
use std::ffi::{c_longlong, CString, c_double};

extern "C" {
    fn atof(p:*const i8)->c_double;
    fn atoi(p:*const i8)->c_longlong;
}

fn main() {

    // Convert 'string float' to float
    let f_string = "123.456".to_string();
    let mut f_cstring: CString =
        CString::new(f_string.as_str()).unwrap();
    let mut f_result:c_double;

    // Convert 'string integer' to long
    let i_string = "123".to_string();
    let mut i_cstring: CString =
        CString::new(i_string.as_str()).unwrap();
    let mut i_result:c_longlong;

    unsafe {
        f_result=atof(f_cstring.as_ptr());   // to float
        i_result=atoi(i_cstring.as_ptr());   // to integer
    }

    println!("{}", f_result);
    println!("{}", i_result);
}
```

Both the atof and atoi functions accept strings as parameters and return either a float or integer, respectively. We create test values as Strings: "123.45" and "123". The CString::new constructor creates CStrings from the String test values. We need CStrings to marshal the function arguments. The as_ptr function converts the CStrings to pointers, which is equivalent to char*. The results of calling the functions are saved to the proper types: c_double and c_longlong.

You can now compile this application as normal. Because of the libc crate, there are no special considerations for building the application.

Structs

Until now, we have focused on interoperability with basic types, such as integers, floats, and strings. However, you often need to marshal compound types, such as structs, as well. System APIs, for example, frequently require structs as a parameter or return value.

For marshaling, compound types require extra consideration. The memory alignment may be different. In addition, the memory layout of C structs can be affected by user-defined packing and memory boundaries. Furthermore, Rust makes no assurances about the memory layouts of its structs. These differences could make marshaling a nightmare. The solution is adopting the C model for structs that will be marshaled. You do this by applying the `#[repr(C)]` attribute to the Rust struct, which will remove the difference in the memory layout between C and Rust structs.

Listing 22.5 shows an example.

Code Listing 22.5.   Rust struct with C memory layout

```
#[repr(C)]
pub struct astruct {
}
```

Structs are marshaled at their most basic level. This means decomposing structs into their constituent parts first. Only then can you determine the correct marshaling. Listing 22.6 is a typical C struct where the constituent parts are the integer fields, where each can be marshaled.

Code Listing 22.6.   C-style struct

```
struct astruct {
        int field1;
        int field2;
        int field3;
};
```

In Rust, the struct could be marshaled as shown in Listing 22.7. The fields are assigned the appropriate FFI types. In this example, the constituents fully describe the composition of the struct, which is required.

Code Listing 22.7.   Rust struct with FFI

```
struct astruct {
    field1:c_int,
    field2:c_int,
    field3:c_int,
}
```

In Listing 22.8, the C source code has a struct. `Person` represents a person and has fields for their first name, last name, and age. In addition, there is a global instance of `Person`, named `gPerson`. There are also `get_person` and `set_person` functions to manage `gPerson`. These are typical getter and setter functions. The `get_person` function returns a pointer to `gPerson`, while `set_person` replaces `gPerson` with its input parameter.

Code Listing 22.8.   C source file that manages the Person type

```
// person.c

#include <stdio.h>

struct Person {
    char *first;
    char *last;
    int age;
};

struct Person gPerson;

struct Person* get_person(){
    if(gPerson.last == 0) {
        gPerson=(struct Person) {"Bob", "Wilson", 23};
    }
return &gPerson;
};

void set_person(struct Person new_person) {
    gPerson=new_person;
}
```

We want to call the get_person and set_person functions in Rust. This will require marshaling the Person struct, as shown in Listing 22.9. The char* fields are marshaled as 64-bit const pointers, which are equivalent. For the age field, C int is marshaled as c_int.

Code Listing 22.9.   The Person type in Rust

```
#[repr(C)]
pub struct Person{
    pub first:*const i8,    // C: char*
    pub last:*const i8,     // C: char*
    pub age: c_int,         // C: int
}
```

Listing 22.10 shows the remainder of the Rust application.

Code Listing 22.10.   Rust application that uses the Person type

```
extern "C" {
    fn get_person()->*mut Person;
    fn set_person(new_person:Person);
}

fn main() {
```

```
let mut person;
let new_person;

unsafe {
    person=get_person();
    println!("{:?}", (*person).age);
    println!("{:?}", CStr::from_ptr((*person).first));
    println!("{:?}", CStr::from_ptr((*person).last));
}

let first=CString::new("Sally".to_string()).unwrap();
let pfirst=first.as_ptr();
let last=CString::new("Johnson".to_string()).unwrap();
let plast=last.as_ptr();

new_person=Person{
    first:pfirst,
    last:plast,
    age:12
};

unsafe {
    set_person(new_person);
    person=get_person();
    println!("{:?}", (*person).age);
    println!("{:?}", CStr::from_ptr((*person).first));
    println!("{:?}", CStr::from_ptr((*person).last));
}
}
```

Here are descriptions of the various sections in the application:

- The extern "C" block imports the get_person and set_person functions from the C library.
- In the first unsafe block, we get and display the default value for gPerson. We call get_person to return the default value, as *Person. We dereference the pointer to access the Person fields, and we convert the first and last fields to string literals with the CStr::from_ptr function. We can then display all three fields within a println! macro.
- Next, we update the Person in the library with the set_person function. We create the individual values for each Person field and then we update a new Person with the values.
- In a second unsafe block, call set_person to update gPerson.
- Finally, we call get_person to obtain the recently updated value, and we display the Person, as shown before.

Bindgen

You can spend considerable time creating the proper FFI binding to marshal data between Rust and C. The process is even more tedious when converting a header file that may contain dozens, if not hundreds, of definitions that require marshaling. Furthermore, if this is done incorrectly, you could spend even more time debugging compilation errors and panics. Fortunately, bindgen is a tool that can automate this process for you.

Bindgen creates the correct FFI binding for C definitions. This saves you from the drudgery of creating the mappings yourself. Bindgen can read a C header file and generate a Rust source file containing the proper bindings for everything. This is particularly useful for portions of the C Standard Library not included in libc.

Bindgen can be downloaded at crates.io. Alternatively, you can install bindgen directly using Cargo. Here is the command:

```
cargo add bindgen
```

In the next example, the application displays the current date and time as a string. We will use time.h, which is part of the C Standard Library. The following `bindgen` command reads the time.h header file, and generates the proper FFI binding, which is saved to time.rs:

```
bindgen time.h > time.rs
```

There are plenty of mappings in the time.rs file. The `tm` struct, as shown in Listing 22.11, is an example.

Code Listing 22.11.   The tm type from the time.h header file

```rust
#[repr(C)]
#[derive(Debug, Copy, Clone)]
pub struct tm {
    pub tm_sec: ::std::os::raw::c_int,
    pub tm_min: ::std::os::raw::c_int,
    pub tm_hour: ::std::os::raw::c_int,
    pub tm_mday: ::std::os::raw::c_int,
    pub tm_mon: ::std::os::raw::c_int,
    pub tm_year: ::std::os::raw::c_int,
    pub tm_wday: ::std::os::raw::c_int,
    pub tm_yday: ::std::os::raw::c_int,
    pub tm_isdst: ::std::os::raw::c_int,
}
```

The application shown in Listing 22.12 relies on the following imported functions and types from time.h:

- The `time64` function returns the number of seconds since January 1, 1970, at midnight (UTC/GMT).
- The `_localtime64` function converts local time, as const `__time64_t`, to a tm struct.
- The `asctime` function converts the time, as tm, to a string.

Code Listing 22.12.   Rust code that uses time.h from the C Standard Library

```
mod time;
use time::*;
use std::ffi::CStr;

fn main() {
    let mut rawtime:i64=0;
    let mut pTime:* mut __time64_t=&mut rawtime;

    unsafe {
        let tm=_time64(pTime);
        let ptm=&tm as *const __time64_t;
        let tm2=_localtime64(ptm);
        let result=asctime(tm2);
        let c_str=CStr::from_ptr(result);
        println!("{:#?}", c_str.to_str().unwrap());
    }
}
```

C Calling Rust Functions

So far, we have focused on Rust applications calling foreign functions, most notably via the C ABI. You may want to reverse direction and call a Rust function from a foreign application. Much of the semantics for marshaling remain the same, including using the FFI.

For interoperability, we precede Rust functions to be exported with the extern keyword.

Rust mangles the name of its functions for a unique identity. The mangled name combines the crate name, hash, the function name itself, and other factors. This means that other languages, unaware of this scheme, will not recognize the internal names for Rust functions. For this reason, name mangling should be disabled on exported functions by applying the no_mangle attribute. This will make the function name transparent.

Listing 22.13 is an example of a Rust function, display_rust, that can be called from another language. Notice the no_mangle attribute and extern keyword that adorn the function.

Code Listing 22.13.   Exported Rust function

```
#[no_mangle]
pub extern fn display_rust() {
    println!("Greetings from Rust");
}
```

To interoperate with other languages, you must build a static or dynamic library for the Rust application. The library will provide other languages access to the implementation of the exported functions. Add a lib section to the cargo.toml file to create a library for the crate. In the crate-type field, staticlib will create a static library. For a dynamic library, set the crate-type field to cydlib. The name of the library will default to the package name. If desired, you can set the name explicitly using the name field.

Here is a snippet of a cargo.toml file that requests both a static and dynamic library for the Rust application:

```
[lib]
name = "greeting"
crate-type = ["staticlib", "cdylib"]
```

To call a Rust function from C, you should create a header with the function definition in C. If there are function parameters and return values, this will also determine the data marshaling that needs to occur. Here is the header file that includes the display_rust function from the previous example:

```
// sample.h
void display_rust();
```

With the header file, you can now call the exported function as a normal function, as shown in Listing 22.14.

Code Listing 22.14.   C program calling Rust function

```
// sample.c
#include "hello.h"

int main (void) {
    display_rust();
}
```

When building the C application, you must include the C source file and link to the library created for the Rust application. In the following clang command-line, that would be greeting. dll.lib:

```
clang sample.c greeting.dll.lib -o sample.exe
```

The result of this command-line task is a C executable, sample.ex.

Cbindgen

We recently looked at the bindgen tool, which we used to create the FFI binding to marshal data between Rust and the C ABI. The cbindgen tool is functionally the reverse of the bindgen tool. The cbindgen tool creates a C header file from a Rust source file that contains the necessary definitions for interoperability. This is done in lieu of you creating the C header file yourself, as shown in the previous example. Cbindgen is found in crates.io.

You can combine the cbindgen tool with build.rs to automate the process. The following example demonstrates this. The max3 function is a Rust function that returns the maximum number among three integers. We want to call the function from C++. Listing 22.15 shows the function.

Code Listing 22.15.   Rust function to be exported

```
#[no_mangle]
pub extern fn max3(first: i64, second: i64,
        third: i64) -> i64 {
    let value= if first > second {
        first
    } else {
        second
    };

    if value > third {
        return value;
    }

    third
}
```

In the cargo.lib file, cbindgen is added as a build dependency. It will be used in build.rs during the build process. We also request that both a static and dynamic library be generated. Listing 22.16 is the final cargo.toml file.

Code Listing 22.16.   Cargo.toml file with cbindgen dependency

```
[dependencies]

[build-dependencies]
cbindgen = "0.24.0"

[lib]
name = "example"
crate-type = ["staticlib", "cdylib"]
```

Next, the cbindgen tool is called in the build file to create the proper C header file. As part of the build process, the C header is automatically updated whenever the Rust source file is updated. Listing 22.17 is the build.rs file that uses cbindgen. We start by creating a new builder, followed by some daisy chained commands. Most importantly, the Builder generates the proper binding, which is written to the max3.h header file, using the write_to_file function.

Code Listing 22.17.   Build file that uses cbindgen

```
extern crate cbindgen;

fn main() {
    cbindgen::Builder::new()
    .with_crate(".")
    .generate()
    .expect("Unable to generate bindings")
    .write_to_file("max3.h");
}
```

Listing 22.18 shows the contents of the max3.h header file. It contains the definition for the max3 function, which is the only function exported from the Rust example. We did not have to create the proper definition; cbindgen performed the task for us. This can be enormously helpful when a number of items are being exported from Rust, not just one, as shown here.

Code Listing 22.18.   The max3.h header file created with the cbindgen tool

```
// max3.h
#include <cstdarg>
#include <cstdint>
#include <cstdlib>
#include <ostream>
#include <new>

extern "C" {

int64_t max3(int64_t first, int64_t second, int64_t third);

}
```

Listing 22.19 shows a C++ application that calls the max3 function. For this purpose, the header file that cbindgen generated is included.

Code Listing 22.19.   C++ program that calls a Rust function

```
// myapp.cpp
#include <stdio.h>
    #include "max3.h"

    int main() {
      long answer=max3(10, 5, 7);
      printf("Max value is:  %ld", answer);
      return 0;
    }
```

The following command will compile the C++ program and link to the Rust library:

```
clang myapp.cpp example.dll.lib -o myapp.exe
```

It's important to note that we can easily interoperate with a C++ application, similar to a C application, as shown.

Summary

Interoperability is important in its ability to expand the universe of capabilities available to Rust applications—at least until crates.io contains every fathomable functionality in the universe!

Interoperability is a broad topic. In this chapter, we focused on the C ABI, which is the most prevalent programming interface. However, Rust can interact with a variety of languages, not just C and C++ ABI.

External functions imported into Rust must reside in an extern "C" block. Because Rust cannot ensure the safeness of functions from another language, you must place any reference to those functions in an unsafe block. For functions exported from Rust, you should prefix the function with the no_mangle attribute and the extern keyword.

A major consideration for interoperability is to correctly exchange data between Rust and a foreign language. The Foreign Function Interface (FFI) provides the interoperable types necessary to successfully marshal data between incongruent languages.

Although the FFI is helpful, marshaling is still dependent on you making the correct decisions. The bindgen tool helps automate selecting the correct FFI binding. The tool consumes a C header file and generates the related FFI binding, saved in a Rust source file.

Cbindgen is the reverse of the bindgen tool. It creates a C header file from Rust source code. The header file can then be included in C/C++ programs to call Rust functions.

Building a Rust crate that interfaces with C can require additional steps and a complex command-line task. Within the cc crate, you will find functionality that will help automate the build process.

23

Modules

Modules help developers better organize their source code. You can organize code hierarchically or based on context. The alternative to using modules is a monolithic approach where the entire application resides in a single source file. This approach becomes cumbersome when an application includes hundreds, even thousands, of lines of source code. Monolithic applications of that size are hard to navigate and maintain. You can reorganize your application into modules to prevent these sorts of problems.

Fundamentally, modules allow you to group related items. These include structs, enums, functions, and globals. However, modules can also be empty. The name of the module hopefully indicates its context. For example, a module named calculus would include algorithms and constants related to that area of math. A solar system module would include information about the eight planets, plus Pluto (long story).

Rust itself relies on modules extensively to group language features and also provide context. Within this book, we have referred to many of the modules. Here are some common modules mentioned thus far:

- The `std::string` module contains items related to strings, including the frequently used String type.
- The `std::fmt` module provides support for the `format!` macro.
- The `std::io` module groups items related to input/output, such as the Stdout, Stdin, and StdErr types.

In the preceding list, the content of the module, as the names indicate, provides the context. The `std::io` module has the input/output context, for example. Rust can also support logical hierarchies using modules, such as the `std::os::linux::net` module path. Modules in a module path use `::` as a separator. For example, `std` is the crate that contains the `os` module. The other two modules are submodules, as shown in Figure 23.1, which is a module tree. The context of the `net` module combines that of its descendant modules, which is OS (operating system) and Linux networking. For that reason, the `net` module includes Linux-specific implementations of the TcpStreamExt and SocketAddrExt types.

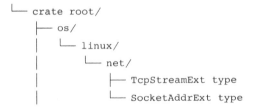

Figure 23.1.   Module hierarchy for the net module

Inevitably, when speaking of modules, many developers make comparisons to namespaces, which is a feature in other languages, including C++, Java, and Python, that has some similarity to modules. However, modules have other capabilities, such as module files, so a direct comparison is not very helpful.

There are two types of modules: module items and module files. A module item is contained within a sources file, while a module file spans a file.

The conversation about modules is made more complicated because of the existence of two models: the *current* model and the *legacy* model. The current model for modules was introduced in Rust 1.30. However, both models remain supported and are widely used, thus adding to the confusion. For that reason, both are included here, starting with the current model.

Module Items

Modules are declared with the mod keyword. You can declare a module item within a source file. Here is the syntax:

```
mod name {
     /*   content ... */
}
```

Within the curly braces, you add items included in the module, such as structs and other items. For visibility outside the module, prefix the item with the pub keyword. The default is private visibility for items. Private items are not accessible outside of the module. Here is the syntax for referring to a public item outside the module:

```
module::item_name
```

In Listing 23.1, the application displays a greeting in English and with an Australian variation. For this reason, we define two hello functions. The first function is in the *root module*, which is the default module. It is also the implicit module. The other hello function is defined in the australian module. In main, we call the default hello function and the hello function found in the australian module.

Code Listing 23.1. Application with `hello` and `australian::hello` functions

```
fn hello() {
    println!("Hello, world!");
}

mod australian {

    pub fn hello(){
        println!("G'day, world!");
    }
}

fn main() {
    hello();
    australian::hello();
}
```

The module tree for this application is shown in Figure 23.2.

```
└── crate root/
    ├── australian/
```

Figure 23.2 Module tree for the `australian` module

In the previous example, notice the `pub` prefix for the `hello` function in the `australian` module. This makes the function visible outside of the module. Consequently, we can call the function in `main`.

Avoiding name conflicts is a key benefit of modules. The `hello` function appears in two modules: the `root` and `australian` modules. However, the modules resolve the name conflict with the `hello` functions. The hello and australian::hello functions present no ambiguity. With applications that have a moderate amount of source code, modules help prevent name conflicts, including with the Rust language.

Modules share the same namespace as structs, enums, and others. For that reason, within the same scope, you cannot share a name with a type and module. Listing 23.2 demonstrates this possible problem.

Code Listing 23.2. Module and struct have the same name.

```
mod example {

}

struct example {

}

fn main(){

}
```

In the application, both the module and struct are named `example`. Because they are at the same scope, this will create the error message shown in the following code:

```
  |
1 | mod example {
  | ---------- previous definition of the module `example` here
...
5 | struct example {
  | ^^^^^^^^^^^^^^ `example` redefined here
  |
  = note: `example` must be defined only once in the
          type namespace of this module
```

You can declare modules within modules. Nested modules are called *submodules*. In this manner, you can create a logical hierarchy within your application. There is no limit to the depth of submodules. When accessing an item, you must precede it with the full module path. Let's assume the `addition` function is found in the `algebra` module, which is declared within the `math` module. Here is the syntax to call the function:

```
    math::algebra::addition(5, 10);
```

In Listing 23.3, we model the solar system using modules. There is a module for the solar system and a submodule for each planet. Each module for a planet will have the `get_name` function, which returns the planet name. The `constants` submodule, within each planet module, contains various constants related to that planet. Notice that the submodules are declared public with the `pub` keyword. This makes the submodules visible outside the parent module. In `main`, we display information on planet Earth.

Code Listing 23.3.   **Modules that model the solar system**

```
mod solar_system {
    pub mod earth {

        pub fn get_name()->&'static str {
            "Earth"
        }

        pub mod constants {
            pub static DISTANCE:i64=93_000_000;
            pub static CIRCUMFERENCE:I32=24_901;
        }
    }

    /* and the other eight */
}

fn main() {
    println!("{}",
        solar_system::earth::get_name());
```

```
    println!("Distance from Sun {}",
        solar_system::earth::constants::DISTANCE);
}
```

Figure 23.3 shows the module tree for the previous code listing.

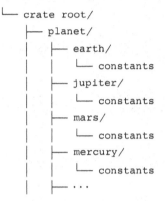

Figure 23.3   Module tree for the solar system application

Encapsulation is another feature of modules. Within a module, you can define a public interface for users while hiding the details. The public items, defined with the pub keyword, form the public interface. Everything else is hidden. This allows developers to better model real-world entities within their application. The results are applications that are more maintainable, extensible, and predictable.

Next, we will model a vehicle. Within the car module, the car struct implements both a public and private interface, as shown in Listing 23.4. The public interface includes ignition and gas_pedal. This exposes functionality readily available to any driver. All other functionalities, such as engine, alternator, and throttle, involve the inner workings of a vehicle, which remain private.

In main, we first create an instance of Car and then call various public functions. However, calling the throttle function, which is private, will cause a compiler error. Without the pub keyword, it is only accessible within the Car module.

Code Listing 23.4.   A module that models a car

```
mod car {

    pub struct Car {}

    impl Car {
        pub fn ignition(&self) {  // public
            self.engine();
        }

        pub fn gas_pedal(&self) {  // public
```

```
                self.throttle();
            }

            fn engine(&self) {  // private
                self.alternator();
                println!("engine started");
            }

            fn alternator(&self) {  // private
                println!("alternator started");
            }

            fn throttle(&self){  // private
                println!("throttle open...");
            }
        }
    }

fn main() {
    let mycar=car::Car{};
    mycar.ignition();
    mycar.gas_pedal();
    mycar.throttle();  // does not work
}
```

Module Files

Module files span an entire file. This is unlike module items module items, where the curly braces set the extent of the module. With a file module, the file sets the scope of the module. For this reason, curly braces are not required. Define a module file with the mod keyword and name. The module file would be *modname*.rs file.

```
    mod mymod;    // mymod.rs
```

Whether a module file or module item, the logical path to the module does not change. You still use :: to separate modules within the module path.

Listing 23.5 shows a module file. In main.rs, the mod hello statement declares a module file, hello.rs. For that reason, this code listing contains two files: main.rs and hello.rs. In the main function, we call the hello function in the hello module.

Code Listing 23.5.   Using hello.rs as a module file

```
// main.rs
mod hello;

fn main() {
    hello::hello();
}
```

```
// hello.rs
pub fn hello(){
    println!("Hello, world!");
}
```

In the preceding example, main.rs and hello.rs reside in same directory. However, you may want to create subdirectories for module files to maintain both a physical and logical hierarchy. With the mod keyword, you can declare *submodule* files inside of module files. Submodule files are placed in a subdirectory based on the module name (i.e., *module*.rs).

This is best demonstrated with an example. We will create an application that displays "Hello, world!" in a variety of languages: English, French, Korean, and Hindi. The application defines the following module tree, as shown in Figure 23.4.

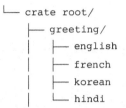

```
└─ crate root/
   ├─ greeting/
   │  ├─ english
   │  ├─ french
   │  ├─ korean
   │  └─ hindi
```

Figure 23.4 Module tree for a module with submodules

The application is shown in Listing 23.6. In main.rs, we declare greeting as a module file, greeting.rs. Both main.rs and greeting.rs reside in the same directory. In the main function, the various hello functions are called using their module paths, as described in the module tree.

Code Listing 23.6.   Accessing the language submodules

```
// main.rs

mod greeting;

fn main() {
    greeting::english::hello();
    greeting::french::bonjour();
    greeting::hindi::नमस्ते();
    greeting::korean::안녕하세요();
}
```

The submodules for each language are declared in greeting.rs, as shown in Listing 23.7. There will be an external file created for each submodule, such as english.rs, french.rs, and so on. Because the parent module is *greeting*, the external files are placed in the greeting subdirectory.

Code Listing 23.7. Defining the submodules in the greeting subdirectory

```
// greeting.rs

pub mod english;
pub mod french;
pub mod korean;
pub mod hindi;

pub fn hello(){
    println!("Hello, world!");
}
```

In the greeting subdirectory, you will find the files for each submodule. The individual files are shown in Listing 23.8.

Code Listing 23.8. Submodules in the greeting subdirectory

```
// english.rs

pub fn hello(){
    println!("Hello, world");
}


// french.rs

pub fn bonjour(){
    println!("Bonjour le monde!");
}

// hindi.rs

pub fn नमस्ते(){
    println!("हैलो वर्ल्ड!");
}

// korean.rs

pub fn 안녕하세요(){
    println!("안녕, 세계!");
}
```

The path Attribute

With the path attribute, you can explicitly set the physical location of a module, overriding the default. You apply the path attribute directly to a module. The attribute names the file for the module, including the directory path and where to find the module. In Listing 23.9, the path attribute places the abc module in the cooler.rs file. In main, the funca function is called from the abc module.

Code Listing 23.9. Using the path attribute

```
#[path =".\\cool\\cooler.rs"]
mod abc;

fn main() {
    abc::funca();
}

// cooler.rs ".\cool\cooler.rs"

pub fn funca(){
    println!("Doing something!")
}
```

Functions and Modules

You can even declare modules within functions. The rationale remains the same. Modules can be used to group items within a function, create a hierarchy, disambiguate items, and so on.

Modules defined in a function have the scope of the application but the visibility of the function. For that reason, you cannot access the module, or its items, outside the function. Items in the module must be public to be accessible outside the module, but within the function.

Variables declared within a module contained a function must be either static or const.

In the next example, funca contains two modules, as shown in Listing 23.10. The modules disambiguate the do_something functions. The correct do_something is called based on the function argument.

Code Listing 23.10. Implementing modules within the funca function

```
fn funca(input:bool) {

    if input {
        mod1::do_something();
    } else {
        mod2::do_something();
    }

    mod mod1 {
        pub fn do_something(){
            println!("in mod1");
        }
    }
```

```
        mod mod2 {
            pub fn do_something(){
                println!("in mod1");
            }
        }


    }
```

The `crate`, `super`, and `self` Keywords

You can use the `crate`, `super`, and `self` keywords, with a module path. Here is the explanation of each keyword:

- The `crate` keyword starts navigation at the `crate` module (root). From within any module, this is a fixed path and will always navigate to the same module node.
- The `super` keyword starts navigation at the parent module. This is a relative path, relative to the location of the submodule module within the module tree. This is typically less brittle than using a fixed path with the `crate` keyword.
- The `self` keyword refers to the current module.

There is a saying, "All roads lead to Rome." With the navigation keywords, that is often the case. It is not uncommon for there to be multiple paths to the same modules. The choice can sometimes be subjective. The two most common criteria are brevity and complexity. This means choosing either the shortest or less-complex path to a module. In addition, relative paths are preferred to fixed paths.

The next example demonstrates navigation using either the `crate`, `super`, or `self` keywords. The module tree, shown in Figure 23.5, is created here.

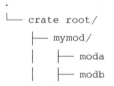

Figure 23.5.   Module tree for the sample application

In Listing 23.11, we create a module hierarchy. In `funca`, the three keywords are used to navigate the module tree.

Code Listing 23.11.   Example that includes the `crate`, `super`, and `self` keywords

```
mod mymod {
    pub mod moda {
        pub fn funca(){
            crate::mymod::modb::funcb();
```

```
            super::modb::funcb();
            self::funcc();
        }

        pub fn funcc(){println!("moda::funcc")}
    }

    pub mod modb {
        pub fn funcb(){println!("modb::funcb")}
    }
}
```

Let's review the module paths presented in this example:

- The `crate::mymod::modb` module path starts navigation at the root module. From there, we navigate to `mymod` and `modb`, where `funcb` is found.
- For the `super::modb` module path, the `super` keyword refers to the parent, which is `mymod`. From `mymod`, we can proceed to `modb` and call `funcb`.
- The `self` path refers to the current module, which is module `moda`. You can then call `funcc`.

Legacy Model

As previously mentioned, a new model for modules was introduced in Rust 1.30. However, the legacy model remains available and is used by some developers. In addition, there is plenty of older Rust code that adheres to this model. For these reasons, it is helpful to be familiar with the legacy model for modules. There is absolutely no difference between a module created with the legacy versus new model, as shown in the first portion of this chapter.

The primary difference between the two models relates to module files and the mod.rs file. For the legacy model, here are the steps for creating a module file:

1. Declare a submodule within a module as `mod` *name*.
2. Create a subdirectory using the module's name.
3. In the subdirectory, place a mod.rs file.
4. Within mod.rs, name all the additional submodules with the `mod` keyword.
5. In the module subdirectory, create a module file for each submodule named previously. The names should be *submodule*.rs.

In the next example, we want to repeat an example similar the greeting where hello is displayed in various languages. Figure 23.6 shows the module tree for the application. Within the `all` module, the `hello_all` function displays the greeting for every language. Each language module, such as `english`, displays "Hello, world!" in that language.

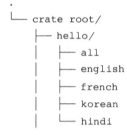

Figure 23.6   Module tree with a submodule for each language

In main.rs, the he11o mod is declared, as shown in Listing 23.12. In addition, we call the hello_all function to display hello in the various languages.

Code Listing 23.12.   Calling the hello_all function that is in a submodule

```
// main.rs

mod hello;

fn main(){
    hello::all::hello_all();
}
```

In Listing 23.13, we create the hello subdirectory for the submodule declared in main.rs. The presence of mod.rs indicates that the directory contains module files. For our example, we list the modules for each language.

Code Listing 23.13.   In main.rs, declaring the he11o module

```
// mod.rs - crate::hello

pub mod english;
pub mod french;
pub mod korean;
pub mod hindi;
pub mod all;
```

Listing 23.14 shows the module file for each language submodule. Each contains a function to display the greeting in that language.

Code Listing 23.14.   Listing the various module files for each language submodule

```
// all.rs - crate::hello::all

pub fn hello_all(){
    super::english::hello();
    super::french::bonjour();
```

```
    super::korean::안녕하세요();
    super::hindi::नमस्ते();
}


// english.rs - crate::hello::englsh
pub fn hello(){
    println!("Hello, world!");
}


// french.rs - crate::hello::french
pub fn bonjour(){
    println!("Bonjour le monde!");
}


// hindi.rs - crate::hello::hindi
pub fn नमस्ते(){
    println!("हैलो वर्ल्ड");
}


// korean.rs - crate::hello::korean
pub fn 안녕하세요(){
    println!("안녕, 세계!");
}
```

Summary

Modules help developers better organize their applications. Instead of a monolithic application, you can use modules to create a hierarchical approach and group related items together. Declare a module with the `mod` keyword. You can access public items in a module using the `module::item` syntax.

There are several benefits to modules:

- Hierarchical organization
- Avoiding name conflicts
- Creating public interfaces
- Grouping items

There are two types of modules. Module items are contained within a source file with curly braces defining the scope. You can even include module items within functions. Alternatively, there are module files where the module spans an entire file.

There are two models for modules. Regardless, modules are modules. There is no difference between modules created in the current model versus the legacy model. The primary difference between the two models is the mod.rs file. The current model does not use the mod.rs file.

Submodules are nested modules. You can have multiple levels of modules. When describing the path for submodules, you separate each module along the path with the :: operator.

A module path can be prefixed with the crate, super, and self keywords. The crate keyword creates a fixed path, starting at the crate's root module. The super keyword starts a module path relative to the parent module. The self keyword refers to the current module.

Index

F

J-K

L